A Dynasty of Water

A Dynasty of Water

*The Story of
American Water Works Company*

by G I L B E R T C R O S S

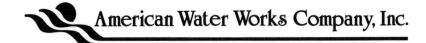 American Water Works Company, Inc.

Library of Congress Catalog Card Number 91–70804
ISBN 0–9619049–1–7 (regular edition)
ISBN 0–9619049–2–5 (deluxe binding)

Printed in the United States of America
10   9   8   7   6   5   4   3   2   1

American Water Works Company, Inc.
1025 Laurel Oak Road
Voorhees, New Jersey 08043

Contents

I

IN THE BEGINNING

II

ENTER JOHN WARE

III

THE ENTERPRISE EVOLVES

IV

A NEW ERA

Foreword

There is a saying that "History is written by the winners." In the case of a company like ours, it could be argued that history is often forgotten by the winners. The present American Water Works Company came into being in 1947, as a result of the reorganization of a predecessor called American Water Works & Electric. AWW&E in turn was created when a new management took control of an even earlier entity, called American Water Works & Guarantee. Meanwhile, over the years these companies acquired control of other companies and groups of companies, which themselves had grown by acquiring still other companies.

In each case the "winners," the new owners or managers, tended to assume that history, at least any history that mattered, began on the day they took control. As a result, the record of what had happened before tended to be ignored and then largely forgotten.

The preparation of this history began in 1986, in anticipation of the fortieth anniversary of the founding of the present company. It is fair to say that those of us who were involved at the start were thinking of the project largely as a commemoration of the events of the previous 40 years. But as the research proceeded, there gradually unfolded, layer by layer, a history covering not 40 years, but more than 100, with beginnings reaching back almost 70 years before that. So in tracing our roots we rediscovered our heritage. And a rich and colorful heritage it turned out to be, with the story of our company and its predecessors interwoven with the major events and forces in the society around it.

It is clear by hindsight that we began this history not a moment too soon. Much of the story of the past half century in our company's affairs came from a series of interviews with John J. Barr, who not only played a key role in the development of our company, but for more than 30 years was a close associate of John H. Ware, Jr., the "founding father" of American Water in its present form. A few months after the last interview, Jack Barr was dead. Two other sources were W. James MacIntosh, the lawyer who in 1947 helped set the strategy that determined control of the present company, and Howard Briggs, an early secretary and treasurer. Before the book was finished, they also were gone.

The original working title of the project was "The Evolution of an Enterprise." But as time passed, it became clear that this is not primarily a story about corporate structures, strategies and programs. Rather, it is a story of people—the people who struggled to build and maintain the early water companies, the people who acquired, developed and defended those companies during the century that followed.

There is no record of how many people were involved in creating the hundreds of local water systems that evolved into the present company. The number of laborers who laid the pipes and built the dams must have been well into the thousands; the number of entrepreneurs and managers who played a part at some point had to be in the hundreds. It was obvious that we could not include all or even a major fraction of those people in our story. The only feasible approach was to be selective: to focus on the careers and contributions of the leading figures of each era, relying as much as possible for the telling on their memories or the memories of those who were participants in or witnesses to their actions. Out of that approach emerged the title, *A Dynasty of Water.*

But this account would not be complete without taking note of others whose efforts have been important to the accomplishments of the leading figures. The names of a number who also contributed significantly to the growth of the present company are included in Appendix C.

Another group deserving particular notice are the members of the present management team, who have played a crucial role in completing the transformation of our company into a modern business organization. Among these is Loren Mellendorf, president of the Service Company. Not only is Loren considered one of the best financial men in the water utility industry today, but he also has emerged as a highly competent general manager. Reporting to him is a talented group of executives, including three senior vice presidents, Jim Barr, George Johnstone and Ed Limbach; and five regional vice presidents, Bill Cobb, Glen Thornburg, Jerry Smith, Dillard Edgemon and Bob Greaves. In March 1991, the Board of Directors selected Mr. Johnstone as president-elect to succeed me upon my retirement in 1992.

The senior group is supported by scores of highly educated and trained personnel—and an ever-increasing number of women and minorities, who keep the company growing. To the members of this new generation belongs not only major credit for our company's recent progress, but also responsibility for its future. Our history tomorrow will be written by these resourceful individuals.

Voorhees, New Jersey
May 1991

J. V. LaFrankie, President
American Water Works Company

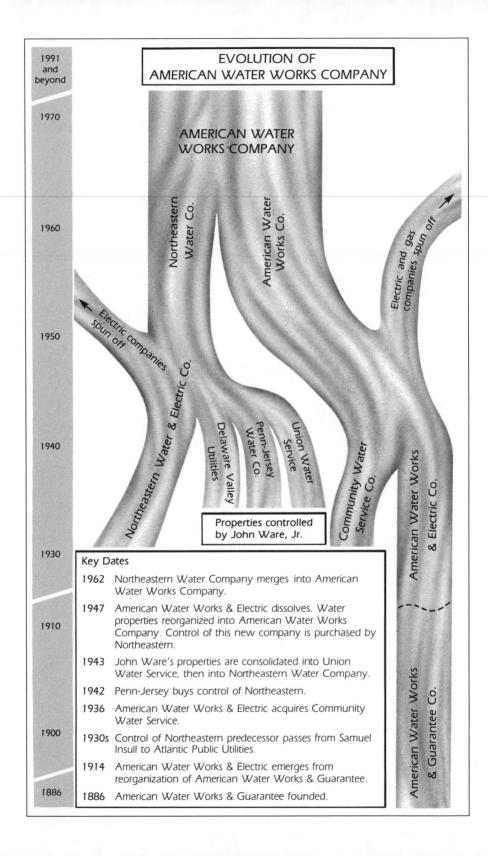

EVOLUTION OF
AMERICAN WATER WORKS COMPANY

1991 and beyond

1970

1960

1950

1940

1930

1910

1900

1886

AMERICAN WATER WORKS COMPANY

Northeastern Water Co.

American Water Works Co.

Electric and gas companies spun off

Electric companies spun off

Northeastern Water & Electric Co.

Delaware Valley Utilities

Penn-Jersey Water Co.

Union Water Service

Community Water Service Co.

American Water Works & Electric Co.

American Water Works & Guarantee Co.

Properties controlled by John Ware, Jr.

Key Dates

1962 Northeastern Water Company merges into American Water Works Company.

1947 American Water Works & Electric dissolves. Water properties reorganized into American Water Works Company. Control of this new company is purchased by Northeastern.

1943 John Ware's properties are consolidated into Union Water Service, then into Northeastern Water Company.

1942 Penn-Jersey buys control of Northeastern.

1936 American Water Works & Electric acquires Community Water Service.

1930s Control of Northeastern predecessor passes from Samuel Insull to Atlantic Public Utilities.

1914 American Water Works & Electric emerges from reorganization of American Water Works & Guarantee.

1886 American Water Works & Guarantee founded.

Preface

When the first settlers arrived on the North American continent, finding water for drinking, cooking or washing did not present much of a problem. If there was no stream or spring nearby, it was easy to dig a well. Later, as waves of emigration moved westward, water still did not usually pose a problem; nobody would think of starting a town or clearing a farm unless there was a good supply at hand.

It was only with the rapid industrialization of the second half of the nineteenth century that providing an adequate supply of usable water did become a problem. As people flocked to the rapidly growing cities to find jobs or make fortunes, nearby sources became polluted, spreading disease. As downtown buildings became taller and more numerous, fighting fires demanded something more effective than a bucket brigade or hand-operated pumper. In the more established cities of the East—Boston, New York, Philadelphia—when demand for water had outstripped local sources, municipal government took over the job of providing a better supply. Not so in many of the newer cities. Local government was weak and inexperienced; demand for municipal services of all sorts—sewers, streetlights, police, public transportation—was overwhelming, and resistance to new taxes was strong. Into this gap stepped an extraordinary group of people—entrepreneurs and organizers, managers and financiers, politicians, eccentrics, and now and then a scoundrel—who not only provided water to meet the needs of an expanding, evolving society, but played a significant role in laying the foundation for the growth of industrial America.

This is the story of those people. In particular it is the account of one succession of individuals who, over more than a century, created and developed a $2 billion enterprise, the American Water Works Company, which today is the largest investor-owned supplier of water in the United States.

Prologue:
The Impossible Dream

In the early summer of 1947 a man named John Ware, Jr., telephoned the prestigious Philadelphia law firm of Morgan, Lewis, & Bockius and asked for an appointment to see William Clark Mason, the senior partner.

The John Ware who arrived to keep the appointment hardly seemed to fit the elegant surroundings of Philadelphia's leading law firm. Plain in appearance, unassuming, almost diffident in manner, he lacked the presence, the elegant tailoring, of the lawyers at Morgan, Lewis. He looked more like a prosperous farmer who had put on his good suit for the occasion, or the proprietor of a small business—say an electrical shop—which in fact he once had been. On the basis of appearance alone, he might not have been able to see the senior partner of Philadelphia's most prestigious law firm; he likely would have been shuffled off to a junior associate.

Appearances notwithstanding, John Ware at this point in his career was not a man to be shuffled off. If his suits had more the look of Sears than Saville Row, it was because he preferred it that way; his net worth was such that he could have afforded the finest tailors of London or New York. Behind the quiet manner lay an ambition and drive that had no discernible limit. And his aw-shucks, country-boy style concealed—sometimes quite deliberately concealed—a near-photographic memory, a versatile and creative intellect, and compelling persuasiveness—when he elected to employ it. His name was not a household word in New York or Chicago, and it still is not today, but it carried enough clout in the Philadelphia of that time to open most doors, including this one.

An eighth-grade dropout who had founded a series of successful businesses, Ware had made a million dollars by the time he was 36, added another million within two years, and now owned a group of small water companies. He was by no means a heavy hitter, even by local standards; he was a relatively small millionaire, as those things are measured, and his money was "new money," which does not command the status and connections old money does, especially in Philadelphia. But small millionaires have been known to become big ones, and new money becomes old money with the passage of time. So Mr. Mason was more than willing to find out what was on John Ware's mind. After they had talked for a few minutes, Mason invited W. James MacIntosh, another partner in the firm and a specialist in public utility law, to join them.

What was on John Ware's mind became clear almost from the moment he sat down. He wanted to buy an entity called the American Water Works Company, which was then being created as a result of the breakup of a public utility empire, and was asking the help of Morgan, Lewis in accomplishing that purpose.

From the standpoint of prudent, sophisticated men like Mason and MacIntosh, this was not a practical proposition. A successful local operator like Ware could not hope to command the resources necessary to purchase a concern like American Water Works, which would be the largest enterprise of its kind in the United States. It was as though a promising player in Triple A ball had suddenly decided that he wanted to start in the World Series. Even with the most generous of credit, it seemed clear that John Ware could not come up with anything approaching the price of the new water company.

But if Ware was short of the money he needed to achieve a goal, that was not exactly news. It had been pretty much the story of his life. On a number of previous occasions it had appeared that he lacked the financing, or the expertise, or one resource or another needed to achieve a particular objective; it had not so far held him back. And if he resembled a successful minor league player determined to star in the big leagues, that was not far from the fact. John Ware was fond of saying that for every obstacle there had to be a way through it, or over it, or under it, or around it. So the issue he posed to the lawyers that day was not "Can I do it?" and certainly not "Should I do it?" but "Find a way to get it done."

After conferences with bankers it became clear that by mortgaging all his holdings, borrowing to the hilt, Ware might hope to command something in the range of $13 million in cash. But this would not be nearly enough to purchase the new American Water Works, whose price might run to $40 million or more. Even to raise the $13 million would result in what is called a "highly leveraged" situation: The interest charges on the loan would be so heavy that any downturn in the business could result in Ware's losing everything. Jim MacIntosh admitted 40 years later, "I thought it was too risky."

But John Ware would not be put off, so MacIntosh suggested that instead of attempting to buy the company outright, he consider bidding for a majority interest, something over 51 percent of the stock, and thus at least obtain voting control.

Ware did not take to that idea. Fifty-one percent was not his notion of control. One hundred percent was more to his taste. In any previous dealing he had never willingly accepted less than sole ownership. But MacIntosh quietly persisted; and Ware, notwithstanding his boundless ambition, his unrelenting optimism, and his characteristic refusal to compromise, was ultimately a realist. When it became clear that the opportunity would pass him by unless he was willing to settle for something less than 100 percent, he reluctantly agreed that the alternative approach should be explored.

The entity John Ware aspired to buy was at that time a division of the American Water Works & Electric Company. AWW&E was a holding company, a concern that does not buy or sell or manufacture anything, but exists simply to own the stocks of other companies. American Water Works & Electric, as its name suggests, owned a controlling interest in a number of electric utilities in western Pennsylvania, West Virginia, Maryland and Virginia, along with 80 or so local water companies supplying cities in the East, South and Midwest.

During the 1920s the public utility industry had boomed, and with it, the fortunes of American Water Works & Electric. After the stock market crash of 1929, many inflated, irresponsibly managed public utility empires collapsed, with losses to investors in the billions of dollars. To prevent any recurrence of the abuses that led to the crash, in 1935 the Congress passed the Public Utility Holding Company Act. One of the objectives of the new law was to simplify the structure of holding companies. Some of them had become so complex, with companies owning companies, which in turn owned other companies, that no one could understand, much less manage them successfully. It can be argued that it was not fair to American Water Works & Electric to be required to change its structure along with the others, since it had not been guilty of the abuses which were the targets of the Holding Company Act. But the rain falls alike on the just and the unjust, and the law was the law. So, to simplify its structure and comply with the law, the management of AWW&E decided to split the company in two. All the electric properties, comprising about 60 percent of the business, were to be consolidated under an existing subsidiary, the West Penn Electric Company. All the water properties, comprising the remaining 40 percent of the business, would be taken over by the new company, which would be called simply the American Water Works Company. Once these transactions were complete, the parent company, American Water Works & Electric, which would no longer serve a purpose, would pass out of existence. It was the new American Water Works Company that John Ware wanted to buy.

Another World

The principal officers of American Water Works & Electric and the soon-to-be-created American Water Works Company were everything John Ware was not. Ivy League–educated, privileged, born to affluence, they belonged to a world that Ware had seen only from the outside. The chairman of AWW&E, H. Hobart Porter, was one of the giants of the American business establishment. A member of the best clubs and the boards of other major corporations, he had long been a leading spokesman for the public utility industry. Scheduled to become president of the new company was Gilbert W. Chapman, a graduate of Yale and a leader in the cultural as well as the business life of New York City. Chapman's second in command was to be Lorenzo Semple, known socially as "Bunny," a product of the U.S. Naval Academy and the Harvard Business School. The families of all three were listed in the New York Social Register.

Once it was agreed that John Ware would bid for control rather than sole ownership of the new enterprise, Ware, Jim MacIntosh, and Ware's chief financial man, a strapping 35-year-old named John J. Barr, caught the train from Philadelphia to New York. There they began a series of conferences with William C. Langley, who was senior partner of his own investment banking firm, W. C. Langley and Company, and George D. Woods, chairman of First Boston Corporation, a major investment banker, in an effort to devise a strategy by means of which Ware could gain control of American Water Works.

In the past when Ware had purchased water properties, the transactions had been straightforward. He would buy all the common stock or all the assets of the entity in question. The American Water Works situation was more complicated. At the time of Ware's talks with the bankers, there was no company to buy, there was no stock to bid on, and the assets as such were not for sale. AWW&E's plan was, first, to create an issue of stock in the new corporation. Bids for the stock would then be solicited from teams of brokers called syndicates. The team with the highest bid would "underwrite" the entire issue. That is, it would buy all the shares at "wholesale," then, through its member firms, offer them at "retail" to investors around the country. The goal of Ware, Barr and MacIntosh was to persuade Langley and Woods to create a syndicate that would bid for the stock of the new company, and then, if

[5]

their bid should prove successful, to turn around and sell enough of the shares—more than 50 percent—to Ware to give him control.

As the conversations proceeded, however, Langley and Woods expressed doubts. The full plan for the financing was this: After the winning syndicate had committed itself to buy the new issue of stock, the shareholders of the old company, AWW&E, would be given an opportunity to buy shares. For each share of the stock of the old company, a stockholder would receive a warrant entitling him to buy one share in the new company, and he would be given 10 days to decide. This freedom to choose introduced a troubling unknown into the situation. Suppose the stockholders of the old company subscribed to more than 50 percent of the shares of the new company. That would prevent Ware from obtaining a majority of the shares. In that event, who would take the remaining shares off the syndicate's hands? Or suppose none or very few of the current shareholders exercised their subscription rights, and as a result the underwriters were saddled with virtually all the shares, more than John Ware could afford to buy. There would then be a risk of loss to the underwriters if the market was not interested in the remaining shares.

Ware, Barr and MacIntosh withdrew from the meeting, then returned and submitted this proposal: Even if the stockholders of the old company should take more than 50 percent of the new shares, Ware would guarantee to take any that were left, up to 40 percent of the total issue. Therefore, there would be few, if any, shares remaining to be sold in the general market, and the underwriters would be protected from loss. On the other hand, in the event the AWW&E stockholders took only a few shares of the new company, Ware would guarantee to take all remaining shares, up to 60 percent of the total issue. The result, again, would be relatively few shares remaining to be sold in the general market, and this also would protect the underwriters from loss.

For the underwriters, this was a sweet deal. They were guaranteed a sale—and a profit—regardless of the outcome. They quickly accepted.

However, it was still necessary to decide what price to bid, and this decision required a delicate balance. The price had to be high enough to have a reasonable chance of outbidding potential competition, but it could not be so high that John Ware would be unable to make good his guarantee to buy up to 60 percent of the total shares.

In a good market, stock in the new company would certainly command a price of somewhere around $10 a share, and perhaps substantially more. However, the economy was flat in late 1947, and profits were down. In this situation there was at least a reasonable prospect that the bidding might go no higher than $7.50 or $8. Finally it was agreed to submit a bid of $8 a share. Eight dollars was a gamble. A stronger bid by another syndicate would close Ware out. But if he won his gamble he would gain control of a very attractive property at a very reasonable price.

Now there was nothing left to do but wait.

While Ware and associates waited, it was a busy time at the headquarters of the old company, 50 Broad Street in New York, which was also to be the headquarters of the new company. The naming of Chapman and Semple as president and vice president of American Water Works had been announced. Remaining staff were being chosen. Offices were being assigned. Records were being set up.

The deadline for bids on the new stock issue, September 25, 1947, was approaching. But this was looked on more as a formality, a paper transaction, than a real event. Not a lot was changing. In the old company the water properties had been a division. Now they would comprise a separate corporation. But life would go on. The staff would be largely the same. Directors would be shared. Many of the stockholders would be the same.

As the deadline for the change approached, these reassuring words were printed in the AWW&E employee newsletter:

> It is not contemplated that the segregation of the water works properties under the new American Water Works Company will result in any marked changes in policy; nor is it contemplated that there will be any change in executive management personnel.

[7]

The Envelope, Please . . .

The bids were due by noon of the appointed day. After that hour had passed, the first reaction at 50 Broad Street was surprise: There was only one bid, from the syndicate headed by First Boston and W. C. Langley & Company. The second reaction was disappointment. The bid was only $8 a share, well below the amount the management had expected. The third reaction was astonishment, shock, outrage. Some interloper, some outsider, some upstart from Philadelphia had stolen—there was no other word for it—he had stolen the new company from its legitimate inheritors.

As one witness recalled four decades later, there were "long faces" at 50 Broad Street. And there was joy in Philadelphia. Through luck, shrewdness, boldness or some combination of the three, John Ware had won his gamble.

Of course, there was still the matter of the warrants that gave the stockholders of the old company 10 days in which to purchase shares of the new company. But now the writing was on the wall. The other investment bankers, who had decided not to bid, knew what they were doing. If they were not interested in bidding, it was because investors were not interested in buying—and the other firms did not have the advantage of Ware's no-lose guarantee. When the 10-day period had expired, on October 6, less than 800,000 shares had been subscribed, 29 percent of the total, leaving a full 60 percent, and firm control, for John Ware. Meanwhile, fewer than 300,000 shares, a bit over 10 percent, remained for the underwriters to dispose of.

The day after the matter of control was settled, William Langley and George Woods arranged a lunch for the principals on each side. This would no doubt have been an appropriate gesture under normal circumstances. Under these circumstances it was a bit cruel. Asking shocked and angry losers to break bread with triumphant winners was like arranging a charming little battlefield ceremony at which the defeated general presents the victor with his sword. But who knew, perhaps the two sides could find a way to work together.

[8]

Any illusion on that point was quickly dispelled. The meal had barely begun when Chapman and Semple announced, in effect, "Mr. Ware, we will have nothing to do with you or your company." Observed Jack Barr, Ware's financial man, "I never saw anybody write their obituary so fast."

Arrangements for the separation would take time, so Chapman and Semple agreed to stay on for a transition period. The following morning a meeting was called of the newly constituted board of directors, consisting of the senior managers of American, and John Ware's company, the Northeastern Water Company, with Ware presiding.* In an effort to break the ice, Ware told what he considered an amusing story. The representatives of Northeastern looked uncomfortable. The aristocratic managers of American sat in stony silence. Nobody laughed. "I felt sorry for him," commented one participant.

There was no cause to waste much pity on John Ware. In the decades that followed, his optimism was vindicated by the greatest economic boom the world had seen, to which his company contributed and from which it profited. For an initial investment of $13 million, he had gained control of assets of $183 million. At the end of his life, in 1963, the total had reached $500 million. By 1990 the company's assets totalled more than $1.8 billion, and it served a population of 5 million in 20 states.

Within a few years Ware was referred to in the press as "the Water King." In 1956 he received the Horatio Alger Award, putting him in the company of such men as Herbert Hoover, Bernard Baruch and Captain Eddie Rickenbacker, as one who had risen from humble beginnings to eminence. He spent the rest of his days shuttling between mansions in Pennsylvania and Florida and handsomely appointed apartments in Philadelphia and Pittsburgh, dreaming dreams, cutting deals and presiding over a blooming brood of grandchildren as patriarch of his clan.

---

*The actual purchaser of the controlling interest in American was the Northeastern Water Company. But since the sole owners of Northeastern were John Ware and his wife Clara, the reins of control were firmly in Ware's hands.

I

IN THE BEGINNING

ONE

The Chicken and the Egg

There has always been a chicken-and-egg relationship between population and water. A growing population demands an adequate supply; a reliable supply encourages population growth. Jericho in the Middle East, one of the world's oldest cities, owes its beginnings and its continued existence over 10,000 years to a gushing spring that to this day creates an oasis of sparkling green in a parched and baking desert.

The importance of organization—of finding a way to bring water from where it is available to where it is needed—has been evident for at least as long. The first great civilizations, on the Tigris, Euphrates and Nile rivers, are called "hydraulic civilizations" because they grew out of the increasingly complex organization required to channel water from the river to the lands beyond, to decide who was to receive it, when, and how much, and to resolve conflicting claims.

The first settlements on the North American continent were situated on water—at the mouth of a river or on the shore of a bay; their goods went to market by water; their grain was ground and their early factories were powered by water. But as long as the United States remained a largely rural society, finding water for drinking, washing or cooking did not present much of a problem. If there was no spring nearby, it was easy to drop a bucket into a river or lake, or divert a stream, or dig a well. It was only as cities began to develop, and small-scale, make-do methods no longer sufficed, that organized water systems began to appear.

The first public water system in North America was founded in Boston in 1652. New York City developed a system of municipal wells as early as 1660. When Benjamin Franklin died in 1790, he left a bequest to the city of Philadelphia to finance a municipal water supply; it began operating in 1801. But it was not until the latter part of the nineteenth century, with its rapid industrial development, that people began flocking to the new centers of trade and manufacturing and the need for organized water systems became acute.

The entities that eventually came to comprise the American Water Works Company originally consisted of more than a hundred small, local water companies, created for the most part between 1870 and the late 1920s. Over time these local systems were consolidated into a few dozen larger companies. These in turn were gathered into a handful of multisystem holding companies, which finally were combined through acquisition or merger to create the company in its present form.

As the Prologue notes, the immediate predecessor of the American Water Works Company was the American Water Works & Electric Company, which existed from 1914 until it was dissolved in 1947.

The predecessor of American Water Works & Electric, the American Water Works & Guarantee Company, existed from 1886 to 1913, and traced its roots to 1882. It is difficult, however, to follow the pedigrees of all the component companies of the American system. The Berwick Water Company, of Berwick, Pennsylvania, the oldest operating company in the system, was founded in 1818 but did not join American until 1936. The Huntington, West Virginia, water company was built by American Water Works & Guarantee in 1886 and has remained a part of the American system ever since. By contrast, the Pekin, Illinois, water company was also built in 1886, was acquired by American Water Works & Guarantee in 1887, was sold to other owners the following year, and did not again become part of the American system until it was purchased by the present company in 1981. The Lexington, Kentucky, water company, on the other hand, was founded in 1862 and remained independent until 1927, at which time it was acquired by a holding company called the Community Water Service Company, which became part of American Water Works & Electric in 1936.

Following are accounts of the early development of a number of the local water companies that are now part of American. The forces that brought these companies into being and the problems that beset their early days are not merely typical of hundreds of other companies started then or since. They reflect the essential realities—social, political, financial—of running a community water business to this day.

The Pride of Lexington

Like the ancient city of Jericho, the modern city of Lexington, Kentucky, owes its beginnings to the presence of a reliable source of good water. And like many modern cities, and doubtless some ancient ones as well, Lexington did not achieve an adequate public supply without considerable controversy.

The first explorers camped beside a spring-fed stream that provided water for drinking, cooking and bathing. The camp grew into a town, the town grew into a city, and for more than 100 years springs, wells and cisterns provided water. But as the city prospered in the years after the Civil War and a growing population placed increasing pressure on the existing water supply, periodic droughts caused recurrent shortages. In addition, over time, buildings became so large that the water in cisterns nearby was not enough to put out fires. Also, as houses clustered together and their outdoor privies polluted wells, outbreaks of typhoid and cholera became common.

Both local newspapers, the *Gazette* and the *Press*, along with many leading citizens, had called for some time for the creation of a public water supply. But as late as 1882 a bill to create a municipal water works was turned down by the voters. Local politicians, among them a Dennis Mulligan, opposed the idea. They argued that the higher taxes required to build and operate a municipal system would drive business away. "Which would do more to encourage the growth of manufactures, and the increase of a substantial population," they inquired, "water works and heavy taxation, or no water works and light taxation?" In addition, people at that time did not understand the connection between water and disease. Dennis Mulligan claimed that typhoid was caused by "overheated young people who cooled off at open windows or on the pavement."

The factor that did most to settle the argument was the need for fire protection. In 1879 the Phoenix Hotel burned; in 1881 seventeen stores were destroyed by fire; in 1883 fire gutted the barn and stables of the street railway, killing the mules and destroying the cars.

The creation of the Lexington Water Company was largely the result of the efforts of one man, Gilbert Hinds King. When the proposal to form a municipally owned system failed in 1882, King and two other Lexingtonians, General William Preston and Colonel R.H.S. Thompson, went to the state legislature and obtained a charter to create a private water system, the Lexington Hydraulic and Manufacturing Company. (There is no evidence that the company ever manufactured anything. The "Manufacturing" in the title was perhaps included to impress potential investors.)

This did not end the debate. A number of prominent citizens criticized the project, claiming that the company's proposed reservoir would be nothing more than a stagnant pool. As a result, the company was unable to obtain local financing, and King had to travel out of town to sell his bonds. The need for a water system became a major issue in the mayoral race of 1883. However, Dennis Mulligan, who opposed the water works, was defeated by Claude Johnson, who favored it.

On December 6, 1883, the city council under Mayor Johnson adopted an ordinance permitting private construction of a water works, and within a week Mayor Johnson had signed a contract granting the Lexington Hydraulic and Manufacturing Company the privilege of constructing and maintaining a water works to supply Lexington with "pure and wholesome water for public and private use."

Even this action did not end the controversy. Local residents complained that convict labor was being used to dig the reservoir. This was a common practice at the time, but people were concerned about the presence of a camp of "sullen and dangerous convicts" just beyond the city limits. Others laughed at the "duck pond" that would be created and claimed its limestone base would never hold water.

As a result of various delays, the charter expired and had to be renewed before construction could begin. However, General Preston, on whose farm the reservoir was to be built, could not be found to sign the papers. Some of the convicts escaped, part of the camp was set on fire, and according to press reports, the city was "in a terror."

Despite these problems, by October 1884 the reservoir was completed. However, the long-fought battle was not without a price. A few weeks later Gilbert Hinds King became critically ill, exhausted by the long effort. Three days later he was dead. Ironically, his funeral arrangements were complicated by the fact that the street where he lived had been torn up for the laying of water mains.

The system was put into operation in January 1885, with a public demonstration, a "Programme of Fire Streams," in the center of town, followed by a dedication at the water works by General Preston. According to a later account,

> With his fine, soldierly figure silhouetted against the water, the old general drew cheers and laughter when he said that they had come to see a duck pond which—it had been predicted—would never hold water and they all wanted to look at the geese who had constructed it. During a burst of rapturous applause, the old gentleman tapped a bottle of Mumm's Extra Dry, drank a toast to the new lake, then dashed some of the Champagne across the sparkling waters below him.

A telegram from the financiers was also read:

Bluegrass, the pride of Kentucky;
Lexington, the pride of the Bluegrass;
may our water works be the pride of Lexington.

The need for fire protection was decisive in bringing water systems to other cities as well. In Muncie, Indiana, as the city outgrew the ability of cisterns in the downtown area to supply water, the members of the volunteer fire department could often do nothing but stand and watch a building burn. After the municipal water system was installed in 1885, a significant dividend was the lowering of fire insurance rates. In Milton, Pennsylvania, on May 15, 1880, a disastrous fire destroyed 640 buildings in 9½ hours, leaving a majority of the population of 4,000 homeless and penniless. As soon as the town had been rebuilt, in 1883, the Milton Water Company was incorporated, primarily to prevent another major fire.

In Washington, New Jersey, on January 2, 1880, the local newspaper, the Washington *Star*, called for the creation of a water company, declaring, with an optimism typical of the times, that "Washington seems to be destined to become a large and important town," but that fire protection would be necessary to support continued growth. Because of the cost of installing a system, however, nothing was done. Then in September 1881, Washington's largest industry, the Beatty Organ Factory, was destroyed by fire. Daniel F. Beatty, owner of the factory and mayor of the town, announced that he would rebuild the factory if the community built a water system to provide fire protection. At a public meeting a few days later, half of the estimated $50,000 required to build a system was immediately subscribed.

"Hurrah for Donahue"

Construction of a local water system depended in nearly every case on effective local leadership: a mayor, a banker, a businessman, a judge. In Davenport, Iowa, efforts to construct a municipal water system failed four times in 15 years because restrictions in the city's charter made it impossible to borrow or issue bonds. Then Michael Donahue, a former mayor, owner of a machine shop and foundry, and according to the local press "one of the most progressive and patriotic of citizens," agreed to invest $500,000 of his own money in building a system, providing the city would give him a 25-year franchise to operate it. This the city fathers were happy to do, granting the franchise in 1872. Donahue, with a keen sense of community relations, announced that he would manufacture the fire hydrants, special castings for street mains, and engines for the pumps, and "do all the work possible" in his own plant "in order to give Davenport men employment."

The water works needed a chief engineer, but in Davenport as in most other cities of that time, there was no one who had any experience along that line. This problem did not deter Donahue. He approached T. N. Hooper, who ran a blacksmith's shop across the Mississippi River in Rock Island, Illinois. Hooper, "tho regarded as a good mechanic, had no knowledge of water works." When invited by Donahue to take the position of chief engineer, Hooper replied, "Donahue, I don't know anything about water works," to which Donahue responded, "Neither do I, Hooper."

Hooper took the job, later became superintendent of the system, then vice president, and finally, with the benefit of extended on-the-job training, president of the company.

Service began in January 1874, to be greeted by an enthusiastic editorial in the Davenport *Democrat and Leader*. Less than two months later, on March 2, 1874, fire broke out in the boiler room of Priester & Moeller's cigar box and mold factory, and the new water system received its first test. It passed brilliantly, as reported by the Davenport *Gazette*:

> Before the alarm was given, the flames had burst from the roof. Rescue Engine Company was soon on the ground with their hose, and then occurred the
>
> FIRST FIRE TEST
>
> of the water works. They attached their hose to the hydrant at Scott and Fifth, and soon a most powerful stream was pouring into the

[19]

burning building. This was soon followed by another stream laid by the same company from Fifth and Ripley streets, which was as full of fury as the first stream. All danger was past now, and in fifteen minutes more, the fire was totally extinguished.

THE BUILDING

in which the fire occurred was of stone, was one story in height, and built as a wing to the factory. . . . It contained the boiler and engine of the factory. . . .

THE LOSS

was comparatively slight—not exceeding $1400, for doubtless the boiler is good yet, and the engine can be repaired. So for the service the works proved a grand success at the first trial. . . .

Despite the conspicuous service Michael Donahue had performed by personally financing and constructing a water works, and the clear benefit this provided in the way of fire protection, and for all his skill at community relations and the enthusiastic support he continued to receive from the press, his water works was unable to attract enough customers to make the venture profitable. Furthermore, Donahue himself was continuously harassed by his neighbors with complaints about the service and arguments about water charges, as well as by the slow payment of bills.

Perhaps in an effort to cultivate public support and generate additional business, in June 1875 Donahue arranged a public display of the capabilities of his water works, to be greeted with the usual outpouring of journalistic enthusiasm. In spite of Donahue's efforts, however, from the time the company was founded in 1874 until his death in 1884, "patronage was so slight," in the words of a later newspaper account, "that the income was insufficient to maintain [the company]. Had it been bonded, it would surely have gone into the hands of the bondholders."

After Donahue died, a new management led by his son, Colonel James P. Donahue, "made a thorough investigation of the water supply question and concluded that the lack of patronage was due to the unfitness of the water during the rainy seasons." As a result of the study, a "fine system of filters" was installed, and at long last enough customers signed up to put the business in the black.

HURRAH FOR DONAHUE!

The Water Works Exhibition on Saturday Astonishes Everybody

Probably never since the water works have been established here was there such a practical and thorough test of their capacity, power, and effectiveness, as was given on Saturday last, in the presence of the 1,300 firemen from Illinois, Nebraska, and Iowa. It was a test which not only astonished while it delighted our visitors, but it was a marvel of surprise even to our own citizens, who had not prepared themselves for any such monstrous display. Every one here knew Donahue, knew what his system of water works has done for our city, and were ready and willing to swear that it was the best known system in the world— but they were hardly prepared to believe our visitors could be made to *believe just as we do in regard to it!* But Saturday's test convinced them, and they all go home praising and praying for the Donahue system in their several cities.

There were thirteen streams playing at one time; two from Brady and Fifth, two from Brady and Third, three from Brady and Second, two from Brady and 4th, one from Brady and Front, and three on Second, between Perry and Main, and the height and length these several streams were thrown, was indeed a surprise to all. Far above the roofs of the highest buildings, did the water ascend, and with only 90 pounds of pressure at the water works, part of the time only 80 pounds. It would be almost impossible to measure the height to which these streams reached, but suffice it to say, it appeared fifty and sixty feet above the highest five story buildings in the city. The nozzles used were from 1 to 1¼ inch. The exhibition was witnessed by the visiting Mayors and aldermen, who expressed themselves so well pleased, that they said "No system for us when we get water works, but the Donahue." Hurrah for the Davenport Water Works, and hurrah for M. Donahue, its father, and the firemen's friend!

Davenport *Democrat and Leader,* June 21, 1875

A Matter of Taste

Providing fire protection was often the immediate objective in starting a water company. However, as the example of Davenport demonstrates, the quality of the water provided—whether it tasted good—was the key to public acceptance, adequate sales and ultimate financial success. In Berwick, Pennsylvania, the citizens were looking for an alternative to the water of the Susquehanna River. So in 1818, 60 residents, including Evan Owen, the founder of the town, organized the Berwick Water Company to provide a supply from a tributary of Briar Creek. In Muncie, Indiana, the everyday source for the local system was deep wells, which provided water of more than acceptable quality. However, when there was a fire the much less palatable water of the White River was pumped directly into the system. As a result, many citizens continued to rely on private wells for drinking water, and sales did not reach a profitable level until this practice was discontinued.

In Milton, Pennsylvania, the White Deer Mountain Water Company, established in 1899, drew its water from White Deer Creek. In the period 1883 to 1900, nine other water companies were formed in the area. However, the appeal of the "mountain water" from White Deer was so great that by 1928 all the other companies had sold out to White Deer, including the original Milton Water Company, started after the disastrous fire of 1880.*

How Quickly They Forget

Although the early water companies performed an essential public service, one the cities themselves would have provided if they could have afforded it—or mobilized the votes to do it—once a private

---

*Interestingly, as cities continued to grow and demand for water increased, towns like Berwick and Muncie found they could no longer rely on wells or springs or mountain streams and had to go to the river for an adequate supply. Fortunately, with improved methods of filtration, it became possible to bring the quality of river water up to acceptable levels.

"This Precious Hydrant"

Fire protection was often the first consideration in starting a water company, and the quality of the water supplied the key to its long-term survival and profitability. But convenience was also a factor, as illustrated by the following from the September 14, 1883, issue of the *Weekly Journal* of Philipsburg, Pennsylvania:

Our man about town thinks, for modern improvements, Philipsburg takes the lead of any other town of its size in the State of Pennsylvania. In the year 1881 a certain class of enterprising individuals imagined that a water company organized in Philipsburg would soon become a paying institution, and after very little thought or consideration on the part of the parties concerned, it was finally decided to organize a stock company whereby our little city should be supplied with cool and sparkling water brought from the everflowing Cold Stream Dam, and not two months later the water works was in a flourishing condition, while everybody seemed well pleased with the freshness of the water, and it was not long until the greater portion of our property holders had the water run into their homes.

At the time if you have a personal interview with such and simply ask them how they are pleased with their water works, the verdict will be, "Indeed we could not possibly do without a hydrant in our homes." Another will say "Away with the old-fashioned mode of getting water when we have such an excellent system."

If you don't believe the above, for an illustration, suppose the water is shut off for a couple of hours, especially at mealtime, and you are about the kitchen where the women folks are busily engaged preparatory to getting you something to eat, and if she happens to be a woman addicted to ill humor, and the like, her angry passions will get the best of her, and with a rip, she will say "get out of my way," fling the coal shovel, the stove pipe takes a tumble, bing! bang! goes the door, and a tear-up in general follows, and calmly wanting to know what the fuss is about, you ask her, when she wildly with a dark and angry frown overshadowing her once-in-awhile sweet countenance, exclaims, "'What's the matter?' you ask! Nough! Here it is suppertime and there is no water, confound it!"

A few minutes after the storm, calmness reigns supreme. The water is again in operation with all its powerful force. The woman's temper changes again and she becomes as gentle as a girl "just sweet 16," and with a beautiful smile majestically playing around her lips, she lovingly exclaims "Oh husband how glad I am! Indeed I couldn't do without this precious hydrant for all the wells in town."

company was in business, many citizens, as the Davenport *Gazette* complained in January 1875, "seemed to act as if the water works were a grinding monopoly, endeavoring to invade their rights, instead of realizing that it is something for which they should be grateful."

These sentiments were echoed by William Snowden, the first president of the Haddonfield Water Company in New Jersey. In offering his resignation in 1890, he wrote, "I can assure you it gives me great pleasure to get rid of the troubles and annoyance that I have been subjected to by the importunities of neighbors and friends."

In short, the customers did as water customers have always done. They took excellent service for granted and regarded any shortfall as the violation of a birthright.

Customer complaints translate into votes. Thus companies which at first were encouraged and welcomed by local politicians were later opposed or ignored. (There was doubtless also an element of "turfing" in this situation. A private company providing a public service is a separate power center and revenue source not subject to the control of city hall. And in politics, especially municipal politics, whatever cannot be controlled is likely to be opposed, and, if possible, eliminated.)

A lack of public-private cooperation was demonstrated more than once in the matter of municipal sewage disposal. Ordinarily, a water system would be built when a city was young. When the river was to be the source of supply, the logical and least expensive thing to do was to run a pipeline directly to the river. Years later, as the city continued to grow and outdoor privies and septic tanks were no longer adequate for sewage disposal, it would become necessary to install a municipal sewage system. Here also, the logical and least expensive thing to do, and the way to save tax dollars, would be to run a sewer line directly to the river. But in a number of instances the sewage outlet was upstream from the water intake—not a desirable situation. In Clinton, Iowa; Huntington, West Virginia; and Chattanooga, Tennessee, that arrangement is exactly what occurred.

In the case of Clinton, by the time the sewer system was built, the water company had drilled wells that provided an adequate supply, so the river intake was no longer needed. But a report by a consulting engineer commented, "It seems unfortunate that the city . . . should have pursued such a shortsighted policy and have by its own act added to the contamination of the Mississippi River water and to the popular prejudice against the use of this water for water supply purposes."

In Huntington, West Virginia, after the city had installed its sewage outlet above the water company intake, the state Department of Health ordered the intake moved upstream. Since the Huntington Water Company was owned by the American Water Works & Guarantee Company, which had ample financing, it had no trouble finding the money needed to comply.

The Chattanooga Water Company was not so lucky. In the 1880s, when the city began to release raw sewage into the Tennessee River above its intake, it lacked the money to relocate the intake. When the company was offered for sale in 1887, the purchaser was the same American Water Works & Guarantee Company, which then provided funds to move the intake.

The Franchise Problem

But municipal hostility or indifference to the water company was expressed in more than matters of sewage. When a private company agreed to build a water system, it was usually given a franchise that granted it the exclusive right to supply water to the city for a specified period of time, usually 20 to 30 years. The income assured by the franchise made it possible for the company, through the sale of bonds or stock, to raise the capital needed to build the system. However, when a franchise expired, the company had to obtain a renewal in order to raise the money needed not only to repay its original bonds, but also to continue expanding the system and replacing equipment. But 20 or 30 years is a long time, and upon the expiration of a franchise, municipal authorities were often not as eager to renew it as they had been to grant it in the first place. In Clinton, Iowa, the same city on the Mississippi River whose government put the sewage outlet above the water intake, the water company franchise expired on April 1, 1914. A contract for a new franchise was presented to the city at that time, but by April 1917, three years later, no action had been taken. The same consulting engineer (hired by the company) who complained about the short-sightedness of the authorities in pumping sewage into the river, commented:

> When a city has elected to delegate the duties which it is bound to exercise, of performing a necessary public service, to a private company . . . good faith demands not only that the company shall perform its duties to the city . . . but that the city and its citizens shall exercise their responsibilities in good faith. . . . While there are occasionally those who would take any undue advantage which they conceive can be taken on the expiration of a franchise, the great majority of thinking people in any community are fair minded and desire what is right, for the desire of a square deal is a fundamental characteristic of a majority of the American people.
>
> The city and the company should get together, either through negotiations or through an expert board, and agree on an equitable basis for the adjustment of these matters.

At long last, in 1923, after a nine-year delay, the city and the company did get together, and the franchise was renewed.

The relationship between the Pekin Water Works Company of Pekin, Illinois, and the municipal government was a classic example of troubled relations between a company and a city. The water plant and distribution system were built in 1886. The following year, however, the municipal authorities complained that the well supplying the system had not been drilled deep enough to tap a "second vein" of water, thus violating a provision of the franchise. A well-digging firm from Chicago was hired to investigate the matter and found that the "second vein" was a myth and the company's wells were located on "a very desirable bed of water-washed gravel." But perhaps because the city lost that argument, the next year, when the water company installed the ice house extension on which three new fire hydrants were set, the city refused to pay for the additional service. (Cities normally pay an annual fee to the water company for fire protection, based on the number of hydrants in the system.)

Two years later, a protracted agitation began for the purchase of the water works by the city. Ten years after that, in 1899, the state legislature passed a law making such a purchase possible, and the proposition was then put to a vote. It did not receive the majority needed to pass, but as a result of the ill will generated during the campaign, the city decided not to authorize any more cast-iron pipe for service extensions, regardless of the demand for water or the needs of the population. So for eight years, from 1901 to 1909, the period of Pekin's greatest growth, no cast iron pipe was laid. The company met demands for new service by installing makeshift extensions of galvanized pipe, which later had to be replaced at considerable expense.

In 1906 the water company's franchise expired. The company had applied for a renewal several years earlier, but meanwhile a group of promoters had asked the city to grant them a franchise to build a competing system. The competing franchise was never granted, but as long as the application was pending, nothing was done about the company's application for a new franchise.

In April 1911, five years after the original franchise had expired, the city granted a new one, to run for 20 years. But in order to obtain the new franchise the company had to agree to forgive 23 years of accrued charges on the fire hydrants on the ice house extension, for which the city still refused to pay. Then a few weeks after the new franchise was granted, the city adopted the commission form of government, and as soon as the new officials took office they announced that the franchise voted by the old city council would have to be approved by the voters before it would be effective. An election was held for that purpose on February 6, 1912, and the franchise was not ratified, so the matter dragged on for another three years. Finally, in 1915, after nine years' delay, a new 20-year franchise was granted.

The Pressure of Growth

Regardless of all other problems, and often compounding them, the principal challenge faced by the struggling companies was growth—a relentless expansion of population and industry that resulted in a continuing increase in the demand for water. In some cases managements provided for future needs. For example, when the Alexandria, Virginia, water company was built in 1850, its founders installed enough capacity to supply a town of 20,000 people, although the population at that time was only 10,000. In most cases, however, at the dedication of a new water company the management and the local press would declare in the most glowing terms that the system was the best of its kind to be found anywhere and could easily supply the city's requirements for the indefinite future. But in a few years there would be a pressing need for extension of mains, expansion of reservoirs, replacement or addition of pumps, and, as time passed and quality and safety problems grew, for filtration and chlorination.

In the late nineteenth century it was difficult, under the best of circumstances, to obtain the capital needed for expansion from dubious investors, unfamiliar with the growing cities of the South and Midwest, who sometimes had been burned by previous experience. When municipal authorities refused to approve the renewal of a franchise or to authorize a needed increase in rates, the difficult became impossible. As a result, the original investors would often try to sell the company to the city. Nearly as often, the citizens would go to the polls and refuse to take on the added tax burden. Or the company might be offered for sale to other local investors or to entrepreneurs from Chicago or the East. In some cases new owners succeeded where earlier ones had failed. More often, no acceptable bid was received, or the new owners, after a few years of similar difficulties, were themselves looking for a buyer to take the white elephant off their hands.

This situation was unacceptable to all concerned—to customers, to investors, to management. But it was a situation for which—in the best free enterprise tradition—the marketplace provided a solution. In the 1870s and 1880s the need for water systems to supply the mushrooming cities was so acute that municipalities ran advertisements in the newspapers asking for bids to build them. In response to this demand, some contractors began to specialize in the construction of water systems. Once a system was built, the builder would sometimes continue to own it. In other cases, ownership would remain with the city or with local investors, but the builder would be given a contract to manage it. In still other cases, ownership and management would be turned over to local people, but after the company got into trouble—as it often did—the original builder would step in and buy it back.

One organization that developed a specialty of building and managing water companies was a partnership called Kuhn Brothers & Company, founded in 1882 in Connellsville, Pennsylvania. The partners were two brothers, James S. Kuhn and W. S. Kuhn, along with Edmund C. Converse, who was also affiliated with the National Tube Works. (There was an obvious benefit both ways for a builder of water systems to have a connection with a pipe manufacturer.)

In its early years the Kuhn Brothers firm built a number of private water systems and acquired others by purchase. However, the partners found, as others were finding, that it was extremely difficult to market the securities of small, independent water companies. So in 1886 they organized the American Water Works & Guarantee Company in McKeesport, Pennsylvania. AWW&G not only continued to build and purchase water systems, but also guaranteed the payment of principal and interest on their bonds. As the company established a reputation for financial strength and for sound management of the local systems, the bonds now found a ready market. Thus American Water Works & Guarantee became one of the first, if not the first, public utility holding companies in the United States.

Within two years, AWW&G owned water companies in a total of 18 communities located as far west as Nebraska and as far south as Birmingham and Chattanooga. To oversee the management of these companies it developed a centralized staff of engineers and operators who specialized in water works construction and operation. This provided to the individual companies a level of expertise which, if they had remained under independent ownership, they would have found prohibitively expensive, if it had been available at all.

In the beginning it had been necessary for companies like AWW&G to buy all the assets of the companies they acquired. However, in 1889 the state of New Jersey modified its laws to permit a corporation headquartered there to own stock in other corporations. This change made it possible for one company to control another by owning no more than 51 percent of its voting stock. That in turn meant that with a given amount of capital, a company could control more subsidiaries than before, thereby paving the way for the enormous development of public utility holding companies that followed. So in 1891, American Water Works & Guarantee moved its headquarters to New Jersey to take advantage of the new law.

As time passed, a number of serious charges were leveled against public utility holding companies; many of the charges were true. In the 1920s and 1930s holding companies as a group contributed a dark chapter to American business history. But it needs to be borne in mind that a holding company is merely a device, and a device that can serve a useful purpose: the consolidation of a great many small, nonviable companies into a larger, more viable entity. Like any other device, it could be—and was—abused. But the device itself was neither good nor evil.

Wider Horizons

For the balance of the 1890s and well into the next decade, AWW&G continued to buy and manage local water companies. Beginning in about 1909, however, its horizons began to widen. In the late nineteenth and early twentieth centuries, while privately owned water companies were springing up everywhere, the same economic and social forces were creating the need for other municipal services. Because growing cities required public transportation, local street railways were founded, at first using horse-drawn cars. Gas companies were also started to provide gas (created initially by burning coal or coke) for lighting and cooking. In time, gaslights were replaced with electric lighting, and horse-drawn cars with electrically powered trolleys, so now there was increasing demand for electricity. This was sometimes provided by gas companies that went into the electric generating business, sometimes by street railways that decided to produce their own power, and sometimes by water companies, using streams and dams to generate electricity.

But small, local transportation and electric utilities suffered from the same problems as small, local water companies: inadequate financing and a lack of competent, experienced management. Therefore, in transportation and electricity as in water utilities, a process of consolidation began.

In southwestern Pennsylvania in 1900 a number of small, isolated street railway systems were merged under the name of the Pittsburgh, McKeesport and Connellsville Railway Company. In connection with a number of these properties, electric light and power were provided, although in a limited way. Then in 1904, in order to promote the expansion of the interurban railway system and to increase the supply of dependable power, a new entity, the West Penn Railways Company, was organized. West Penn then proceeded to acquire all the properties of the Pittsburgh, McKeesport and Connellsville Railway Company.

However, the expanding demand for interurban railroad service and the increasing use of electric power constantly required large sums for additional plant and equipment, and, as always, new capital was hard to come by. In 1910 the American Water Works & Guarantee Company stepped in and acquired control of West Penn Railways. Part of the purchase agreement was an understanding that the Guarantee Company would provide money for continuing expansion.

Soon after that, AWW&G became interested in the possibility of hydroelectric power development in the territory adjacent to its holdings, and acquired a large amount of land for that purpose. In 1911 it created the Black River Water and Power Company, which in 1912 changed its name to the West Penn Traction and Water Power Company. West Penn Traction and Water Power then took control of West Penn Railways, along with an electric company which AWW&G already owned.

Between 1909 and 1913 the Guarantee Company also expanded its activities into nonutility fields. It acquired a controlling interest in the United Coal Company, whose mines provided fuel for its electric generators in Pennsylvania and Virginia. It also became involved in so-called "Carey Act" irrigation projects in Idaho and California.

The Carey Act, passed in 1894 and named for Senator Joseph M. Carey of Wyoming, provided for transfer to the states of federally owned lands in the West on the condition that they be irrigated and then sold to settlers for 50 cents an acre, plus the cost of water rights. The prospect of rapid development of thousands of acres of rich soil created a land-boom mentality, and corporations and individuals rushed to share in the promise of new wealth. The Guarantee Company invested heavily in a number of irrigation projects in southern Idaho, in hydroelectric properties to supply the power to operate the projects, and in a railroad to help with their development. It also made substantial commitments to irrigation projects in California.

By early 1913, these were the holdings of American Water Works & Guarantee: There were 30 water and electric lighting companies serving 80 municipalities in 14 states. There was the West Penn Traction Company, operating one of the largest interurban railway systems in the country and supplying electric power to 125 communities in three states. There was the Pittsburgh Coal Company, the largest producer of bituminous coal in the United States, operating more than 50 mines in the Pittsburgh area. And there were major irrigation, transportation and electric generating properties in Idaho and California, along with a sales office in San Francisco and a hotel in the Sacramento Valley to house prospective buyers of the newly irrigated land.

The annual report of the company for 1913, published in June of that year, reflected its size and diversity, its aggressive program of diversification, and its mood of buoyant optimism. The cover of the report was embossed in three colors on richly textured paper. It was illustrated by more than 100 dramatic photographs, along with six full-page maps. It was, by the standards of the time, probably the most elegant report ever published by a company bearing the American Water Works name.

The financial picture was glowing. Net earnings for the fiscal year were $1,704,500, an increase of 36 percent over the previous year, and 14 percent above the company's own forecast of a year earlier. Profits for the following year, 1914, were projected at better than $2 million, a further gain of 17 percent. The report suggested that this trend

> indicates the remarkable growth and development of the towns, cities and communities in which your company's subsidiaries conduct their operations.
>
> A consistent policy of providing for present requirements and future growth has been adhered to. All properties are substantially built and equipped to more than fulfill contract obligations. Relations with consumers are harmonious, as attested by the high praise given . . . by commercial clubs and civic organizations. A steady expansion in population and the character of the services rendered . . . practically assures a rising ratio of earnings from year to year, which is an unusually attractive feature as bearing on permanency of income from investment securities.

The report waxed particularly eloquent about the company's irrigation projects:

> Prosperous and flourishing cities and towns have arisen like magic. Excellent schools, churches of different denominations, places of amusement abound in what was recently only a desert waste. . . . The optimistic spirit of the people is justified by present conditions and future prospects.

There was only one cloud on this otherwise bright horizon. American Water Works & Guarantee had not only invested $10 million of its own resources in the irrigation projects, but following the practice in its other businesses, it had also guaranteed principal and interest payments on some $20 million of irrigation bonds, assuming that these obligations would be covered by payments from the settlers who purchased the land. However, the payments fell short of expectations. As a result the Guarantee Company was unable to meet its obligations on the bonds. On July 7, 1913, *only 26 days* after its glowingly optimistic report had been released, the United States District Court for the Western District of Pennsylvania, upon petition of a group of no-doubt-angry investors, put American Water Works & Guarantee Company into the hands of receivers. After a year-long investigation, in April 1914 a new company, called the American Water Works & Electric Company, was created under entirely new management, and American Water Works & Guarantee was no more.

It is difficult to believe the management of AWW&G did not know their actual financial condition at the time their optimistic report was issued. In fact, it is reasonable to assume they did know, and that their colorful prose represented an all-too-human attempt to deny reality, as well as a last-ditch effort to rescue a deteriorating situation. Such a report, issued today, might well land its issuer in jail, and helps explain the laws for the protection of investors that were passed a few years later.

In any case, the downfall of AWW&G was brought about by a mistake made by many companies then and since: a failure to understand the real nature of the business they were in. A common denominator between the municipal water business and the irrigation and land reclamation business was water, and both businesses employ dams and pumps and pipes. Therefore, the management of AWW&G assumed that a company experienced in developing and managing a system of small and stable municipal water companies over time would be competent to manage large and risky irrigation projects being built in a hurry.

As the outcome demonstrated, this assumption was by no means valid.

Second Time Around

As soon as it became clear that American Water Works & Guarantee would be unable to meet its obligations—perhaps even before its falsely optimistic report was issued—those with a financial stake in the company got busy. A Stockholders' Protective Committee was formed, along with committees representing bondholders, banks, and other creditors. One of the first actions these groups agreed on was to commission the New York engineering firm of Sanderson and Porter to make a detailed analysis of the company's railroad and electric utility holdings. One of the principals in the firm was H. Hobart Porter. After the study was completed and the decision had been made to replace the previous management and organize an entirely new company, the job of president and chief executive of the new company was offered to Porter, and he accepted. It was a good choice. Over the next two decades Porter presided over an era of expansion and growth in which the new company, American Water Works & Electric, became one of the leading public utility holding companies in the United States.

H. Hobart Porter was an aristocrat of American business. Born in New York City in 1865—just as American industry was entering its period of rapid growth—he graduated from Columbia University with a degree in mining engineering in 1886, the same year American Water Works & Guarantee was incorporated. After a few years as a young engineer on mining projects in Mexico and the southwestern United States, he returned to the East and went to work for the Westinghouse Electric and Manufacturing Company as an engineering salesman. That was either a very wise choice or a very lucky one, because just at that moment the demand for electric power was beginning to boom. In 1896, ten years after he left Columbia, Porter joined another engineer, E. N. Sanderson, to form the consulting firm of Sanderson and Porter, which soon gained a reputation for its work in the field of electric utilities. This led Porter in 1914 to the presidency of American Water Works & Electric.

It is worth noting that mining engineering—providing the resources to supply the needs of a rapidly industrializing nation—was a popular field of study for an ambitious young man in the 1880s and 1890s. A case in point was a young fellow named Herbert Clark Hoover, who graduated from Stanford University in 1895 with a degree in mining engineering. Like Porter, Hoover spent his first few years after graduation working on mining projects in the Southwest. Then, like Porter, he also moved on. Unlike Porter, he did not go east but headed further west, to Australia and then to China. Later he became secretary of commerce and president of the United States.

As American Water Works & Electric emerged to prominence on the American business scene, so did H. Hobart Porter. He came to hobnob with the rich and powerful of his generation. He joined the best clubs and became a director of banks, insurance companies and mercantile concerns—whose leaders in turn became directors of his company: The membership of his board read like a Who's Who of the American business establishment. He hunted big game in Africa, like Teddy Roosevelt, to be interviewed on his return by the New York City newspapers.

However, when Porter became president of the newly formed American Water Works & Electric in 1914, all of that lay in the future, and the future at that point not only was clouded but from all indications would be brief. In fact, Porter's role, as initially conceived, was more that of an undertaker to bury the past than an architect to build for the future. He was expected to preside over a "caretaker government" to protect the company's assets until they could be sold off in a gradual and orderly way, thereby realizing the best price and reducing as much as possible the loss to investors

[36]

and creditors. (Because of the imminence of World War I, conditions in the financial markets were too disorganized in 1914 to permit an orderly liquidation.)

Between April 1914 and April 1917, as the American economy was stimulated by wartime demand from Europe, the company's situation improved to a point where it could begin to pay off the accumulated dividends on its first preferred stock. From 1917 through 1921, under the impact of war-induced inflation and the recession of 1920, earnings declined again, although the company was able to continue paying dividends on the first preferred. By 1922, however, as the economic boom of the 1920s began to gather momentum, the outlook had improved to the point where the directors gave up the idea of liquidating the company, and instead began a program of renewed expansion.

Once the decision had been made to expand the business, the management moved aggressively. In less than two years it acquired six major electric utility properties, which it proceeded to develop further through construction, consolidation and acquisition. It moved more gradually in the water utility field, but it moved steadily, acquiring no fewer than 25 local water companies between January 1923 and December 1929.

By February 1935, when American Water Works & Electric published a major review of its holdings, the company's water business consisted of more than 40 operating companies serving 442,000 customers in 16 states and Cuba. The electric utility business served a total of 312,000 customers in an area covering parts of Pennsylvania, Maryland, Virginia, West Virginia and Ohio.

At that point, however, there was a major difference, indeed a radical difference, between the water business and the electric utility business. The water business had undergone its period of infancy and rapid growth in the late 1800s. By the 1920s it had largely settled down. New water companies were still being started, but not at the same rate. The primary challenge now was to provide the technical and management skill and the financial resources needed to meet the demands of continuing growth on the part of existing companies, and American Water Works & Electric was well equipped to do that. Thus the water business provided a solid, reliable financial base—it was the "cash cow," to use the modern term—while the rest of the company, led by H. Hobart Porter, focused on the "go-go" business of the day, the more exciting and rapidly developing electric utility business. (It was not without foresight that the new company had been renamed, in 1914, the American Water Works & *Electric* Company.)

Before the old company, American Water Works & Guarantee, began to diversify in 1910, its total electric holdings consisted of three small electric light and power companies whose operation was incidental, almost accidental, to the water business. In the same way, the electric utility operations of the West Penn Railways Company, which AWW&G acquired in 1910, had been developed primarily to supply the needs of electric street railways. But as time passed and demand increased for electric power for residential lighting and manufacturing, the generation of electricity became a major industry in its own right, far outstripping the other two.

By the 1930s the electric utility side of the American company's business had a structure as complex as that of the water business was simple. For the average reader—and indeed the average writer—of a history like this one, the redundant and ever-changing names of electric utility companies, as they flowered during the period 1910 to 1929, are at best confusing and often incomprehensible. The subsidiary that held all of AWW&E's electric properties was the West Penn Electric Company. The three principal subsidiaries of West Penn Electric were the West Penn Power Company, the West Penn Railways Company, and the Potomac Edison Company. West Penn Power in turn owned the Monongahela West Penn Public Service Company.

To complicate matters further, one of the three principal electric subsidiaries, West Penn Railways, was also the owner of 31.2 percent of the common stock of another principal electric subsidiary, West Penn Power. Meanwhile, Potomac Edison owned, among other things, Potomac Light and Power and South Penn Power, while West Penn Power owned Potomac Transmission and West

Penn Appliance; Monongahela West Penn Public Service owned
Monongahela Water and Electric; West Penn Railways owned Penn
Transit and Pan Handle Traction; West Penn Power owned West
Virginia Power and Transit and West Penn West Virginia Water
Power; and West Penn Electric owned West Virginia Public Service
Company.

All this is about as informative, at least to an outsider, as reciting
the "begats" in the Bible, and as exciting as watching through a
microscope as primitive, one-celled life-forms separate and join. It
is easy to imagine a utility executive of that era saying to his secretary, "Miss Kilowatt, take a letter to the president of West Penn
Electric, I mean West Penn Power, I mean South Penn Power, I
mean Pan Handle Traction. Oh, forget it."

Easy to imagine, but unlikely to have happened. The distinc-
tions between many of the companies existed primarily on paper.
The president of a number of them was often the same person,
and may well have been the fellow in the office down the hall (who
perhaps had an oversize hat rack to hold his many hats). Underlying the seeming confusion was a rational, logical and conceptually
simple design—originally proposed by Sanderson and Porter and
executed under the leadership of H. Hobart Porter. It called for
the creation of an integrated system of street railways and electric
utilities, with associated transmission lines and generating facilities,
covering the major industrial area of southwestern Pennsylvania,
parts of eastern Ohio and northern West Virginia, northern Virginia, and most of western and central Maryland. The spaghetti-
like tangle of holding companies which held holding companies
which in turn held holding companies served as a kind of "geologic
record" of the acquisitions and consolidations (not at all unlike the
activities of primitive, one-celled life forms) that had created the
system. It also reflected, as the company was to claim in a later
defense, the need for separate corporate entities to deal with a variety of local regulatory bodies and governing jurisdictions. (Hindsight suggests that the latter claim may have been overstated. When
the simplification of the structure of holding companies was later

mandated by law, all the companies, including AWW&E, managed to comply without apparent loss of efficiency.)

The fact that the structure of the electric and street railway businesses was more complex than that of the water works business reflected another fundamental difference between the two. Once a water company is established to serve a given community and has perhaps acquired a few small, uneconomic companies in the outlying areas, the system is largely complete. The remaining challenge is to expand the service as the community grows, to provide increased supplies and improved facilities as appropriate, and to replace worn out or obsolete equipment. From a day-to-day operating standpoint, it makes no difference whether a given system is owned by local investors or a holding company a thousand miles away. Nor does it necessarily matter whether the owners hold only this one property or several dozen others—although, as American Water Works & Electric, along with its predecessor and successor companies, have argued persuasively, the holder of multiple small water systems is probably better equipped to provide efficient management than the owner of a single, freestanding enterprise.

By contrast, an electric light and power or railroad company is not limited to a single community or area by the nature of its operations and, in fact, can benefit greatly, both in efficiency and quality of service, if it is connected to and integrated with a number of other companies across a wider region. The original purpose of the Pittsburgh, McKeesport and Connellsville Railway Company, which later became West Penn Railways, had been to combine a number of small, isolated railway properties in the coke-producing region of southwest Pennsylvania into a unified, integrated system. The Potomac Edison Company was the product of the consolidation of 33 smaller electric, gas and railway companies. The several dozen electric light and power companies that were merged to form the West Penn Power Company were themselves the result of previous mergers and consolidations, so that the new company rep-

resented the consolidation of no fewer than 497 individual enterprises.*

Furthermore, as the technology of electric generation and
transmission galloped ahead, the opportunities and pressures it
created virtually dictated not only a continuing process of consolidation of existing companies, but the creation of entirely new ones
to build and manage large central generating facilities and region-
wide transmission lines.

A "Seismic Fault"

Thus, as time passed, the water business, which had been the dominant factor—indeed, the name of the game—for the old American
Water Works & Guarantee Company, came to play a secondary
role, while the electric utility business, which not many years earlier
had been little more than a sideline, emerged as the center of attention and the primary source of growth. Meanwhile, not only was
the structure of the two segments of the business different, their
"cultures"—their ways of thinking and working—were evolving
differently as well. The electric business had its own engineering
staff, with its own focus of attention and its own specialized knowledge and skills, while the Water Works Division, as it came to be
known, had another; each group had its own chain of command,
its own ladder of promotion, its own standards of recruiting, and
its own style of managing.

The two entities continued to operate within the same corporate structure; their rates were set by the same regulatory bodies;

---

*The street railway business of AWW&E continued to prosper until the early
1920s, when it was dealt a fatal blow by the development by Henry Ford of the
Model T, an automobile so inexpensive that ordinary people could now jump
into the family car instead of taking the trolley. However, the growth of the company's electric utility holdings during the 1920s more than made up for the loss
of its street railway business.

they drew their funding from the same financial markets. None-theless—to use a geologic term again—there now existed within the AWW&E organization what amounted to a "fault line." In case of some future "seismic event"—an economic or political shock, let us say—the company could quite conceivably split along this line into two separate, stand-alone businesses.

But only time would tell.

John H. Ware, Jr.,
in the 1930s.

W. James
MacIntosh, John
Ware's lawyer and a
long-time director
of American.

Poster promoting the Lexington Water Company's inaugural fire stream display.

INAUGURATION AND DISPLAY
OF THE
Lexington Water Works!

Friday, January 30th, 1885.

PROGRAMME OF FIRE STREAMS.

10:30 A. M., SIX SIMULTANEOUS STREAMS

From Hydrants at the corners of Winchester and Race, Limestone and Seventh, Georgetown and Third, Broadway and Bolivar, Maxwell and Rose and Court House.
Run thirty minutes.
After a test at Limestone and Seventh, a change of stream will be made to Hamilton College.

1:20 P. M., TEN ONE-INCH STREAMS

On Main street, bet. Dewees and Spring streets.
Run twenty minutes.

2:10 P. M., TWO ONE-INCH STREAMS
Through
500 feet and 1000 feet of hose,
On Main street, near Court House.
Run twenty minutes.

2:30 P. M., ONE TWO-INCH STREAM
Through
Siamese Attachment
At Court House.
Run thirty minutes.

C. G. HILDRETH,
President, Lexington H. & M. Co.

M. KAUFMAN,
Chairman. Water Works Committee.

An old newspaper photograph of Michael Donahue, founder of the water works in Davenport, Iowa, in the 1870s.

Drawing of a filtering system installed in Chattanooga, Tennessee, in the 1890s.

This handsome old pumping station of the Peoria (Illinois) Water Company, built in the 1890s, is listed in the National Historic Register. The roof holds four gargoyle sculptures that were restored by a local artist in the 1980s.

Facing page, top: A pumping station at Belleville, Illinois, that typified local water company facilities at the turn of the century.

Facing page, bottom: A clarifier under construction at the Hays Mine Station in South Pittsburgh in 1924. This unit was still in use in the 1990s.

East St. Louis Water Company workers extend a pipeline across a creek in Granite City, Illinois, in 1930.

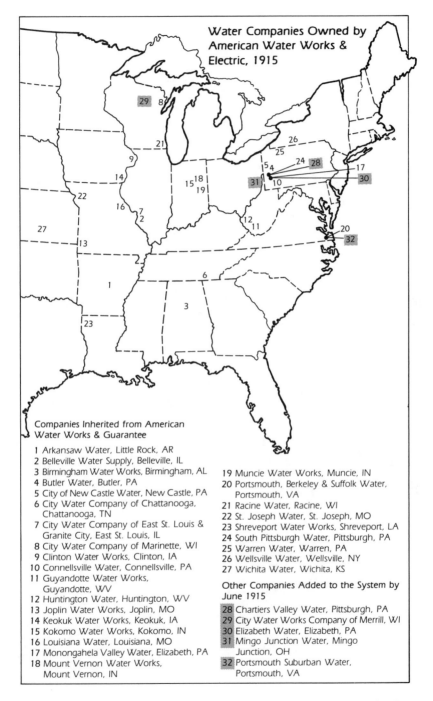

Water Companies Owned by American Water Works & Electric, 1915

Companies Inherited from American Water Works & Guarantee

1 Arkansaw Water, Little Rock, AR
2 Belleville Water Supply, Belleville, IL
3 Birmingham Water Works, Birmingham, AL
4 Butler Water, Butler, PA
5 City of New Castle Water, New Castle, PA
6 City Water Company of Chattanooga, Chattanooga, TN
7 City Water Company of East St. Louis & Granite City, East St. Louis, IL
8 City Water Company of Marinette, WI
9 Clinton Water Works, Clinton, IA
10 Connellsville Water, Connellsville, PA
11 Guyandotte Water Works, Guyandotte, WV
12 Huntington Water, Huntington, WV
13 Joplin Water Works, Joplin, MO
14 Keokuk Water Works, Keokuk, IA
15 Kokomo Water Works, Kokomo, IN
16 Louisiana Water, Louisiana, MO
17 Monongahela Valley Water, Elizabeth, PA
18 Mount Vernon Water Works, Mount Vernon, IN
19 Muncie Water Works, Muncie, IN
20 Portsmouth, Berkeley & Suffolk Water, Portsmouth, VA
21 Racine Water, Racine, WI
22 St. Joseph Water, St. Joseph, MO
23 Shreveport Water Works, Shreveport, LA
24 South Pittsburgh Water, Pittsburgh, PA
25 Warren Water, Warren, PA
26 Wellsville Water, Wellsville, NY
27 Wichita Water, Wichita, KS

Other Companies Added to the System by June 1915

28 Chartiers Valley Water, Pittsburgh, PA
29 City Water Works Company of Merrill, WI
30 Elizabeth Water, Elizabeth, PA
31 Mingo Junction Water, Mingo Junction, OH
32 Portsmouth Suburban Water, Portsmouth, VA

This map and the one on the next page illustrate the rapid growth of American Water Works & Electric.

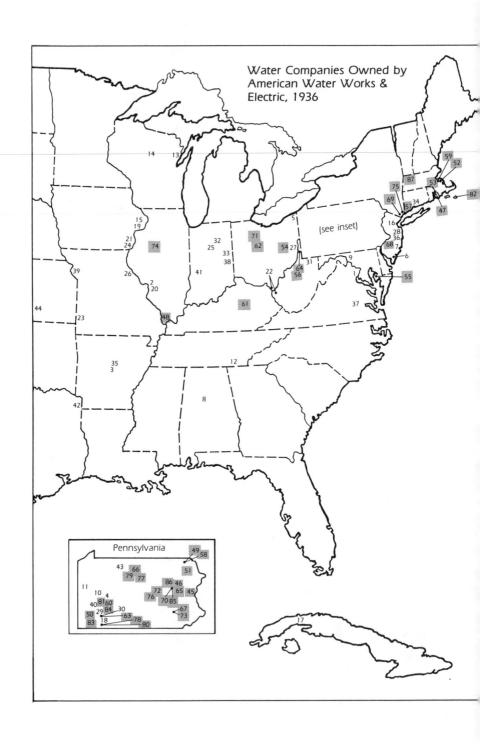

Water Companies Owned by
American Water Works &
Electric, 1936

(see inset)

Pennsylvania

Holdings Before Acquisition of Community Water Service

1. Alexandria Water, Alexandria, VA
2. Alton Water, Alton, IL
3. Arkansaw Water, Little Rock, AR
4. Armstrong Water, Kittanning, PA
5. Ashtabula Water Works, Ashtabula, OH
6. Atlantic County Water Company of New Jersey, Pleasantville, NJ
7. Bay Head Water, Bay Head, NJ
8. Birmingham Water Works, Birmingham, AL
9. Braddock Heights Water Company of Frederick County, Maryland, Braddock Heights, MD
10. Butler Water, Butler, PA
11. City of New Castle Water, New Castle, PA
12. City Water Company of Chattanooga, Chattanooga, TN
13. City Water Company of Marinette, WI
14. City Water Works Company of Merrill, WI
15. Clinton Water Works, Clinton, IA
16. Commonwealth Water and Light, Millburn, NJ
    Bernards Water, Summit, NJ
    Commonwealth Water, Millburn, NJ
    Millington Water, Summit, NJ
    Stirling Water Supply, Summit, NJ
17. Companía de Acueductos de Cuba, Havana, Cuba
18. Connellsville Water, Connellsville, PA
19. Davenport Water, Davenport, IA
20. East St. Louis and Interurban Water, East St. Louis, IL
21. Fort Madison Water, Fort Madison, IA
22. Huntington Water, Huntington, WV
    Lawrence County Water, Chesapeake, OH
23. Joplin Water Works, Joplin, MO
24. Keokuk Water Works, Keokuk, IA
25. Kokomo Water Works, Kokomo, IN
26. Louisiana Water, Louisiana, MO
27. Mingo Junction Water, Mingo Junction, OH
28. Monmouth Consolidated Water, Long Branch, NJ
29. Monongahela Valley Water, Elizabeth, PA
30. Monongahela Water and Electric, Monongahela, PA
31. Morgantown Water, Morgantown, WV
32. Mount Vernon Water Works, Mount Vernon, IN
33. Muncie Water Works, Muncie, IN
34. Noroton Water, Darien, CT
35. North Little Rock Water, North Little Rock, AR
36. Ocean County Water, Lakewood, NJ
37. Old Dominion Water, Hopewell, VA
38. Richmond Water Works, Richmond, IN
39. St. Joseph Water, St. Joseph, MO
40. South Pittsburgh Water, Pittsburgh, PA
    Chartiers Valley Water, Pittsburgh, PA
    St. Clair Water, St. Clair, PA
    Whitaker Water, Whitaker, PA
41. Terre Haute Water Works, Terre Haute, IN
42. Texarkana Water, Texarkana, TX
43. Warren Water, Warren, PA
44. Wichita Water, Wichita, KS

Companies Acquired Through Merger with Community Water Service, 1936

45. Bangor Water, Bangor, PA
46. Berwick Water, Berwick, PA
47. Bristol County Water, Bristol, RI
48. Cairo Water, Cairo, IL
49. Canawacta Water Supply, Susquehanna, PA
50. Citizens Water, Washington, PA
51. Clark's Summit Water, Clark's Summit, PA
52. Cohasset Water, Cohasset, MA
53. Dedham Water, Dedham, MA
54. Dennison Water Supply, Dennison, OH
55. Dorchester Water, Cambridge, MD
56. Glendale Water, Glendale, WV
57. Greenwich Water, Greenwich, CT
58. Hallstead Water, Susquehanna, PA
59. Hingham Water, Hingham, MA
60. Hyde Park Water, Apollo, PA
61. Lexington Water, Lexington, KY
62. Marion Water, Marion, OH
63. Monongahela City Water, Monongahela, PA
64. Moundsville Water, Moundsville, WV
65. Mountain City Water, Frackville, PA
66. Mount Jewett Water, Mount Jewett, PA
67. Myerstown Water, Palmyra, PA
68. New Jersey Water, Haddon Heights, NJ
69. New Rochelle Water, New Rochelle, NY
70. Northumberland Water, Milton, PA
71. Ohio Cities Water, Tiffin, OH
72. Osceola Water Supply, Osceola Mills, PA
73. Palmyra Water, Palmyra, PA
74. Peoria Water Works, Peoria, IL
75. Port Chester Water Works, Port Chester, NY
76. Ramey Water, Houtzdale, PA
77. St. Marys Water, St. Marys, PA
78. South West Water, Uniontown, PA
79. Spring Water Company of Kane, PA
80. Uniontown Water, Uniontown, PA
81. Vandergrift Water, Vandergrift, PA
82. Wannacomet Water, Nantucket, MA
83. Waynesburg Water, Waynesburg, PA
84. Westmoreland Water, Greensburg, PA
85. White Deer Mountain Water, Milton, PA
86. Williamsport Water, Williamsport, PA
87. Williamstown Water, Williamstown, MA

The office of the Muncie (Indiana) Water Company in the 1930s—a good example of offices in the small cities throughout the American System.

Facing page: The structure of American Water Works & Electric in 1945, two years before the company dissolved and John Ware gained control of the water properties.

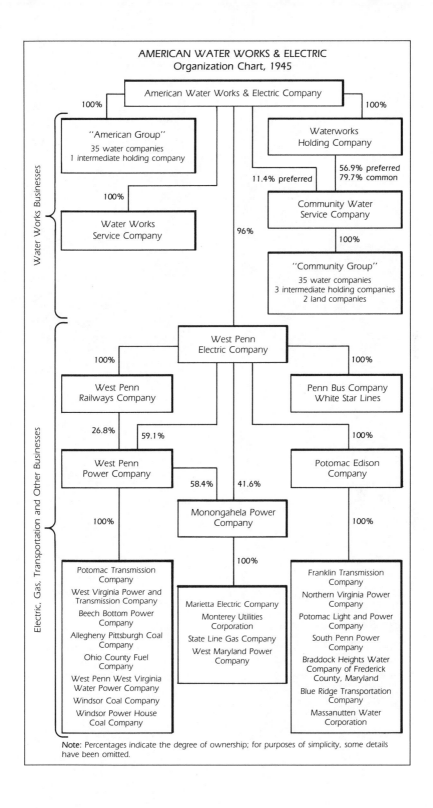

AMERICAN WATER WORKS & ELECTRIC
Organization Chart, 1945

Water Works Businesses

Electric, Gas, Transportation and Other Businesses

American Water Works & Electric Company

100%

100%

"American Group"
35 water companies
1 intermediate holding company

Waterworks
Holding Company

100%

56.9% preferred
79.7% common

11.4% preferred

Water Works
Service Company

96%

Community Water
Service Company

100%

"Community Group"
35 water companies
3 intermediate holding companies
2 land companies

West Penn
Electric Company

100%

100%

West Penn
Railways Company

Penn Bus Company
White Star Lines

26.8%

59.1%

100%

West Penn
Power Company

58.4%

41.6%

Potomac Edison
Company

100%

Monongahela Power
Company

100%

100%

Potomac Transmission
Company

West Virginia Power and
Transmission Company

Beech Bottom Power
Company

Allegheny Pittsburgh Coal
Company

Ohio County Fuel
Company

West Penn West Virginia
Water Power Company

Windsor Coal Company

Windsor Power House
Coal Company

Marietta Electric Company

Monterey Utilities
Corporation

State Line Gas Company

West Maryland Power
Company

Franklin Transmission
Company

Northern Virginia Power
Company

Potomac Light and Power
Company

South Penn Power
Company

Braddock Heights Water
Company of Frederick
County, Maryland

Blue Ridge Transportation
Company

Massanutten Water
Corporation

Note: Percentages indicate the degree of ownership; for purposes of simplicity, some details have been omitted.

Samuel Insull (*top left*), a turn-of-the-century utilities tycoon, came to symbolize the abuses of the industry in the 1920s. (Photo courtesy of UPI/Bettmann.)

Debonair, energetic H. Hobart Porter (*top right*) headed American Water Works & Electric Company.

John H. Murdoch, Jr. (*bottom left*), was a lawyer and vice president of American Water Works & Electric. After that company dissolved in 1947, he stayed on to serve the water company until 1956.

Birth of a Boom

At the time that American Water Works & Electric made its decision to expand, other public utility holding companies were doing the same. Some of the others were, like AWW&E, soundly conceived, rationally organized and responsibly managed. Others were not. The period of the 1920s was a time of growth—uncontrolled, seemingly unlimited growth—of unsound, randomly organized and irresponsibly managed holding companies, and their fortunes—and misfortunes—would ultimately have a decisive effect on the destiny of AWW&E.

The public utility holding company surge of the 1920s was a product of what one historian has called "the Age of Edison." The start of the Age of Edison was marked by the development in 1879 by Thomas A. Edison of the first practical electric light bulb, which revolutionized the lighting of homes, offices and streets. The next major step was the completion in 1882 of the Pearl Street electric generating station in New York to provide electricity to power the new bulbs. Pearl Street, the first central-station power plant in the United States, later became the Consolidated Edison Company; Con Ed in turn became the prototype for the thousands of other power companies that sprang up all over the nation. To provide the generating equipment needed by the new power companies, Edison organized several manufacturing companies, which in time, through a series of mergers, became the General Electric Company of today.

As noted previously, many of the early electric companies—like many of the early water companies—were short of money. In order to sell equipment to them, GE took stock in the companies as payment. As a result, GE became so heavily involved in financing electric utilities that it almost went bankrupt in the depression of the 1890s. Since it did not wish to operate permanently as financier and investment banker, in 1905 GE created a subsidiary called the Electric Bond & Share Company, to which it turned over all its utility holdings. It was originally intended that EB&S would strengthen the utility companies with good management, then sell them off at a profit—a plan very similar to the original plan of American Water Works & Electric in 1914. However, as the boom of the 1920s gained momentum, Electric Bond & Share, like American Water Works & Electric, decided that instead of selling off its holdings it would retain and expand them. General Electric divested itself of Electric Bond & Share in 1924 by distributing its stock to the GE shareholders. And just as Consolidated Edison became the prototype for other electric utilities all over the United States, Electric Bond & Share was the prototype for the enormous proliferation of utility holding companies that followed. But although the organizing principle of AWW&E had been to create an integrated regional power system, the purpose behind the accumulation of holdings of EB&S had been simply to finance the sale of electric generating equipment wherever there was demand. The result was a conglomeration of holdings across the United States with no functional basis or rationale. And many of the other utility holding companies— there were hundreds—that grew up at that time did not even have the initial justification of Electric Bond & Share. The promoters would simply organize a holding company, buy up a few electric utility properties, sell shares in the holding company to the public at a profit, then create a new holding company which in turn would acquire a controlling interest in the original one. The new holding company would then buy more operating companies; its shares would be sold to the public at a further profit; still another company would be created on top of the first two; and so on. The result was pyramids of holding companies on top of holding companies on top of holding companies, in some cases as many as 12 layers deep.

In 1916 the 16 largest public utility holding companies controlled about 30 percent of the electric generating capacity in the United States. By 1925, nine years later, the 16 largest companies controlled 53 percent of capacity. By the mid-1930s, 57 holding companies controlled 90 percent of all capacity in the country. During this period of increasing concentration, two of the largest concerns were Electric Bond & Share and the public utility empire of Samuel Insull.

Just as Con Ed became the prototype for the new electric utilities, and Electric Bond & Share the prototype for the utility holding companies, Samuel Insull came to epitomize the promoters of the holding company boom.

Insull was an Englishman with a head for numbers and a talent for management. As a young man he had gone to work for Thomas A. Edison's London representatives. His ability was soon recognized, and in 1881 he was brought to America to become Edison's private secretary. When it became apparent that the new electric utilities were having trouble financing their purchases, Edison organized the T. A. Edison Construction Department to assist them, and placed Insull in charge of it. When General Electric was created in 1889, Insull became a vice president. In 1891 he became president of the Chicago Edison Company.

By 1907 all of Chicago's electricity was provided by Insull's company. By 1917 his power system extended to most of Illinois and parts of neighboring states. (During the reorganization of 1914, Insull became a director of the new American Water Works & Electric Company. However, he left the board shortly afterward, pleading the pressure of war work, and was not heard from again so far as the company was concerned.) Meanwhile, Insull had created a holding company, Middle West Utilities, which by 1929 controlled holdings valued at more than $4 billion. The enterprise was structured in such a way that an investment of one dollar by Samuel Insull in the top tier of the company controlled no less than $20,000 worth of assets at the operating level.

Since the supply of operating companies was limited, while the demand for holding company stocks continued to rise, the promoters paid increasingly high prices for available properties. These inflated prices were then covered by writing up the value of the assets of the operating companies, and the inflated costs in turn were passed on to customers in the form of higher electricity rates. Meanwhile, there were other opportunities for profit. A parent company could borrow money at low rates and lend it to a subsidiary at higher rates, pocketing the difference. Or the parent company could borrow money from the subsidiary at a low rate and invest it at a higher rate, again pocketing the difference. The holding company could take additional profits from the operating companies by charging inflated prices for engineering, construction, management services, or supplies.

Many of the holding companies had no purpose other than to reap the profits of financial manipulation. In the case of Samuel Insull and some of the others, the initial assumptions had been that large operations would result in economies of scale and that the growth of the market would support the continued expansion of the system. But randomly assembled holdings did not provide the same opportunities for savings as integrated systems, particularly when the operating companies were being systematically exploited by their corporate parents. Furthermore, the expected growth in demand for power did not materialize. As a result, when the bubble of speculation finally burst in 1929, the whole structure, consisting largely of paper companies showing paper profits, came tumbling down, with losses to investors in the billions of dollars.

In the aftermath of the stock market crash, angry investors began to haunt the Insull offices in Chicago, seeking compensation for their losses. But Insull remained at his sumptuous estate in nearby Libertyville, protected night and day by 36 full-time security guards, as he worked to save his empire through new loans and manipulations. Finally, in 1932 he gave up and left suddenly for Europe, resigning 85 directorships, 65 chairmanships and 11 company presidencies.

Testifying before a committee of Congress that year, Owen D. Young, the chairman of General Electric, said of the Insull empire:

It is impossible for any man to grasp the situation of that vast structure . . . it was so set up that you could not possibly get an accounting system which would not mislead even the officers
themselves. . . . I believe Mr. Samuel Insull was very largely the vic-
tim of that complicated structure which got even beyond his power,
competent as he was, to understand it.

"The true significance of the career of Samuel Insull," commented Donald Richberg, a long-time critic of Insull's in Chicago,
"is that his sins were *not* exceptional, save in the sweep of his ambitions and the extent of the injuries he inflicted."

After repeated attempts to avoid deportation from a self-
imposed exile in Greece, Insull was finally returned to the United
States in 1934. He was tried three times on charges of using the
mails to defraud, embezzlement, and violating the bankruptcy acts,
but was acquitted each time. After an unsuccessful attempt at a
business comeback in 1936, he retired to live quietly on a pension
of $15,000 a year, and died of a heart attack in a Paris subway sta-
tion in 1938.

To Regulate a Rattlesnake

In the days that followed the collapse of the holding companies, investors began demanding reform of the laws that had permitted such widespread abuse. As the depression wore on, cries for reform came from other sources. Despite the decline in economic activity and the long lines of unemployed, electric rates, which were controlled by state utility commissions—which in turn were under the control of the utility companies—were kept high in an effort to protect the profits of the companies in the face of declining sales. So the voices of consumers were added to those of investors in calling for reform.

Action on public utilities was going to have to wait, however, until the new administration under Franklin Roosevelt took care of more urgent matters. In the first days of the New Deal, programs were pushed through to resolve the banking crisis, to provide relief for the unemployed, to deal with the problems of farmers, to clean up fraud and abuse in securities markets generally, and to attempt to jump-start the stalled economy.

By early 1935, with those matters out of the way, the time had come to address the holding company question. That effort would create the greatest legislative battle of the New Deal, and leave behind a legacy of bitterness that lasted for a generation.

When President Roosevelt delivered his State of the Union message to the Congress on January 4, 1935, the prepared text of the speech spoke of restoring sound conditions to the public utility field through "abolition of the evil features" of holding companies. When he actually delivered the address, however, he read that line as "the abolition of evil holding companies." In a later press conference he insisted that he had meant to speak of "the evils of holding companies," and certainly did not intend to say that everything about holding companies was evil. "Nonetheless," wrote the historian Arthur Schlesinger, Jr., "Freud was right, and there was much truth in the slip."

The president's advisers were unanimous in the view that regulation alone would not be enough to solve the holding company problem. Previous attempts to regulate the companies had been consistently frustrated; something more was needed. As to what that something more should be, there were two schools of thought. One group of advisers, which included the "brain trusters" Benjamin Cohen and Thomas P. "Tommy the Cork" Corcoran, favored a drastic restructuring of the holding companies to eliminate multiple layers of ownership and scattered and miscellaneous holdings that made no geographic or economic sense. After restructuring, according to this approach, the entities that remained would be put under strict regulation at the federal level to eliminate abusive practices. The other group of advisers, centered in the Treasury Department, favored the immediate and total abolition of the holding companies by means of a stiff tax on payments between corporations.

A few days after his State of the Union Message, Roosevelt called both groups to a meeting at the White House to consider a bill for dealing with the public utility holding company problem. The bill, drafted by Ben Cohen, reflected the Cohen-Corcoran approach: drastic restructuring followed by strict regulation. It soon became apparent, however, that the president, regardless of what he said at his press conference, favored complete abolition. He seemed to feel that if the holding companies survived at all, sooner or later they would use their money and influence to win their way back to power. Ben Cohen argued that his bill went as far as was politically feasible at that time: that it would require the breakup of the complex and unwieldy holding company empires, and would supplement too-often inadequate regulation at the state level with national supervision with teeth. As to whether the holding companies should be allowed to survive in the longer term, that decision could be left for later.

The outcome of the meeting was a peculiar compromise. In terms of substance, the group adopted the Cohen approach. In terms of tone, it went along with Roosevelt. Although the actual provisions of the bill required only restructuring followed by regulation, its language was harsh and vindictive, and the stated objective of the administration was the eventual elimination of all public utility holding companies. The word was put out that the goal was to eliminate the holding companies within five years.

Out of that meeting also came the provision that was quickly labeled the "death sentence" clause. This clause provided that as far as possible the reorganization of the companies was to be voluntary. Their plans for reorganizing under the guidelines provided by the bill were to be submitted for the approval of the newly-created Securities and Exchange Commission. However, the clause gave the SEC the power to compel the breakup of any company that did not submit a satisfactory reorganization plan.

To an outside observer, this provision might not appear unreasonable. It simply gave the SEC power to enforce the law. It put teeth into what otherwise would have been a toothless bill. But perhaps because it did so, and also because of the inflammatory language of the bill and the hostile attitude on the part of the administration, the utilities regarded that provision as a pistol pointed at their heads and mobilized their considerable forces to defeat it.

The Wheeler-Rayburn bill, as it was called, was introduced in the Congress on February 6, 1935. The terms were strict. No public utility holding company would be allowed above the "second degree"—two layers of ownership above the operating companies. No holding company would be allowed to control more than a single geographically integrated system. No electric utility would be allowed to sell gas; no gas utility would be allowed to sell electricity. (By implication, no energy company would be allowed to sell water, as American Water Works & Electric had long been doing.)

The holding companies were not slow to respond. On the day the bill was introduced, a statement was released to the press, signed by the heads of ten leading public utility holding companies. The second name on the list was that of H. Hobart Porter, president of American Water Works & Electric. The statement declared:

> We have seen in this morning's newspapers of the proposed bill to destroy public utility holding companies. We have not yet had the opportunity to study the bill itself. The official summary, however, indicates that it is based on the assumption that public utility holding companies perform no useful function, that they are not only unnecessary, but actively pernicious and solely evil, and that they must not be permitted to live.
>
> To this assumption we do not subscribe. And the facts do not warrant such assumptions. We do not believe it is necessary to destroy these companies in order to prevent a recurrence of abuses, many of which have already been corrected.

In the days that followed, the battle raged. One by one the leaders of the industry stepped forward to make their individual statements. On February 17, it was Porter's turn. The holding company bill, he declared, threatened bureaucratic control of all business by the federal government and the crippling of the nation's electric and gas service. It would lead, he added, to the breaking up of all public utility holding companies, possibly to be followed by the destruction of non-utility holding companies, including industrial and commercial enterprises, and the destruction of the value of securities held by millions of investors. Porter concluded:

> The holding company has played a most important and beneficent part in the development of American industry, and has been responsible not only for the extraordinary development of the light and power business but of the American industrial system as a whole.

What is noteworthy, not only in the Porter statement but also in the entire debate, is that the water business was not mentioned. Although water had been the foundation on which American's business was built, and "Water Works" still preceded "Electric" in the company's name, the water business over the past generation had been neither the source of explosive growth nor the area of abuse and scandal. It was by no means "a poor relation" to the electric utility business. In fact it was the steadier money-maker: Its customers were primarily residential, not industrial, and even when people are unemployed they usually pay their water bills. But in the battle over the holding companies, the water business was somewhat in the situation of the wallflower at the party, a canary caught in a badminton game.

Two days after the Porter statement was released, on February 19, 1935, American Water Works & Electric published a 200-page "white paper," describing in great detail the company's history, structure and policies and declaring:

> The facts contained herein justify unquestionably the economic ne-
> cessity of this Company in the past, its present usefulness for the
> benefit of the public good, and the absolute necessity to the utility
> customers served by its operating subsidiary companies of the con-
> tinuance of this organization in the future.

At about the time the AWW&E white paper was released, it appeared that the administration might be having second thoughts about the wisdom of its all-or-nothing, take-no-prisoners approach. On March 2, 1935, less than a month after the legislation was introduced, a member of the Securities and Exchange Commission told a congressional committee that the administration was considering amendments to the bill that would allow companies that were "economically and geographically sound" to continue in business after the five-year period set for abolition.

Ten days later the president himself, in a message to Congress, picked up the same theme. After once again attacking holding companies in general as "a private socialism of concentrated private power" which must be eliminated, he made an exception for the type of company "necessary to the continued functioning of a geographically integrated operating utility system."

This made considerable political sense. The initial announcement of the holding company bill not only had amounted to a mortal threat—a death sentence in a very real sense—to *all* public utility holding companies, but was also an insult to the responsible leaders of the industry. The more moderate approach, while unlikely to attract the support of these elements, might at least hope to reduce the intensity of their opposition.

There was more than political sense to the new approach. It also made economic sense. The electric utility business had become increasingly regional, with giant distribution networks extending across state lines. At the same time, the regulation of rates continued to be conducted on a state-by-state basis. So regardless of the name given to it, some sort of holding company structure was probably the most rational way to continue to run the business. Local entities would deal with local authorities on the matter of rates, under the control of a broader organization that provided not only regionwide coordination, but also the efficiencies made possible by central management, purchasing and engineering services.

The most prominent spokesman for the power companies was Wendell Willkie, a reputable, responsible executive of a reputable, responsible holding company that had not been guilty of the abuses of many of the others. (Largely as a result of the prominence he gained during the holding company debate, Willkie became the Republican candidate for president in 1940.) In an appearance before a congressional committee to oppose the holding company bill, Willkie was asked what alternative he would propose, and agreed to offer a plan. On April 1, he submitted a substitute, which would have continued to rely primarily on state regulation.

The sponsors of the administration bill dismissed the Willkie approach. Thomas Corcoran declared:

> You just cannot handle it that way. It is a sheer problem of arithmetic. How much money have you against how much money? How many good lawyers have you against how many good lawyers? These are the actualities of the regulatory process—the drip, drip, drip of pleasure and influence; the out-maneuvering, the out-braining, which will simply make it impossible to handle these aggregations of power.
>
> The only regulation for 100-ton trucks going up a village street is that you cannot have them going up a village street at all.

Senator Hugo Black of Alabama put his reaction more succinctly: "I have no more sympathy in the attempt to regulate them," he said, "than to regulate a rattlesnake."

For the next two months the debate continued. On June 11 the death sentence clause came up for a vote in the Senate. It barely survived by a vote of 45–44. Then the bill itself, with death sentence included, passed by a margin of 56–32.

Now the battle shifted to the House. John J. Connor, the chairman of the House Rules Committee, advised a compromise on the death sentence clause. Roosevelt refused. A week later the Commerce Committee reported the bill to the full house, but eliminated the death sentence. Roosevelt stood firm. "It is not a death sentence," he declared, "but an emancipation proclamation."

The public utility lobby had never been more active. According to one estimate it had more representatives in Washington (660) than there were members of Congress (527). One enterprising advertising man wrote to the chairman of Electric Bond & Share suggesting "a whispering campaign designed to create popular suspicion that the 'new dealers' and especially the 'New Dealer-in-Chief' are either incompetent or insane." His letter received no reply, but the campaign began. By mid-July *Time* magazine reported that Washington newspaper reporters were being plagued by queries from their hometown papers asking whether the president was not on the verge of mental collapse. In the words of the *Time* article, "He had, according to the tales roaring through the country in whispers, grown mentally irresponsible. Hadn't you heard that during a press conference he had a fit of laughter, had to be hurriedly wheeled out of the room? Why, his intimates were taking the greatest care not to have him make a spectacle of himself on public occasions." After one legislative setback, the president was alleged to have succumbed to a "violent fit of hysterics."

The utility companies relied increasingly on pressure from the folks back home. On June 27 and 28, Representative Denis J. Driscoll of the Twentieth Pennsylvania District received 816 telegrams from the borough of Warren. Looking them over, he noticed two things. The names appeared mostly to begin with the first four letters of the alphabet; and, though he knew Warren fairly well, he had never heard of most of his correspondents. Where he did recognize names, he sent letters explaining why he was supporting the Wheeler-Rayburn bill. On July 1, people began to reply that they had sent him no such telegrams. Meanwhile, he was receiving new bundles of telegrams against the bill from the town of Meadville. Driscoll now sent wires to a few of the Meadville names. Western Union reported that their addresses were unknown.

The Senate appointed a special committee, headed by Senator Black, to investigate the matter of the telegrams. Black called before the committee the manager of the Warren, Pennsylvania, office of the Associated Gas and Electric Company. The manager told how he had been ordered by his headquarters to send at least a thousand telegrams to the congressman. He had come into the Western Union office for an hour or two a day to dictate the telegrams, taking the names of senders from the city directory, or paying a messenger boy three cents a name for any he could provide.

Early in August, Black reported to the Senate that the utilities had spent at least a million and a half dollars to generate a storm of apparently spontaneous protest that had produced 250,000 telegrams and perhaps 5 million letters.

The administration had counted on the disclosures produced by the Black investigation to swing congressional opinion in favor of the death sentence clause. But now the mood in the Congress was changing. When Roosevelt had originally taken office, the nation was in a state of shock; there was fear of economic collapse and political revolution. The president reassured the country that there was nothing to fear but fear itself, and the country, including the business community, was willing to support almost anything he proposed as an alternative to disaster. But now the threat had eased. The patient was no longer critical and, as recovering patients often do, was starting to complain. In particular, some businessmen were beginning to chafe at the restrictions placed on them by the New Deal programs. Now instead of broad support for whatever the president saw fit to do, congressmen were getting conflicting signals. As one columnist wrote, politicians were "staring frantically in the dark amid fiery eyes shining at them from every side. . . . They began to wonder if the time to jump was not approaching . . . and they wanted to know which way to jump."

Pressures from the utility lobby were relentless. Pressures from the White House were no less intense. The debate became bitter. Congressmen became angry. Willingness to defy the president increased. Finally, in an atmosphere of great tension the House rejected the death sentence clause by a vote of 216–146, and the following day an essentially toothless bill was approved. Now the bill went to a House-Senate conference committee, which would attempt to iron out the differences between the two versions.

On August 1, Congressman Sam Rayburn of Texas returned the bill to the floor of the House and moved to have the House instruct its conferees to accept the death sentence clause. But the House held firm, rejecting it by a vote of 210–155. For the next two weeks the conference committee settled down to a tedious wrangle. On August 17 the *New York Times* reported that there was every indication that the bill would die before adjournment. In the White House, Professor (later Supreme Court Justice) Felix Frankfurter had been working on a compromise designed to save the bill. By mid-August, however, he suggested that the matter be allowed to go over into the next session of Congress to give the congressmen a chance to find out whether or not their constituents wanted a bill with teeth.

But Senator (later Vice President) Alben Barkley continued to press for the Frankfurter compromise. The Senate version of the bill would not have permitted any holding company that controlled more than a single integrated utility system to survive. The Frankfurter compromise directed the SEC to allow a holding company to control more than one integrated system if the additional systems could not economically stand alone and were not so large or so scattered as to impair the advantages of localized management, efficient operation or effective regulation. (Such a provision might easily have permitted an electric utility like American Water Works & Electric to continue to own water companies.) Reluctantly, Roosevelt accepted the compromise. The House, with great relief, agreed to the formula. On August 26, after nearly seven months of battle, the president signed the Public Utility Holding Company Act of 1935.

A Holding Action

Under the new law the procedure for reforming the holding companies was this: First, the companies would be required to register with the Securities and Exchange Commission, thereby acknowledging the commission's authority over them. Then they would be expected to submit for the commission's approval a "voluntary" plan for reorganization within the guidelines provided by the law. Only if a company refused to submit a plan, or was unable to come up with a plan the SEC would approve, would the provisions of the "death sentence" be invoked, and its restructuring compelled by the SEC.

However, while the battle over public utility legislation was raging in the Congress, another struggle was coming to a head. On May 27, 1935, three months before the holding company bill was passed, the Supreme Court struck down the National Industrial Recovery Act, one of the centerpieces of the New Deal economic program, on the grounds that the degree of government regulation of business it required was unconstitutional. This sent a clear signal to the public utility industry: Whatever they lost in the Congress they might well win back in the courts.

The deadline for registration was December 1, 1936. On November 27, three days before the deadline, the North American Company, a major public utility company, filed suit to enjoin the administration from enforcing the new act. The following day American Water Works & Electric did the same, citing as its reason the "enormous damage" complying with the act would do to the company and its subsidiaries. Then, on the ground that the matter was now in litigation, North American and AWW&E, along with every other holding company in the country, refused to register as required by the new law.

[57]

But then a peculiar thing happened. On December 5, just a week after his company had filed suit to overturn the law, H. Hobart Porter of American traveled to Washington for conferences with officials of the SEC. "In utility circles it was reported," according to the New York Times, "that Mr. Porter came here to discuss the status of some of the subsidiaries of his company . . . and readjustments in the setup of the system, but no information was made available at the SEC."

An outside observer might have wondered whether Porter was not hedging his bets, "working both sides of the street"—attempting on the one hand to strike down the new law, while at the same time seeking to arrange the best terms possible in case that effort failed. (As the saying goes, "A good general always has his eye on an avenue of retreat.")

At this point, however, it seemed increasingly likely that the lawsuit would succeed, and the Holding Company Act would be struck down. On January 6, 1936, a month after Porter's trip to Washington, the Supreme Court rejected another keystone of the administration's program, the Agricultural Adjustment Act. As the columnist Arthur Krock wrote at the time, this was "a decision so broad that few of the New Deal Acts before the courts seem to have any chance of being upheld."

But before the two companies could have their day before the highest court, their suits would have to find their way through the tedious processes of the lower courts. So in October of 1936 they asked the Supreme Court to jump their cases to the head of the line, ahead of other pending litigation, in order to get the constitutional issue resolved.

The government, not surprisingly, did not respond with enthusiasm to the idea of helping its opponents, who were already defying the law, to move into a better position from which to destroy the law. In a brief filed with the court, Attorney General Hugh Cummings almost snarled:

> It is a novel suggestion that those who violate a statute . . . should have the right to dictate to the government against which violator

the government should proceed for the purpose of testing the constitutionality of the statute.

In this instance the justices sided with the government and told the companies they would have to wait their turn. So the two cases dragged on.

But this delay created a problem on another front. The financial markets did not look kindly on the securities of a company which might or might not—no one could be sure—be in existence a few years hence. (As they say on Wall Street, "the market discounts uncertainty.") As a result, the companies were having trouble selling their bonds in order to retire existing debt when it came due and to maintain their facilities.

Meanwhile, the administration was not about to accept the view of the Constitution then being applied by the Court. To do so would have amounted to conceding the defeat of most of its major programs and being branded a failure by history. In early 1937, after being reelected by a landslide, Roosevelt mounted his highly controversial effort to "pack" the court with justices more favorably inclined toward his views. The effort was eventually defeated—but the company could not have known that outcome in advance. At that point, however, Porter had an abrupt change of heart—or else he was continuing a two-pronged strategy. On February 26, 1937, despite the fact that its lawsuit to overturn the Holding Company Act was still pending, American Water Works & Electric announced that it would go ahead and register with the SEC, as required by the act, the first holding company in the country to do so.

Although Roosevelt's court-packing attempt did fail—in a bitter defeat for the president—the effort nonetheless appeared to have had an impact on the Supreme Court. In April 1937 the Court broadened its view of constitutionality and approved the Wagner Labor Relations Act. Now the prospect had changed. Now there was a distinct possibility that the Holding Company Act would be upheld.

While the record does not show it, it seems probable that H.

Hobart Porter's quiet trips to Washington continued. In any event, on August 26, 1937, four months after the court upheld the Wagner Act, American Water Works & Electric became the first holding company in the country to submit a plan for reorganization to the SEC, and on December 30, the SEC announced, with obvious satisfaction, that it had approved the plan.

As to the nature of the plan the SEC had approved, there was good news. The company would be required to sell its real estate holdings in California—which, after all, were only a souvenir of a mistake of the distant past. But it would be allowed to keep its other holdings, including its 80 or so water companies, being required only to simplify its structure so that there would be no more than two levels of holding companies above the operating properties.

As the press reported, "The commission's decision is regarded . . . as a milestone . . . because of its demonstration that the commission was kindly disposed toward even the largest holding companies if they showed a cooperative attitude."

This was a far cry from the bitterness and fear, the dogma and defiance, of only two years before, and it showed the desire of the commission to ease the relationship between the regulators and the regulated.

The day after the SEC's approval was announced, H. Hobart Porter declared it "most satisfactory." "The Commission and its staff," he added, "have shown an eminently constructive and cooperative attitude throughout the proceedings."

There would be a price to pay for the settlement: In order to execute its reorganization plan, the company would have to raise an estimated $60 million in new money to pay off the obligations of the holding company layers that would be eliminated. However, even though the restructuring had now been agreed to, it would not be necessary to execute it immediately. Furthermore, the lawsuits still pending might even yet make the whole exercise unnecessary.

A short time before the SEC's approval of the restructuring plan was made public, Porter gave up the post of president of AWW&E, after 23 years in the job, and took the newly created title of chairman of the board. His successor as president was Earle S. Thompson, a product of the electric utility side of the business.

Porter had reason to be satisfied with the job he had done. In 1914 he had taken over the leadership of a company about to go under, and had led it through a period of spectacular growth, to become one of the leading concerns in its field. Then, with shrewd timing and considerable diplomatic skill, he had piloted it safely through a time of convulsive change.

A week after the reorganization was approved, Porter was honored by being named a "life trustee" of his alma mater, Columbia University. A short time later, however, the news was not as happy. AWW&E announced that because of a reduction in its earnings resulting from the recession, along with "uncertainty for the future," the company's board of directors had decided to omit the regular quarterly dividend on its common stock.

The major uncertainty for the future continued to be the lawsuits, still pending, aimed at overthrowing the Holding Company Act. As a result of the shift in the Supreme Court's attitude, the prospect of winning was now far less bright than it had been. But as long as the suits were pending, investors could not be sure whether or not the Holding Company Act would be enforced, and no one could know what the future shape of the company would be.

In 1939 and 1940 American again passed the dividend on its common stock. After the United States entered the Second World War in 1941 and price controls were imposed, limiting rate increases and maintaining pressure on earnings, the company continued to omit the dividend. Finally, in 1943 the Supreme Court agreed to hear the holding company cases. But by now most of the justices were Roosevelt appointees and the prospects for striking down the law, already dim, had become dimmer. At this point, any decision would have been a blessing, removing the cloud of uncertainty hanging over the company.

But in accordance with Murphy's Law, which holds that whatever can go wrong *will* go wrong, no sooner had the Court agreed to hear the cases than four of the nine justices disqualified themselves from sitting on it. As a result the Court lacked the needed quorum of six, and the case was once again put on hold.*

The two cases remained stalled until May 1945, when Chief Justice Harlan Stone (perhaps at the urging of the utility industry) reversed himself and decided that he was eligible to sit on the case. Then, however, Justice Owen J. Roberts resigned and the Court again lacked a quorum. Finally, Justice Roberts' successor, Justice Harold Burton, decided he was eligible to hear the case, so the Court at last had a quorum, and the case was scheduled for argument in November of 1945. The decision was at long last handed down in early 1946: the Holding Company Act was found to be constitutional.

In early 1945, President Thompson of AWW&E had told the stockholders that the company would continue to be reluctant to restore the dividend until its status under the Holding Company Act had been clarified. But by that time all the utility companies could see the writing on the wall and began to prepare for the inevitable reorganizations.

American's management reviewed the plan the SEC had approved in 1937. But with the company's record of skipping dividends for the previous eight years, and with the uncertainty facing the American economy in the early postwar period, investors could hardly be expected to bid eagerly for the $60 million in new securities that would have to be sold in order to execute the original plan. So despite the long struggle to keep the organization intact, the only feasible course now appeared to be to sell off the "cash cow," the steady, reliable water works business, in order to finance the reorganization. In February 1946 the company asked the SEC to approve a revised plan permitting it to sell the water business.

---

*Chief Justice Stone had previously been a partner in the New York law firm of Sullivan and Cromwell, which had long represented a number of utility companies, including American Water Works & Electric. Justice William O. Douglas had been Roosevelt's first chairman of the SEC, so he could scarcely be considered objective. Justices Frank Murphy and Robert H. Jackson had been FDR's attorneys general, so they also had addressed the issue in public.

Meanwhile, it began to reorganize its electrical holdings in preparation for the change.

But Murphy's Law was still in force. As part of its reorganization plan, the company made an offer to certain minority shareholders of cash or shares in the new water company in exchange for their holdings. But the stockholders objected, saying they were entitled to more, and filed suit to block the reorganization plan. With time passing and lawyers' fees mounting, the company in June negotiated an agreement with a group of the dissident shareholders to increase the payment for their shares. However, it was necessary for the SEC to review this agreement, and in December 1946 the commission rejected it, saying it was not fair to other shareholders. In January 1947 the company offered a new set of terms, and in February the SEC approved it.

Even this was not the end. Now it was necessary to wait several months for clarification by the Internal Revenue Service of the tax issues involved in the exchange. Finally, on August 31, 1947, twelve long years after the Holding Company Act had been passed, the SEC authorized the company to go ahead with its revised reorganization plan. The date of September 25 was set as the deadline for underwriters to submit bids for the common stock of the new American Water Works Company.

II

ENTER JOHN WARE

A Different Breed

John Ware, Jr., read the newspapers. When it was announced in early 1946 that American Water Works & Electric was planning to divest itself of the largest collection of water companies in the United States, it is unlikely that he would have missed the story. (Even if he had, the staff in Philadelphia was instructed to clip and forward to him, wherever he might be, any item of possible interest.)

In the 18 months between the first announcement of the divestiture plan and final go-ahead, it is easy to imagine Ware quietly watching the progress of events, as his fertile imagination toyed with various stratagems for conquering this final summit, this Everest of local water supply. Finally, in the summer of 1947, as arrangements for the separation moved toward a conclusion, it was time to make his move. Ware placed the call to the law firm in Philadelphia that put into motion his bold takeover effort.

"The Kid Millionaire"

John Haines Ware, Jr., was of a different breed from anyone involved before or since in the history of the three companies that have borne the American Water Works name. Like some of his predecessors he had started successful businesses. Like others he had built them into larger systems. He had also proven himself a capable manager, although with his restless temperament, day-to-day minding the store was not his favorite activity. But at root John

Ware was an innovator and entrepreneur of the peculiarly American type that over the previous hundred years had created and fueled the country's industrial growth. He did not achieve the spectacular wealth of a Rockefeller or a Carnegie, nor the breakthrough innovation of a Ford or an Edison. But he was one of their breed; he was cut from the same cloth.

A number of studies have been made of the entrepreneurial personality, and they have identified a set of common traits. A few have come from backgrounds of wealth or at least affluence; most have not; most were raised in poverty or something close to it; many were either orphaned immigrants or had fathers who were irresponsible or failures or who suffered serious financial reverses. And while not all were overtly religious, and some were downright irreligious, in a high proportion of cases they were raised by mothers who put strong emphasis on religious or ethical values and were ambitious for their sons—ambitious perhaps to have them achieve the success their fathers had not.

In each case there was tremendous drive and appetite for work, a high tolerance for risk, indomitable, unrelenting optimism—what someone has called "an extraordinary gift for hope"—and the ability to perceive opportunities in ordinary situations that most people overlook.

There are interesting parallels between John Ware's career and that of Thomas A. Edison. Edison's father was, in the words of one historian, "an easy-going optimist who liked whiskey, women . . . and his independence," who late in life had fathered three illegitimate children. Edison's mother was "a pious, strait-laced woman . . . demanding, strict and stern, eager to imbue him with the morals and culture his father so conspicuously lacked," pouring into her son her ambitions for herself and her family.

Edison left school at age 12—a common pattern of behavior in those days for the sons of families like his. He patented his first invention when he was 21, but it was not commercially successful. By age 29, however, he had developed an improved stock ticker and three improvements on the telephone, which he sold for nearly $400,000 (almost $5 million in 1990 dollars). This income enabled him to establish his famous laboratory in Menlo Park, New Jersey, where in 1879 he perfected the incandescent light bulb, and the Age of Edison was born.

John Ware, Jr., was born in Philadelphia in 1888 and grew up the poor relation of an old family. An ancestor, Joseph Ware, had landed in New Jersey in 1675. One branch of the family, from the late eighteenth through the early twentieth century, made spindle-backed household chairs, known as "Ware chairs," that are prized by antique collectors today.

John Ware's father, John, Sr., made a meager living traveling through the South selling and repairing commercial scales—the kind used for weighing merchandise. In the summer months he pieced out his income by operating the merry-go-round at Cape May, New Jersey. During school vacations young John would travel to Cape May to help his father.

John's parents were divorced, which in that era not only carried considerable social stigma, but also aggravated the family's financial problems. John would later recall that there was no greater luxury in his early life than a milk shake, and he enjoyed very few of those.

By all accounts, John's mother was both an extremely difficult woman and an exceedingly religious one, who would go to church "whenever the door was open," as one relative puts it. She also suffered from deafness, the same kind that afflicted Thomas Edison. As John Ware told the story later, Edison himself once appeared at the Ware home in North Philadelphia to adjust Mrs. Ware's hearing aid. After the device had worked particularly well, Edison burst forth with a colorful stream of the profanity for which he was notorious, profoundly scandalizing the deeply religious Ware household.

Like Edison, young John was a tinkerer; like Edison his bent was electrical. From an early age he earned pocket money by doing assorted repairs in the neighborhood. In 1902, at age 14, he earned $100 ($1,400 in 1990 dollars) installing an electric motor to run the elevator in a Philadelphia wool packing plant. On the strength of this achievement, young John quit school and became an electrician. By age 15, as he told it later, he was the sole support of his family. At 16 he was running the J. Elliot Shaw Electric Company at 632 Arch Street in Philadelphia. At 18 he won a contract to wire a Pennsylvania Railroad power station.

To impress a skeptical contractor, the story goes, he lied about his age. Apparently the contractor was not the only one impressed. The following year, at age 19, John Ware married Clara Edwards, the contractor's daughter. John's marriage, in contrast to that of his parents, was a particularly happy one, with diminutive, unflappable Clara serving as a balance to impulsive, sometimes stormy John.

The panic of 1907—the year he married—hurt Ware's electrical business, so he answered an advertisement in the *Philadelphia Bulletin* for someone to sell subscriptions door to door to *Collier's Magazine.* He did very well. On one occasion in Penn's Grove, New Jersey, he sold $28 worth of subscriptions between the 11 o'clock and 4 o'clock trains, and he was offered a job as manager of the local sales office. With a combination of magazine sales and electrical work, John was able to save enough money to move to Lancaster, Pennsylvania, his wife's hometown, and start his own electrical shop. Combining his electrical know-how with his demonstrated selling ability, he traveled the countryside persuading farmers to let him bring electricity to their homes.

At that time the newly established electrical companies were concentrating their efforts on the easy profits of providing service in cities and towns. John Ware recognized that there was also profit, and no competition, in bringing electricity to the country; he later boasted that he had established the first rural electrification program in the United States.

Ware would wire a farmer's house and barn for electricity, but true to the breed of the entrepreneur, he recognized an opportunity for more than a one-time fee. Shrewdly, he retained ownership of the poles and lines that brought power to the farm—according to one account, he would sometimes hang the wires from the branches of trees. Then around the beginning of World War I, "with a big mortgage and a lot of hope," he purchased an old water-driven flour mill, Hunsecker's Mill on the Conestoga River, and installed an electric generator there. While the mill continued to grind the farmers' grain and John's two young sons, John 3rd and Willard, dug trenches and played war in the yard, the generator produced electricity to light the farms, and now John Ware owned an electric company. (It is said that the miller was terrified of electricity. If the power failed while John was on the road selling, John's wife, Clara, would go out and adjust the generator.)

Not long after that, according to the story as John Ware told it later, he had electrified 17 out of 21 townships of Lancaster County. By 1924, when he was 36 years old, he had developed his holdings to a point where he was able to sell them to a syndicate of investors for a profit of $1 million, and Philadelphia newspapers were calling him "the kid millionaire." However, when the new owners had trouble operating the power system, they asked John Ware to come back and manage it for a fee. Ware refused, saying he was not a hired hand. The owners sweetened their offer, offering to give him all the common stock in the company in return for managing it, while they held on to the preferred. Ware agreed and ran the enterprise successfully until it was sold two years later to the Philadelphia Electric Company, netting John Ware, at age 38, a profit of another million.

At that point he could have retired, but Ware was not the retiring type. In 1933, when a banker friend named Edwin Herr asked him to take over management of the faltering National Water Works Company, headquartered in Philadelphia, Ware agreed. Now he was in the water business.

National was in bad shape. Its facilities were run down, and it had virtually no cash. One Christmas Eve, at the depth of the Depression. Ware called the members of his organization into his office. After reporting the deplorable state of the business, he led them to a nearby five-and-dime store, where they exchanged ten-cent gifts. But Ware worked as hard as any subordinate—harder than most—and had the capacity to communicate enthusiasm and optimism, as well as to inspire loyalty and reward it. He also showed a knack throughout his career for picking competent people.

Gradually he turned the business around. And in the 1930s as in the 1880s, the successful management of one faltering utility company served as a springboard for taking over other faltering companies. Over time he also gained control of the Union Water Service Company, the Delaware Valley Utilities Company, and the Penn-Jersey Water Company, all of whose properties were located in eastern Pennsylvania and New Jersey.

Then, in 1942, Ware learned that a company called the Northeastern Water & Electric Company, which controlled a total of 37 local water utilities, along with two electric companies and one water-electric company, was up for sale. Northeastern had originally been part of the empire of Samuel Insull. After Insull's collapse, control had passed to a holding company, Atlantic Public Utilities of Boston. When Atlantic also failed, after a series of receiverships and reorganizations, John Ware was able to buy the company, a property then worth nearly $4 million, for a reported down payment of $50,000. Thus the number of his operating companies increased from seven to 54, and the assets he controlled rose from $5 million to $26 million.

The following year Ware consolidated his properties. He merged Penn-Jersey Water into Union Water Service. A few months later he sold off the electric properties he had acquired with Northeastern Water & Electric, then combined that company with Union Water Service and Delaware Valley Utilities to form a new company, called simply the Northeastern Water Company, whose owners were John and Clara Ware.

A Gentle Man

John Ware's normal style of dealing with people was remarkably low-key. He would address bellboys as "sir," and when he summoned a subordinate to his office, he would inquire gently, "Could you spare a few minutes?" or, "Would you mind coming down?" In the words of one associate, "It was almost as though he was working for you, rather than the other way around." As gently as he might express them, however, it was clear that his wishes were orders, and his orders were to be obeyed. He was known to everyone as "the Boss."

And if Ware's manner in dealing with people was ordinarily gentle, it was by no means so in every situation. On one occasion a very aggressive banker came to see him with the intent of buying one of his water companies. "Mr. Ware," said the banker, "I'm going to make you rich."

"There is no need to do that," John Ware responded. "I *am* rich. You get out."

Just as he would not willingly acknowledge that any obstacle could not be surmounted, Ware would not tolerate opposition in any form. Once, in the late teens or early 1920s, as his electric company was beginning to pick up momentum, he received a summons to Chicago to see none other than the legendary Samuel Insull. He arrived at Insull's headquarters to find the great man seated behind a large desk at the far end of a long office. Against the wall behind him stood a splendid grandfather clock.

"Mr. Ware," Insull announced, after young John had completed the long and presumably humbling walk to his desk, "I want to buy your company."

"I'm sorry, Mr. Insull," John Ware is said to have replied, "My company is not for sale."

"Then I will *take* it," responded the strong-willed Insull.

"You will *not* take it," replied the no less strong-willed Ware, "and some day *I* will sit behind that desk, and *I* will own that clock."

A dozen years later, after Insull's empire had collapsed and Insull himself had fled to Europe in disgrace, an auction was held in Chicago to liquidate his assets. Sure enough, as he told the story later, Ware showed up at the auction, made it a point to be high bidder, and went home with the desk and clock. (The fact that Northeastern Water & Electric had also once belonged to Samuel

Insull quite possibly whetted his appetite to own that as well.) Fifty years later, Samuel Insull's clock occupied a place of honor in the Ware mansion in Florida, while the desk used for many years by the corporate secretary was said to be the one that had once belonged to Insull.

The Outsider

As John Ware's electric business prospered, he expanded it eastward and bought the Oxford Electric Company, which was headquartered in the little farming community of Oxford, Pennsylvania, about 50 miles southwest of Philadelphia. (He later boasted that he had quadrupled the business of Oxford Electric in the first year—perhaps by electrifying farms.) He also moved his family to Oxford, where he bought a handsome 20-room house, one of the largest in town.

The kitchen stove and water heater in the house were gas operated. After the family had lived there for a time, Ware asked the local gas company to supply him with gas for the furnace, as well. The company refused. Ware promptly bought the gas company and ordered a pipe installed to supply his furnace with gas.

The oldest families in Oxford had settled the area in the late 1700s and were now the social, cultural and business leaders of the community. They did not respond favorably to this brash newcomer, with his conspicuous wealth and lack of inclination for small talk. "We did not know anything about them," recalled one oldtimer with genteel snobbery, speaking of the newly rich, newly arrived Wares.

At the time that Ware bought the gas company, it was also providing steam for heat, through pipes laid under the street, to many of the houses in town. (As noted earlier, in those days the gas sold by a gas company was produced by burning coal. The heat from the coal would in turn be used to create steam, which could also be sold.) The amount of the heating bill for each house was determined by the quantity of water, condensed from the steam, that collected in a little cup attached to the pipe. It appeared, however, that some of the bills were oddly out of line. Upon investigation, John Ware discovered that a number of people, including a few leading citizens and one Sunday school teacher, were cheating on their heating bills by draining water from the cup before the meter reader came around.

He promptly terminated the heating business, which required many of his neighbors to go to the expense of installing furnaces of their own. It seems unlikely that this added to his popularity in Oxford.

In 1931, after Ware had lived in Oxford for several years, a disagreement arose concerning his house. No one is quite sure what the problem was. Some say the town assessor abruptly raised his taxes. Others say the road in front of the house created a dust problem, and he wanted to reroute it behind the house, but the neighbors refused to go along. Still others say the problem was an unpleasant neighbor. In any case, the matter was deadlocked, with ill feelings all around. Then John Ware took action.

In connection with one of his electrical properties, he owned a street railway in Pittsburgh. So he brought in a crew of railway workers who jacked up the house, placed it on timbers, installed tracks, attached a small locomotive, and proceeded to move it half a mile, across a small valley and up a hill, to a new location.

After the house had been jacked up but before the actual move had begun, the town was abuzz with rumors about what this fellow Ware was up to. Ware played along with the rumors. It happened that one day he brought in a large dump truck and backed it up to the garage under the house. In response to a query from a reporter, Ware responded solemnly that because the truck was a few inches too high to fit into the garage, he was jacking up the house to make room for it. At that point, according to one account, the town fathers considered holding a hearing to have him declared insane. He reportedly answered, "You can hold your hearing if you want to, but I'm still going to move my house."

It took six weeks to complete the move, going at a rate of about one foot a minute. Tracks were laid out ahead of the house and picked up behind it, with John Ware involved at every step, advising, supervising, tinkering, troubleshooting—and enjoying himself immensely.

During the entire time the house was in passage, the family continued to live there, with water, gas and electricity supplied. The Wares even gave a party, billed in the invitation as "The Flittin' of the Wares." The guests at the party had no idea what they were in for until they arrived to find the home in transit. They were also unaware that the house would continue to move while the party was under way. After the party was over, the house had moved far enough that some of the guests were unable to find their cars.

Reflecting afterward on the motive for the move, one long-time associate commented, "I think he just wanted to live at the top of the hill."

Some years earlier, John Ware had also bought a mansion in Florida, on a man-made island between Miami and Miami Beach, within eyeshot of Al Capone's palatial winter residence and just down the street from the house of Hetty Green, reputedly the richest woman in America, known as "the witch of Wall Street." Later there was a problem with the Florida house as well: the place had termites. John Ware's response was equally direct. He ordered the house torn down to its foundation, with nothing left but a marble floor on a concrete slab, along with two bathrooms, one on top of the other, then had a new house built from scratch.

It is said that John had neglected to tell his wife Clara what he was doing to the Florida house until the work was well along, when he happened to mention it in a telephone call to Oxford. Her only response was "Oh, I wish you had told me sooner. I always wanted a bigger dining room." He immediately ordered the work stopped, the wall knocked out, and the house extended four feet to accommodate the larger dining room his wife desired.

Wintering in Florida did have one interesting result. It afforded Ware an early look at someone who was to have an important influence on the future of the public utility industry. He later recalled:

> Franklin Roosevelt belonged to the same boat club. He was an awful Mama's pet. She paid all his bills.
>
> I had him sized up from the start. He hated everybody who could do anything well. My goodness, I certainly never thought he'd get to be president.

New Challenges

Although John Ware's primary concerns throughout his working life were first electricity and then water, his restless imagination was continuously searching for other opportunities. At one point in the early 1930s he heard that natural gas could be used instead of gasoline to power internal combustion engines. It occurred to him that he could use the gas from his gas company to power the pumps for his water companies at a considerable saving over the cost of running the coal-fired steam pumps then in use. He immediately ordered a large storage tank for natural gas installed at one of his pumping stations in New Jersey. After considerable tinkering he managed—at 4 o'clock one morning—to get the gas to run an engine. However, as the price of electricity dropped and the efficiency of electric motors rose, electric pumps rather than gas-powered ones eventually took the place of steam.

After Ware had spent time in Florida and had seen the damage hurricanes could do, it occurred to him that a house made of reinforced concrete, employing reusable steel forms, would be cheap enough for ordinary people to own and sturdy enough to resist hurricanes. He built a number of those houses, both in Oxford and Miami. Several still survive. They were cheap and obviously durable. From a marketing standpoint, however, there were two problems: The houses were ugly, and they all looked the same. As it turned out, there was not a strong demand for large numbers of identical ugly houses. But if John Ware's idea was ahead of its time, and if his execution lacked something in aesthetic quality, the concept was sound and foreshadowed the development homes and prefabricated structures of today.

To rebuild his own house and to construct his concrete houses, John needed windows, and wooden window frames not only required considerable labor to assemble, but in Florida tended to attract termites. So he started a company to manufacture windows of aluminum. For many years the company produced windows, not only for Ware's concrete houses and his utility plants around the country, but for the commercial market as well. Shortly after World War II, the Prudential Insurance Company sponsored a large housing development in southern California. They tested all aluminum windows then on the market and declared the Ware windows the best of the lot.

At some point Ware also heard that it might be possible to make wallboard or particle board for his buildings out of fallen palm fronds, of which Florida has a plentiful supply. He ordered an experimental processing plant constructed on property he owned near the Miami airport. This experiment was also not a commercial success. But here again the concept, while ahead of its time, was sound: Witness the various kinds of fiber board and particle board on the market today.

When World War II began there was tremendous demand for war materials of all kinds. One of the most critical shortages was of high-precision optical lenses for bombsights and other military devices. Before the war the lenses had been supplied by German optical companies, but that source was now cut off. John Ware decided that his contribution to the war effort should be to manufacture the lenses so desperately needed. The fact that he had absolutely no experience in the field did not deter him—perhaps it even attracted him.

The officer in charge of lens procurement at the Frankford Arsenal in Philadelphia was John L. Plummer, an engineer recently graduated from Louisiana State University. As Plummer recalled it:

I first met John Ware in 1942. He came to my office with his son Willard and said that he understood there was a shortage of optics for military purposes, and was interested in getting into the business. I talked to them for a while and found out they didn't know anything at all about optics. But Mr. Ware explained that he was a man of some financial means, and would be able to make the project go if I wanted him to.

After talking to him for a while longer I told him I thought his interest and the interest of our government would best be served if he took his money and put it into war bonds.

Mr. Ware left without getting any commitment from me. But it wasn't very long—maybe a couple of weeks—before they were back and Mr. Ware said he still wanted to pursue the matter and felt he could do something. In the meantime I had done a little checking and found out that he was indeed a very wealthy man. So I showed him a little more respect when he came back the second time than I did the first.

Finally, at John Ware's insistence, I asked the Birmingham Ordnance District to give him a contract to produce lenses in Miami. We had nothing to lose. We didn't put any money down. We gave him an order and said, "Let's see what you can do."

At the start they didn't even have a plant. Mr. Ware started sending photos of the building as it went up. First a hole in the ground, then the foundation, then the walls, and then a roof. It took a very short time to put up a small building and they got started in optics.

We gave them as much technical help as we could, allowing their people to come up to Frankford to see the optical shop in operation, but they went through the agonies of hell, I would guess, in getting the thing started.

Mr. Ware brought his brother, Charlie Ware, down from Pennsylvania to help set up the plant. Charlie was crippled with arthritis, but he turned out to be a mechanical genius.

They needed equipment so fast I couldn't afford to divert them as much as they wanted. So Charlie got the idea to go to auto junkyards and buy rear axles to get the differentials, which he made into lens-grinding machines. They couldn't get heavy castings to mount the machines on, so they'd dig a hole in the plant floor and set them down and pour concrete in. That was fine and dandy until they had to remove the machinery at the end of the war. It was a helluva job.

Despite the problems, the Delaware Optical Company, as it was called, soon became the most efficient producer in Plummer's optics production group. New orders poured in until it became necessary to build a larger plant. Before the war ended, the company had received "E for Excellence" awards from both the Army and the Navy, and John Ware had not only served his country, but had earned a respectable profit in the bargain.

"He had no more business getting into optics than a jackrabbit," as John Plummer summed it up. "The only thing he knew was that the country needed optics, and when he got something like that in his head he was going to do it or bust a gut."

After the war John Plummer remained in the optical business, founding the Plummer Precision Optics Company, which became a leading manufacturer of precision optics. But Ware himself, satisfied that he had met the challenges of the field, liquidated his optical company and moved on to other things.

Into the Black

The mid-1930s were a difficult time for John Ware. He had entered the water business just as the depression was taking hold, and then proceeded to expand his holdings, using borrowed money, to buy other systems that had fallen on hard times. Thus income was low and debts were high. In the words of Jack Barr, Ware's chief financial man, "We struggled along, and I mean struggled. There were days when you had to scratch to see if you could meet the payroll.

There were days when we scratched to meet the interest on the bonds."

However, at about that time the Pennsylvania state legislature passed a bill making it possible for a municipality or other local body to set up a "public authority" that would have the power to construct a new water system or purchase an existing one. This arrangement would not only give the community greater control of its affairs, but, because the bonds would be tax-free and therefore carry a lower interest charge, would presumably reduce water bills to consumers as well. However, after the authorities bill had been passed, little if any use was made of it. Local communities did not show much interest in borrowing the money required to build or buy a water company and then taking on the headaches of running it. And given the long history of management and financial problems of local water systems, public or private, investors were not exactly lining up to lend them money with which to do this. Then, as often happened, John Ware saw an opportunity that other people had missed. With Jack Barr in tow, he would approach the leaders of a community where one of his water properties was located and propose that they create an authority to buy the local system on the following terms: A major part of the purchase price would be provided by an issue of what Ware called "A bonds," conventional tax-free municipal bonds offered to outside investors. For the balance of the purchase price, Ware agreed to accept and hold what he called "B bonds," at the remarkably low interest rate of 1¾ percent. Under the agreement, the interest on the B bonds would be paid to John Ware only after the obligations on the A bonds had been met. Furthermore, the terms of the B bonds included a provision that they would be paid in full only if revenues from the water system in question remained above an agreed-upon level. If revenue fell below the target sum in any given year, a certain number of B bonds would be canceled. Meanwhile, to assure that the system would be run efficiently and the revenues, and the water, continue to flow, Ware would take a management contract, and receive a management fee, for the term of the bonds—40 years.

Like the proposal he presented to the investment bankers 10 years later in his successful effort to acquire control of American Water Works, Ware had devised a no-lose proposition. The local community gained control of its water system, along with the prospect of lower rates, with no outlay of taxpayers' money and no management headaches. Meanwhile, the management contract, along with Ware's continuing commitment represented by the B bonds, made the A bonds attractive to outside investors. At the same time, through the device of the B bonds, he would receive a good price for the property—substantially more than he could have obtained in the open market—along with a long-term management fee and tax-free interest on the bonds.

There was an element of risk for Ware. If revenue fell below the agreed-upon level, some or all of the B bonds would be canceled. But risk had never bothered John Ware. And as Kenneth Gemmill, one of his lawyers, recalled many years later, "I don't think there was ever a default on the B bonds. Never! Never!" And several of the management contracts negotiated in the 1940s were still in force in the late 1980s.

Between 1938 and 1942, Ware sold six local water companies to authorities in Pennsylvania, thereby raising cash with which to pay his debts. "By that means," in the words of Jack Barr, Ware's financial man, "by 1941–42 we'd gotten around to where you could stick your head out and look around." In looking around, Ware spotted the Northeastern Water & Electric Company, borrowed to the hilt once again to buy it, and the cycle of debt and repayment started again.

However, as noted earlier, the Northeastern purchase included three electrical properties. Within a year Ware had sold those off and used the proceeds to retire part of the debt. Meanwhile, he continued selling water properties to authorities; the profits from his wartime optical business were substantial; and his aluminum window business also contributed, as did his natural gas company. By 1947, John Ware had once again reached the point where he could "stick his head out and look around." This time it was the soon-to-be-created American Water Works Company that caught his eye. Now his energy, imagination, and boundless ambition were focused on this new goal.*

What Happened?

Although it could never be proved, it seems clear that the circumstance that made it possible for Ware to win control of American was management's plan to give stockholders of the old company, American Water Works & Electric, first refusal on buying the shares of the new one. As the underwriters pointed out in their first discussions with Ware, the uncertainty about how many shares would be subscribed by the existing shareholders made it impossible to predict how many shares would remain to be offered to the public. This in turn made it difficult if not impossible for potential underwriters to know what price they could safely bid. It was John Ware's willingness to protect his underwriting team from loss by guaranteeing to buy the bulk of the remaining shares, regardless of how many there might turn out to be, that enabled them to submit the winning bid—the only bid as it turned out—on the new shares.

And yet curiously—ironically—the management of the old company had anticipated precisely this situation and had made provision to deal with it in case it arose. AWW&E filed its plan for disposing of the water properties with the SEC on February 21, 1946. Eleven months later, on January 21, 1947, after the long delay resulting from the dispute with the minority stockholders regard-

---

*Interestingly, once he had disposed of the electric utility holdings of Northeastern, John Ware applied for, and was granted, an order from the SEC declaring that Northeastern was no longer a holding company under the terms of the Public Utility Holding Company Act of 1935—which was directed primarily at electric and gas utilities. Thus, at a time when companies such as American Water Works & Electric were struggling to accomplish the restructuring required by the law, Ware was now free to wheel and deal as he chose.

ing the terms for exchanging their shares, the company filed an amended plan. This plan authorized the directors of American to withdraw the offer to existing stockholders of first refusal on the new shares if the situation in the financial markets at that time made it advisable. Following is the explanation that was offered.*

> At the time of the filing of the Plans in February of 1946 investment bankers were willing to underwrite issues of securities which stockholders were to have the prior right to purchase . . . the underwriters agreeing to purchase at an agreed price . . . all shares so offered to stockholders and not subscribed by them. However, due to the marked changes in the securities markets occurring since that time . . . American is advised by representative investment bankers that, under market conditions now prevailing, it would probably be impossible today for Water Works Holding Company to obtain satisfactory bids, or possibly any bids at all, from reputable underwriters for the proposed issue of its common stock, if subscription warrants therefor are to be issued, and that there can be no assurance that similar conditions will not prevail at such future time as Plan I is to be consummated. American is also advised that, even under circumstances which would render it impossible to secure a satisfactory underwriting of the common stock of Water Works Holding Company where such stock is first being offered to stockholders of American, it may well be possible to secure an underwriting of such stock on favorable terms if the prior offering to stockholders is eliminated and the common stock is sold directly to the underwriters under arrangements which will permit its immediate and unrestricted sale by them. . . .
>
> Accordingly, provision is made in the amended Plan . . . for carrying out the Plan without such prior stockholders' rights if, in the opinion of the Board of Directors of American, market conditions then prevailing make it impractical or inadvisable . . . to issue transferrable subscription warrants to its common stockholders.

There it is in black and white, in the careful language of well-paid lawyers: the situation the company's own underwriters

---

*"Plan I" was the plan to create the new water company and sell off its shares. "Plan II" was the plan to liquidate the old company, AWW&E. "Water Works Holding Company" was the interim name of the new company; it would later be changed to "American Water Works." "Subscription warrants" were the documents which would grant the right of prior purchase to the stockholders of AWW&E.

warned them about in January of 1947, and the situation John Ware's underwriters immediately recognized a few months later. And yet despite the warning, despite the escape clause built into the revised plan, the company went ahead with its underwriting and fell into the trap it could have known—should have known— was there.

The question has to be asked, Why? Why did not the management of AWW&E recognize that the situation they had been warned against was now likely to arise, and take the action needed to avert the problem by canceling the first-refusal plan?

A possible explanation is that the matter had dragged on so long that when the time came to execute the plan, someone just pulled it out of the drawer, dusted it off and went ahead, without considering whether or not the earlier assumptions still applied.

A related possibility is that people were simply busy—the electric people with reorganizing the electric business, the water people with setting up the water business—and everybody thought somebody else was taking care of the financial side. So when the offer came, when the blow fell, it caught everyone by surprise.

What is evident in any case is that there was total miscalculation. The shock and surprise at 50 Broad Street when the bid was opened make that plain. Perhaps the thought—if there was a thought—had been that if the market did not take to the original plan, there would be no bids at all, at which point the plan could have been modified and bids solicited again. In any case it was assumed that the stock, whenever and however issued, would be widely held, leaving effective control of the company in the hands of management. What no one imagined was that a shrewd and determined outsider would quietly structure a deal whereby a majority of the new shares would simply fall into his lap.

The record does not show at precisely what point the underwriters broke the news to the management of AWW&E that their bid included a commitment to sell a controlling interest in the new company to Ware. It is possible that they decided to say nothing at the time the bid was opened. The terms of the offering allowed the company two hours, from noon till 2 P.M. on September 25, 1947, in which to accept or reject any or all bids that might have been submitted. The underwriters might have feared that breaking the news at that moment would have queered the deal. Perhaps they waited until the following day to ask for a meeting at which, as gently as possible under the circumstances, they informed the sellers of the strings attached to their bid.

However, even after the company had accepted the underwriters' offer, it was free to change its mind. The terms of the offering also reserved for the seller of the shares the right to cancel the underwriting at any time before the subscription warrants for the new stock had been mailed to the holders of the old shares—and that process would have taken at least a day or two. The company could thus have canceled the underwriting, withdrawn the first-refusal terms, and offered the stock for bid again with that impediment removed.

But that was not done. Again the question has to be asked, Why? Why was the bid not rejected? Or, failing that, why was the underwriting not canceled when the management learned of its unwelcome terms? Conceivably, the people at AWW&E thought the Ware offer was the best they could get. And yet if they had received a bid of $8 a share despite the uncertainty created by the first-refusal terms, it seems reasonable to assume that they would have obtained one at least as good without it. The document they filed in January made that assumption clear.

Or perhaps, after the long ordeal, all participants were simply tired and wanted to put the matter behind them and get on with their lives. However, the shock and anger of Chapman and Semple, the president and vice president of the new water company, suggest that if they had had any say in the matter, they would have rejected Ware's offer out of hand.

But it seems unlikely that they had any say. It appears more probable that it was the electric utility people, who had long been dominant in the organization, who were calling the shots. H. Hobart Porter's major contribution to the company had been to build up the electric utility side; his successor as president was Earle S. Thompson, an electric utility man, and Thompson had been slated

Sentence of Death

The passage below, consisting of no fewer than 254 words gathered into one enormous sentence, will never be praised for its clarity nor compared to Shakespeare for its poetry. Nonetheless it is a classic of sorts, for it embodies the terms which persuaded the investment bankers to submit the bid that enabled John Ware to lift control of American Water Works out of the hands of its shocked and astonished managers:

> Pursuant to the foregoing provisions of the Agreement Among Underwriters, the Representatives propose to enter into an agreement on behalf of the several Underwriters with Northeastern Water Company, a Delaware corporation (hereinafter called Northeastern), as soon as the Post-Effective Amendment to the Registration Statement shall become effective, pursuant to which the several Underwriters will agree to sell to Northeastern, when, as and if issued to the several Underwriters, and Northeastern will agree to purchase from the several Underwriters, at the initial public offering price set forth on the cover of this Prospectus, either (a) 1,379,281 shares of Common Stock of the Company (with the option to Northeastern to purchase up to but not exceeding 270,447 additional shares of Common Stock), if the number of Unsubscribed and Unexchanged Shares of Common Stock to be purchased by the several Underwriters from the Company shall equal or exceed 1,379,281 shares of Common Stock, or (b) up to but not exceeding 1,081,789 shares of Common Stock of the Company, if the number of Unsubscribed and Unexchanged Shares of Common Stock to be purchased by the several Underwriters from the Company shall equal or exceed 811,342 shares but shall be less than 1,379,281 shares of Common Stock, it being understood that, within the limits stated above, Northeastern shall be obligated or shall have the option to purchase and the several Underwriters shall be obligated to sell all the Unsubscribed and Unexchanged Shares of Common Stock which the several Underwriters shall purchase from the Company pursuant to the Purchase Contract.

not only to become president of the surviving electric company, but also chairman of the board of the water company, after the reorganization was complete.

While the electric utility people had obviously hoped to get a better price for the water business than they did—all proceeds from the sale of the water company were to go to the electric company after the expenses of reorganization had been deducted—it appears the priority for them at that point may have been simply to get the deal done. If some outsider had appeared out of nowhere to take control of the water business, that was regrettable, especially for Chapman and Semple, who would likely lose their jobs. But that was the luck of the draw. Those things happen. The important thing now was to close the matter out and get back to the business of selling electricity. Thus John Ware's offer was accepted.

While the reorganization plan was making its halting progress toward execution, a melancholy episode occurred. Late in 1946, H. Hobart Porter, now 81 years old and still chairman of the board of American Water Works & Electric, was on his way to lunch at the University Club in New York. When an elevator door malfunctioned, Porter's leg was crushed. After a lingering and painful stay in the hospital, he died of his injury on February 9, 1947, an undistinguished end for a very distinguished man.

The event was symbolic: An important and colorful era, presided over by a talented and effective leader, was coming to a close. And come to a close it did, a little more than seven months later, when American Water Works & Electric, like American Water Works & Guarantee before it, passed out of existence, and a third incarnation of the enterprise bearing the American Water Works name came into being in the hands of another talented but very different individual named John Ware.

John Ware (*left*) and his younger brother, Charles, in Philadelphia about 1896.

Ware family members identify this house as John and Clara Ware's first home in Millville, New Jersey.

Clara Edwards Ware, whose steady nature helped to balance her husband John's more impulsive temperament.

Below: Clara Ware with her sons Willard (*left*) and John 3rd in the early 1920s.

One of the "Ware chairs" built by a branch of the Ware family between the late eighteenth and the early twentieth century.

Below: John Ware's winter home (bottom center, white roof) on Star Island in Biscayne Bay eventually became the home of his son Willard and Willard's wife Rhoda. This view is looking northeast, toward Miami Beach.

The Ware homestead in Oxford, Pennsylvania, as it was being moved from one hill to another.

Facing page, top: This verse by a friend, with accompanying sketch, appeared in the Wares' invitation to their house-moving party.

Facing page, bottom: A poured-concrete house in Oxford, Pennsylvania, characteristic of the ones John Ware built in the 1940s.

THE BALLAD O' THE FLITTIN'

Sure, the rumor's false, and wholly unfair!
It's only the house, and not John Ware,
    That's on the skids.

Believe it or not, with nowhere a crack,
The Homestead is slipping down the track,
    To a distant hill.

Yes, living as usual goes on within!
Plus a bit more dirt and quite some din.
    But such is life!

Don't think he's crazy, causing all this jam—
Johnny simply-doesn't-give-a-damn!
    So what the hades!

But on to Oxford and see the steel groove
That Johnny has built for this latest move—
    Regardless of cost!

The moral, dear friends, of this here flittin'—
If discontented, why don't stay sittin'—
    Move your house along!

—ZIM

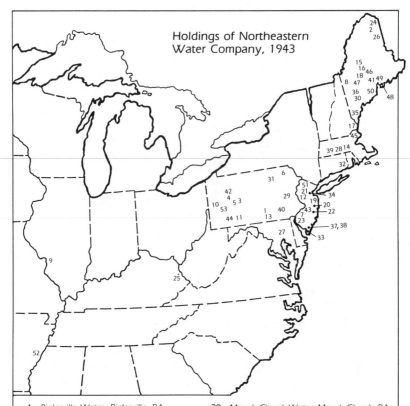

Holdings of Northeastern Water Company, 1943

1 Biglerville Water, Biglerville, PA	29 Mauch Chunk Water, Mauch Chunk, PA
2 Caribou Water Works, Caribou, ME	30 Mechanic Falls Water, Mechanic Falls, ME
3 Citizens Water Service, Philipsburg, PA	31 Morris Water, Morris, PA
4 Clarion Water, Clarion, PA	32 Mystic Valley Water, Mystic, CT
5 Clymer Water Service, Clymer, PA	33 Neptunus Water, Cape May Court House, NJ
6 Consumers Water Company of Montrose, PA	34 New Jersey Water Service, Little Falls, NJ
7 Delaware River Water, Palmyra, NJ	35 North Berwick Water, North Berwick, ME
8 Eastport Water, Eastport, ME	36 Norway Water, Norway, ME
9 Edwardsville Water, Edwardsville, IL	37 Ocean City Sewer Service, Ocean City, NJ
10 Ellwood Consolidated Water, Ellwood City, PA	38 Ocean City Water Service, Ocean City, NJ
11 Everett Water, Everett, PA	39 Oxford Water, Oxford, MA
12 Frenchtown Water, Frenchtown, NJ	40 Parkesburg Water, Parkesburg, PA
13 Gettysburg Water, Gettysburg, PA	41 Penobscot County Water, Brewer, ME
14 Grafton Water, Grafton, MA	42 Punxsutawney Water Service, Punxsutawney, PA
15 Greenville Water, Greenville, ME	43 Riverton and Palmyra Water, Riverton, NJ
16 Guilford Water, Guilford, ME	44 Riverton Consolidated Water, Lemoyne, PA
17 Hampton Water-Works, Hampton, NH	45 Salisbury Water Supply, Salisbury, MA
18 Hartland Water, Hartland, ME	46 Sangerville Water Supply, Sangerville, ME
19 Ideal Beach Water, East Keansburg, NJ	47 Skowhegan Water, Skowhegan, ME
20 Jamesburg Water, Jamesburg, NJ	48 Southwest Harbor Water, Southwest Harbor, ME
21 Junction Water, Hampton, NJ	49 Stockton Springs Water, Stockton Springs, ME
22 Lakewood Water, Lakewood, NJ	50 Waldoboro Water, Waldoboro, ME
23 Laurel Springs Water Works, Laurel Springs, NJ	51 Washington Water, Washington, NJ
24 Limestone Water and Sewer, Limestone, ME	52 West Helena Water Works, West Helena, AR
25 Louisa Water, Louisa, KY	53 West Penn Water, McDonald, PA
26 Mars Hill & Blaine Water, Mars Hill, ME	
27 Maryland Water Works, Bel Air, MD	
28 Massachusetts Water Works, Millbury, MA	

Facing page: The holdings of Northeastern Water Company after John Ware consolidated his smaller water companies under the Northeastern name.

A distribution crew at the South Pittsburgh Water Company (part of the American System) in 1940.

An age-old problem: plants that treat river water, like this one at Peoria, Illinois, are often susceptible to flooding.

Pipe-laying by the South Pittsburgh Water Company in 1951, a few years after John Ware acquired the American System. Notice the absence of hard hats in that era.

Winners Take All

Only hours after his control of American had been confirmed, Ware walked into the company's headquarters in New York, accompanied by his chief lieutenants, Lawrence T. "Bill" Reinicker and John J. "Jack" Barr. The employees at American, who awaited their arrival with understandable apprehension, found them friendly, informal, approachable—and decisive. One by one the newcomers talked to the members of the staff. Who are you? they wanted to know. How long have you been here? What do you do? Then they would decide, almost on the spot, whether the employee would stay or go: We won't be needing you; we'll arrange for severance. We need you; we want you to stay around. However, most of the departures were near the top. There was no mass housecleaning, no "Saturday night massacre." Once the decisions had been made as to who was to leave and who to stay, Ware and his people moved quickly, through formal meetings, informal chats and chance encounters in the hallway, to reassure the remaining employees that they were needed. The management that emerged, in fact, contained four American people to only three from Northeastern, although there was no question about who occupied the catbird seat.

The Northeastern Water Company retained its separate existence as a corporation for more than a decade—that is, as long as John Ware was actively involved with the company—no doubt reflecting his reluctance to merge an entity he fully controlled with one in which there were still substantial outside holdings. However, the two companies shared many of the same officers and directors;

American Water Works Company, Inc.
Officers, 1948

From Northeastern Water Company:

John Ware, Chairman of the Board and President
Lawrence T. Reinicker, Vice President
John J. Barr, Vice President

From American Water Works Company:

Clarence H. Dickey, Vice President
Marshall A. Anderson, Treasurer
Howard H. Briggs, Secretary
L. Edward Sharpe, Comptroller

---

employees were transferred freely between them; and the problems and decisions were the same. Thus, the separation existed largely on paper.

Starting that October, Bill Reinicker and Jack Barr took up residence in the Commodore Hotel in Manhattan, commuting home to the Philadelphia area on the weekends. John Ware continued to live in Oxford, but kept an office at American's headquarters in New York.

The summer after he took control of American, Ware found his New York office unbearably hot. Despite the severe postwar shortage of such items, he somehow managed, in typical John Ware fashion, to lay his hands on an air conditioner, and now his office was comfortable and cool. Then he began to feel guilty because he had taken care to make himself comfortable, while his associates continued to swelter in the heat. He located four more air conditioners, and one hot July evening set out to install them. As was typical of Ware, he was directly and personally in charge, stripped to his undershirt, sweating in the heat, issuing orders that tools and stepladders be obtained from whatever source. But these were not the usual gentle requests. The night was hot; the hour was late; Ware wanted to finish the job. Finally, after midnight, the conditioners were installed.

Although their offices were now cool, the senior people at Northeastern/American still had reason to feel uncomfortable. They had no roots in New York, nor did they feel any ties, social or financial, to the life of the city. Not surprisingly, once the organization had settled down, the operating headquarters of the combined companies was moved back to home ground: Philadelphia. The staff was located on the eleventh floor at 121 South Broad Street. Ware kept a suite of offices on the floor below, along with an apartment at the Ritz-Carlton Hotel nearby. (He now had five residences: the house in Oxford, the house in Florida, the apartment in Philadelphia, another apartment at the Carlton House in Pittsburgh, and a third at the Penn Albert Hotel in nearby Greensburg. He also kept an office in Greensburg, close to a number of the company's operations.)

While in Philadelphia, Ware could be seen in his office, wearing the green eyeshade of an old-fashioned bookkeeper, along with the headset of a telephone operator, so that his hands would be free during numerous and protracted telephone calls. He also sometimes wore the elastic "sleeve garters" favored by bartenders and barbers in the nineteenth century. He usually had an afternoon snack of milk and cookies.

Parking was difficult near the Philadelphia office, but not for John Ware. His chauffeur would pull the car directly in front of the building, in an area liberally posted with "no parking" signs. But the policeman on duty, who had been tipped regularly and generously, would not only greet Ware but would hurry over, hold the door for him, and then stop traffic to allow him to depart.

Just as the headquarters of American Water Works took on the stamp of John Ware, so did its board of directors. The annual report for 1947, the year he took over, listed Ware as chairman of the board, and Gilbert Chapman and Lorenzo Semple, the senior members of the previous management, as president and vice president, respectively; the following year they were gone. The early boards also included Oliver B. Merrill, a partner in Sullivan and Cromwell, the prominent New York law firm that had been involved in the takeover negotiations, and George D. Woods, chairman of the First Boston Corporation, one of the lead underwriters of the stock that Ware purchased. Within a few years they were gone as well.

Ware's chief lieutenants, Bill Reinicker and Jack Barr, were members from the start. As time passed, Ware also named his two sons, John 3rd and Willard, to the board, along with John Plummer, the former Army procurement officer who had made it possible for Ware to set up his optical business, and other friends and business associates from Philadelphia.

William Langley, the other investment banker who had been instrumental in the takeover of American, and earlier had assisted in financing Northeastern, was also a member, and remained until he retired in 1952. Jim MacIntosh, the lawyer who had played a key role in formulating the strategy of the takeover, was also on the board from the beginning. Later, Ware named another lawyer from Philadelphia, Kenneth Gemmill, to the board.

Thus, despite the fact that 40 percent of the common stock of American continued to be publicly held, the makeup of its board soon became that of a closely held, family-owned company, dominated by a single individual: John Ware.

Whether in Florida, Oxford, Philadelphia or Pittsburgh, Ware was kept informed of the operational and financial progress of his companies and participated in all significant decisions. He also kept track of people, showing a particular interest in employees who had started, like himself, without educational advantage. When he saw that someone was willing to work and able to produce, he took care to see that his career moved ahead, regardless of formal schooling.

But Ware did not involve himself in the day-to-day operation of his enterprises. The water companies he left to his lieutenants, Reinicker and Barr. His gas company in Oxford he put in the hands of his elder son, John Ware 3rd. To his younger son, Willard, he had entrusted the aluminum window business in Florida, along with his wartime venture in optical lenses. Meanwhile, Ware himself was occupied as always with dreaming dreams, cutting deals, and hands-on involvement with whatever project lay immediately to hand. If a piece of property was being considered as the site for a new office building, Ware would inspect it. If there was an opportunity to sell a water company at a profit, he would make the contact and conduct the negotiations. If a major construction project was under way, he could be counted on to show up and offer advice. If an extension of an existing water system was contemplated, he would travel the back roads himself, counting potential customers with a hand-held clicker to estimate demand.

John Ware normally presided at meetings of the boards of directors of American and Northeastern. However, if a meeting began to bore him—a not uncommon happening—he would excuse himself and go back to his office to continue an endless series of telephone calls relating to some pending deal. As Jack Barr put it later, "He was the phone company's best customer."

Meanwhile, Back at the Water Works . . .

The life of an entrepreneur does not always end happily. Too often after spectacular success based on boundless energy, unshakable confidence and brilliant innovation, he sees the enterprise fail or slip from his control because of a lack of inclination for day-to-day managing, or an unwillingness to choose competent managers and delegate to them, or simply because, in his search for new worlds to conquer, he neglects the existing business or takes unacceptable risks. An exception to this pattern was Thomas A. Edison, who started one company after another on the basis of his inventions. Then as soon as feasible, he would put competent managers in charge and go back to his laboratory to invent something else.

John Ware was another exception. During his career he might not show up at the office for weeks at a time, while off pursuing or promoting some new venture. Meanwhile he left the water business in the hands of people he trusted—and rewarded—who over time had proved themselves competent to manage successfully. Starting in the 1920s, his principal deputy was Bill Reinicker, a graduate of Cornell University with a degree in engineering, to whom he assigned not only the day-to-day management of the water companies, but such other important responsibilities as orchestrating the move of his house in Oxford. (Ware did not draw a clear line between business matters and personal concerns. Whether he wanted to move a house, buy or sell a company, or build a reservoir, he deployed whatever talent was available to get the job done.)

In the late 1930s, Jack Barr also became a key member of Ware's management team. As time passed, and Reinicker retired and John Ware faded from the scene, Barr emerged not only as the dominant figure in the American Water Works Company, but also as the giant of the investor-owned water utility industry.

It is a truism that there are two kinds of people in the water business. There are operations men whose primary concern is keeping the system running and providing reliable service. And there are financial people, the money men, whose chief preoccupation is the bottom line. Needless to say, there is a kind of built-in tension between the two. It is not unheard of for operations people to complain that money men have neither the heart nor the conscience to care about serving the customer, while financial people have been known to observe that operations people do not have the inclination, if indeed they have the intelligence, to pay attention to the bottom line. A combination of the two is obviously necessary. As between John Ware's lieutenants, Bill Reinicker was the operations man; Jack Barr, emphatically, the money man.

When Ware acquired control of American Water Works in 1947, Reinicker, who was then 53, and Jack Barr, who was 33, were named vice presidents of the company, while Ware took the titles of chairman of the board and president. Six years later, in 1953, Reinicker, now 59 years of age, was promoted to president, and John Ware, then 65, continued as chairman. The following year Reinicker was elevated to the newly created rank of vice chairman—the next year he retired—while Jack Barr, at 40, became president. Ware continued to be chairman and, at least nominally, chief executive. However, for practical purposes, Jack Barr now ran the company.

In the late nineteenth century, while the water business was in its infancy, engineering could fairly be described as the dominant discipline in the field. To the extent that they had any formal training at all, the builders and operators of early water companies tended to be engineers. In the early twentieth century, H. Hobart Porter, who took over management of the new American Water Works & Electric Company, had also been trained as an engineer, and engineering dominated the company for the next 30 years. When it was separated from AWW&E in 1947, the American Water Works Company boasted the largest engineering department in the water supply industry—125 professionals. But in the years that followed, with the huge investments required to keep pace with the growth of the postwar American economy, with the rate increases needed to support those investments, and with the need to pay off the debts John Ware had incurred in buying Northeastern and then winning control of American, the key not only to success but also to survival was a money man. And that was Jack Barr.

Tall, handsome, athletic—he is still remembered as the "dynamite third baseman" of the Oxford, Pennsylvania, town baseball team—Barr hardly seemed the financial type. "He was so good looking," recalls one old-timer, "people tended to underestimate him. They didn't allow for the fact that there was a very keen mind at work there."

Jack Barr did indeed have a good head for numbers. But he had not originally intended to become a money man, nor had he necessarily thought of entering the water business until he found himself in it. Here is his story as he told it:

I got out of high school in Palmyra, New Jersey—across the river from Philadelphia—in 1931, in the depth of the depression. My grandparents raised me; my dad passed away when I was four years old. I started college but had to give up after the first semester for financial reasons. I had worked at a drug store part-time since my second year of high school. Having given up college, I was still working in the drug store. One day Gene Hargett came in. He was what we later termed a division manager [for the Riverton-Palmyra Water Company, Ware's local operating property] whom I had gotten to know coming in and out of the store. He was a great Coca-Cola drinker.

Gene Hargett walked in one day and said, "What are you doing?" I said, "I'm working here at the drugstore." He said, "You're not here all the time?" I said, "No." He said, "Well, do you want a job?" I said, "What doing?" He said, "What the hell do you care?"

That's how I started with the Riverton-Palmyra Water Company. It was in the spring of 1932. I started out trying to collect delinquent bills. Like all other companies at that time, accounts had run up. They hadn't been too strong enforcing collections, and we had a terrible list of delinquent accounts. So I walked door-to-door extracting 50 cents when I could, a buck when you could get it. I did that for a year, and then started working in the office with Gene Hargett, keeping the customers' accounts.

In 1934 the treasurer of the company, Clyde McAdee, came over to make an audit, to see whether anybody was holding some cash out of the accounts and so forth. That's how I met him, and he was a great character. We walked door-to-door for about a week checking customers to see how much they owed and if that agreed with our records.

About two weeks after he left, McAdee called me up and said, "How about coming over and working in Philadelphia in the main office?" So I started over there in early '34. And then I started going to the University of Pennsylvania at night, studying accounting.*

---

*It is interesting that Jack Barr, like John Ware, grew up without a father in the house; Barr, like Ware, did not have a college degree; and Barr, like Ware, continued his education at night. In interviews late in life, Ware made a great point of the fact that he had dropped out of school at age 14. However, after he left high school he actually studied engineering part-time at the Drexel Institute in Philadelphia.

It was shortly before he moved to the Philadelphia office that Barr first met John Ware, and that encounter very possibly had something to do with the invitation to move to Philadelphia. Here is his memory of that event:

John Ware had become involved in natural gas properties in western Pennsylvania, related to the gas company that he owned in Oxford. That led to his discovery that some people were undertaking to fuel gasoline engines with natural gas. So he came up with the idea that we build a new pump station over at the Riverton-Palmyra Water Company and the pumps were to be run with natural gas. And of course the natural gas was to come out of his well fields in Western Pennsylvania.

I'll never forget the day they called the Palmyra office and said that there was a truck down at the toll booths at the Tacony-Palmyra Bridge [over the Delaware River] that had a great big damn tank on it, and the driver didn't have any money to pay the toll. And he was supposed to be coming to the Riverton-Palmyra Water Company. I was alone at the office at the time, but I finally got Gene Hargett on the telephone. He came rushing in and told me to take $100 out of petty cash and go down and get the guy through, which I did. He had the biggest damn tank that you ever saw in your life.

So he pulled this great big trailer up on the river bank at Palmyra. And this was in the late afternoon—he hadn't had any sleep for 48 hours or so—so he just up and left. But the next day, Bill Reinicker and two engineers that Mr. Ware had retained showed up to supervise the unloading of this tank. We started calling them the Three Wise Men. First of all they rolled the tank off the truck onto timbers and then the guy was supposed to jack one timber at a time here, and then jack the other down there, to lower it gently to the ground. This went on until one o'clock, and then the Wise Men left for lunch. They weren't gone ten minutes until the driver showed up. He just took his truck around, backed it up against the tank and rolled it onto the ground.

So they got the tank all hooked up finally, and the pumps going, but they couldn't get the motors to cool. As soon as they turned the motors up to pump the water they would heat up and kick out. So one afternoon about two o'clock, Gene Hargett called me in and he said, "I want you to take the car and go over to the Packard Building in Philadelphia to pick up Mr. Ware. He's coming over here to show them how to make these pumps run."

Boy, I was living then. He was nothing but a name to me and a big, big man. So I went over to the Packard Building. I was to be there at 3 o'clock and he came out at a quarter after five. He said, "Hi, son," and so forth, and was ready to go. Meanwhile, they had a crew standing around waiting for him.

By about 10 o'clock that night I was out getting different plumbers to open up their shops to try to get some kind of fittings to hook up a special water line for cooling. Finally about three or four o'clock in the morning he got the damn thing running. By the time I got him back to his hotel in Philadelphia he was calling me the "redheaded Irishman," I never knew why. And that was how I first met him.

After that, with due modesty, I sort of became Mr. Ware's fair-haired boy. I was closer to him than anybody, and I traveled with him up through the hills when we sold companies, down in the mines and God knows where. . . .

Over the course of the 1930s, Ware relied increasingly on Barr:

For some reason he was not too close to or fond of McAdee, the treasurer. And he could never tolerate the chief accountant, Gary O'Mann. Gary was the old, green-visored bookkeeper. He just couldn't vary from that straight line, however hot the water, and that didn't appeal to Mr. Ware.

Within two years after I moved to the main office, a couple of people left, and I moved up a bit. Then in 1936 McAdee left. That opened things up a bit more. Some time later, I guess it was very early '38, Gary O'Mann, who had taken over for McAdee, decided he would resign, and we were left with nobody resembling the chief bookkeeper other than myself.

So Barr, then age 24, was named treasurer of Delaware Valley Utilities, joining Bill Reinicker as the second of John Ware's principal deputies.

John Ware favored Jack Barr in more than matters of promotion:

One thing I never will forget him for. I got married in 1937, when Social Security came in the first of the year. We had had a pension plan going in the company for about two years, where they would take money out of your paycheck, little that it was. When Social Security came in, they terminated the pension plan and I think I got something like $200 back, and that was enough for Peggy and me to get married. I got a weekend for the honeymoon, and when I came back to work, Mr. Ware had come in that day—he was spending quite a bit of time in Florida then. He called me in the office and handed me a check for $1,000. That was really something. I was making $75 a month at that time. I've never forgotten it. Then when my first son was born, he gave me another thousand.

Shortly after his marriage, Jack Barr moved to Oxford, where John Ware's principal residence was located. There he encountered a hallmark of the Boss, his desire to talk things over in the evening:

He might call anywhere from six to eleven o'clock at night. "Come over," he would say. "Just to look at something. I want to talk."

Some of his ideas, I had to say, "Oh God, you can't do that. We can't afford that."

"By God, Jack, we'll find the money."

"They Worked Really Well Together"

While there was never a formal division of responsibility between Reinicker and Barr, there were differences in personality as well as background, and these helped determine their roles. According to Howard Carlock, for many years the chief design engineer of American:

Bill Reinicker and Jack Barr were opposites. Bill Reinicker was a quiet, pipe-smoking gentleman, the easy going, fatherly type, who would sit and listen to your problems. Jack Barr was all business, definite, made decisions.

When you talked to Jack Barr and he said no, you knew it was no. When Bill Reinicker said no, you could sit there and reason with him and maybe get him to say yes.

It was like husband and wife. One is firm and says no, and you go to the other one, who maybe will listen to your story. It still may be no, but at least they listen to the whole story. So they worked real well together, and there wasn't any question who the bosses were. It was just those two. The others really worked for them.

Marshall Anderson, treasurer of the organization for many years, recalls,

Bill Reinicker was a quiet guy. When things would go wrong he would chew the end of his pipe and not say much, although you knew that he was thinking a lot. Jack Barr was more outspoken. You knew what he was thinking. He was also very meticulous, right down to the last nut and bolt, and he always knew more than anybody else.

In 1956, Raymond T. Wendell, who had been part of the Northeastern organization when John Ware acquired it in 1942, was transferred to headquarters and gradually emerged as the third member of the senior management team. When Reinicker retired in 1959, Ray Wendell replaced him as the chief operations man— "the dirt and muddy boots guy," in Wendell's words. In contrast to Barr, Wendell had always wanted to be in the water business. Unlike Barr, he made his start elsewhere. Here is his story:

My intention when I got out of school, if I had one, was to get into water works for some reason. I had never had anything to do with it, so I don't know why I had that in mind, but that is what I had in mind.

Wendell graduated from the University of Maine in 1931 with a degree in civil engineering. He took a job as an assistant sanitary engineer with the Department of Health and Welfare of the State of Maine.

> I did a lot of inspection work at restaurants, hotels, and following up on complaints of people being sick from drinking polluted water. My occupation for the first year or so also included working for the director of the Bureau of Health. He was an old country doctor in his 80s, and boy, I'm telling you, that guy had more energy than I did. He took a liking to me some way or another, because I could drive a car on ice. By God, I'm telling you, we drove the state of Maine on ice, in snow, in thunderstorms, and he knew the state of Maine; I don't know how he got to know it, but he knew it. He was a real country doctor, the kind who would get into a rowboat and go out to an island and stay until the mother and baby were stabilized, and then go back home.
>
> I loved that old man, but I hated to have him call me to drive, because I knew it was going to be one hell of a trip.

After two years of making inspections and driving "on ice, in snow, and in thunderstorms," the state of Maine "very nicely" sent Ray Wendell to the University of Michigan for a master's degree in public health engineering.

> I came back from the University of Michigan in the spring and they sent me out inspecting boys' and girls' camps. Maine has about 200 boys' and girls' camps, and I spent about two summers doing that. In the winters I inspected reservoirs and hunted up complaints. All the while I was keeping my eyes on all of the things going on in Maine, and I got a couple of trips with an engineer assigned to water works. So I kind of got tied up with him, making trips with him. Then in 1939 this job became available in Skowhegan, Maine, in the division office of what was then the Northeastern Water & Electric Company. They had a division engineer and he resigned. So Pat Paterson, who was division manager at the time, started hunting around and he came

[101]

to me somehow or another, offered me the job, and I took it. That's how I got into the water works.

Not long after he took the job at Northeastern, Wendell learned that things were not run the same way there as they had been at the Health and Welfare Department.

> The first thing that hit me after I started work—maybe a couple or three months afterward—word came down from headquarters, "Okay, here's your paycheck, but until you guys collect some bills and get some money in the bank, these checks are no good."
> I thought, "Jeez, I'm going into a nice job."

Northeastern Water & Electric had been created out of Atlantic Public Utilities following its bankruptcy. As a result, not only was it short of cash and its facilities run down, but its policies were a carryover from the days before the crash of 1929. As Wendell recalled:

> They were concerned to declare dividends and not pay too much attention to the properties. God, everything run down to hell and gone and no money. You'd have your board of directors meetings every three months and you damn well declare dividends. That's about all you had on the agenda.
> When I went to work for Northeastern, they were still being run by the old guard. The president in New York, Boyd Bennett, he didn't know his ass from third base about running a water company or anything else.
> They sent their chief engineer, who was the only engineer that Northeastern had at that time, to Maine a few times. He loved to come to Maine and stay with my wife and me, and he'd move right in with us. His wife was a society belle in New York, and poor old Pres Mailer was anything but society. He liked to come up and stay with us and visit all the Maine properties.
> Well, he was a steam engineer, and all the water works he knew was getting water in the boilers to make steam. But he and I had some interesting times.

Northeastern's generous dividend policy had a predictable outcome: The company ran out of money in 1942. This gave John
Ware the opportunity to buy it. His first move was to put his lieutenants in charge. According to Wendell,

> Jack Barr and Bill Reinicker were trying to take over without
> upsetting things too much, except they were having a hard
> time to stop the way the old outfit was running things. It was
> kind of a touchy situation. They didn't get along. I would
> get crossed up with the people in New York and Bill Rein-
> icker would learn about it and pat me on the back and say,
> "Give it to them. You're right."
>
> As I say, Boyd Bennett didn't know a damn thing about
> water works or anything else. He's the guy I got crossed up
> with, and Bill Reinicker got interested in me by the copies
> of the letters I wrote Boyd Bennett objecting to things and
> demanding that, damn, we have to *do* something!

Bennett was not Ray Wendell's only problem. Jack Barr did not
share the old management's attitude toward declaring dividends,
but with the financial situation as it was, he too had no great enthusiasm for spending money. So Wendell faced a double hurdle:

> First Bennett says you couldn't do it, then Jack Barr ends up
> telling you you couldn't do it, too.
>
> My first real bump-up against Jack Barr—we had to sub-
> mit work orders from Maine for every bit of capital ex-
> penses, even installing a fire hydrant. We had to send the
> work orders down to the general office and get approval
> before we did it.
>
> Well, my first bump-up against Jack Barr, we had a hy-
> drant broken off in the middle of winter in Caribou, Maine,
> in one of the principal intersections in the business district.
> Now, this is a wooden town. They had a few brick buildings,
> but mostly it is a wooden town, and a fire in the high winds
> they have up there and the whole place would go up. Well,
> that hydrant got broken off and I replaced it and sent a work
> order through afterward. The work order came back dis-
> approved. Well, I had to indicate to Bill Reinicker, who was

my best contact at that time, that dammit, we had to replace that hydrant and you have to tell Jack that this work order has got to be approved.

He said don't worry about it. I don't know how he straightened it out, but he did; and later I got a blistering letter from Jack Barr.

Wendell had other ways of getting work done when he had to:

We had some emergencies up in Aroostook County in the northern part of the state. I remember one where we had a particularly aggravating leak which ended up to be a total of 15 feet under frozen ground. I mean frozen ground. In the daytime we were there with hand chisels, and overnight the damn ground would freeze as fast as they dug it. What an experience that was. I'm up there keeping 'em going, and Pat Paterson and I, to pay the crew, took advances on our expense accounts. If Jack Barr had ever found out about that, he would have blown the lid off the state of Maine.

However, while Ray Wendell had his "bump-ups" with Barr, he is generous with praise:

This Jack Barr was something. The guy was unbelievable. I got crossed up with him so many times on things that I knew we had to do and he said we can't do 'em. But Mr. Ware would not have made a go of this water works without Jack Barr or somebody equal to him, and I'm not kidding a bit.

SEVEN

Uneasy Mix

After John Ware took control of American, the first task confronting the new managers was to blend two very different groups of people into an effective team. At the upper levels of the organization the transition was reasonably smooth. According to Howard Briggs, who was named secretary of American shortly before the takeover and remained with the company afterward, "So far as I was concerned, there wasn't a great deal of difference. I got along with one group. I got along with the other group." (It is worth noting that the four corporate officers of American who survived the first few months remained with the company for many years; three continued in some capacity until they retired.)

At the lower levels of the organization there was a certain amount of muttering at the start. People from the American side were heard to comment that "The tail [Northeastern] is wagging the dog [American]," and to observe darkly, "Well, we'll just have to wait and see," suggesting that if things didn't work out they could always look elsewhere for employment. But in fact things did work out. In the words of Ken Earnhardt, who was assistant manager of one of the American properties at the time of the takeover, "There was no great upheaval that I recall. Everyone with whom I was associated was very comfortable."

But if there was no great upheaval, there was resentment. William S. Harris, who later became a vice president of the service company, joined American as a young engineer in 1950—three years after the takeover—and thus was not identified with either group. However, his first assignment was in western Pennsylvania, which had been largely American territory. A year later, Harris was transferred to the New Jersey Division, whose manager, Tony Greco, was from the Northeastern side. One day, Greco and Harris visited the Monmouth Water Company in New Jersey, whose manager, Oscar Newquist, came from American.

As Bill Harris recalled it,

> When I walked in the door—this was the first time he saw me—he said, "You American or Northeastern?"
> I said, "I don't know."
> He said, "Where did you come from?"
> I said, "Pittsburgh."
> He said, "You're American."
> For the rest of the day he wouldn't talk to Tony. He would only talk to me.

Resentment at the lower levels faded in time. However, at the middle levels of the organization, particularly in operations and engineering, the transition was more difficult. The contrast between the two groups in background and experience and in ways of working and thinking could hardly have been greater. Furthermore, while jobs at the top and bottom of the company were fairly well-defined and reasonably secure, the jobs in the middle were anything but. A corporate secretary is a corporate secretary; where there is a corporation, there is likely to be a secretary. By the same token, a local plant manager is a local plant manager. As long as there is a local plant, it will presumably have a manager.

At the middle levels, the situation was less clear. Supervision over a group of operating companies could be assigned and authority delegated in a variety of ways, depending on the philosophy of the management. And there was no established set of qualifications, especially in a time of change, for filling a given job.

Furthermore, the problem of adjustment was not a one-time thing; it was simply the latest phase of a continuing process. American Water Works and Electric had acquired the Community Water Service Company in 1936, and the assimilation of the Community people into the American organization was not complete in 1947 when John Ware appeared on the scene. Meanwhile, Ware's Delaware Valley Utilities had acquired Northeastern in 1942, and the adjustment pangs of that relationship were still being felt at the time that Ware acquired control of American.

As for the difference between the two organizations, "The American group was larger, more sophisticated," according to Tom Earl, who was chief engineer of American from 1961 to 1976:

> Each man had more of a specialty and they prided themselves on knowing down to the last inch what they knew in their field. The Northeastern men had been working in smaller operations. They had to cover broad areas, and you couldn't expect them to know each part as well. They ran things more from the seat of their pants.

In the view of Howard Briggs, the corporate secretary, "There was more of a personal relationship between the Northeastern people; they grouped together a little bit. On the defensive, I'd say, even though they were in the driver's seat."

Nowhere was the contrast between the two "cultures" more stark than in the matter of centralization or decentralization of authority. John Ware had historically given his subordinates remarkable latitude—and let them sink or swim on that basis. Nor was he a believer in job descriptions. It was not unheard of for him to hire a bright youngster and say to him, "Go out to the plant and see if you can find a way to make yourself useful."

That was *not* the way they did things at American. According to the 200-page "white paper," prepared in 1935 as part of American's effort to persuade the SEC not to break up the company:

> The complete management of the group of subsidiary [water] companies, is centered at this [the New York] office, [which is] eminently fitted ... by virtue of the experience and training of its personnel and its location in the principal national financial market [to perform that function].
>
> The Chief Engineer, who is a man of national prominence and unique experience in the Water Works industry, supervises the activities of the entire group. . . . Four men [on the staff of the Chief Engineer in New York] are designated as Plant Managers, to each

one of which is assigned a group of subsidiary water companies. Each of these Plant Managers . . . maintains an intimate knowledge of the affairs of the companies in his group. . . .

The personnel [of the General Engineering Department] are always available when accidents or emergencies arise . . . and by correspondence, telephone or trips to the plant render assistance . . . which, by reason of their technical training and wide experience, is of immense benefit in overcoming the trouble.

Jack Barr's idea was different:

It was almost ridiculous, the way they operated at the time we took over, when I speak of the overall power of the engineering department. Hell, the guys out in the field would hardly turn a pump on without calling up New York to see if they should.

I'll never forget being down in Lexington, Kentucky, one time. The manager down there was Jake Jacobsen, one of God's finer people. They had a reservoir system down there, 1, 2, 3 and 4 reservoirs. 1, 2 and 3 were really just sections of one big one, but Number 4 was somewhat removed, and it was always a question at what time you start to take water out of Number 4 and let it go down to the lower ones— whether or not it was going to rain. I remember going into the office one morning there, sitting with Jake, and he said, "Say, before we start I want to call Guy Waldrop"—he was an engineer in New York—"and see if I ought to take some water out of Number 4." It didn't really hit me at first. Then I sat there and listened to his telephone conversation where Jake was telling him what it looked like, whether it was going to rain, whether he should take water out of Number 4. Well, they finally decided that they should. When they hung up, I said, "God Almighty, you mean you have to call up New York to find out if you can take water out of that reservoir?"

"Oh, yeah," Jake said, "Oh hell yeah. I'm not going to risk that. Hell, they'd kick me out of here if I didn't check."

Now that was no part of my way of doing business.

At the time of the acquisition of American, the engineering department was headed, in Barr's words, by "a couple of guys who had run the company from an engineering standpoint for years," who "weren't much given to fitting into the new management." In less than a year, not surprisingly, the old timers had retired, and the job of chief engineer was turned over to Elwood H. "Spike" Aldrich, a man more given to fitting in. Then in January 1949, 16 months after Northeastern took control, the company was reorganized. Following the pattern that had existed at Northeastern, the operating subsidiaries were grouped into four geographic divisions, with a resident manager located in each division, rather than in New York. The new division managers reported not to the engineering department but to Reinicker and Barr. (In the style of John Ware, there was, as noted earlier, no precise definition as to which of them was in charge of what. As Ray Wendell put it, "There really was no boss between the two of them.") In the years that followed, the management made a continuing effort to push authority and responsibility down the line, not simply to the division managers (later called regional vice presidents) but to the local plant managers as well.

The reorganization provided an opportunity to move some of the Northeastern people closer to the mainstream of the business. Justus W. "Pat" Patterson, the Northeastern division manager who had originally hired Ray Wendell, was named the head of the eastern section of the Pennsylvania division. Ray Wendell, who by then had become a division manager in Maine, was made head of the western section.

These changes created problems, however. Although he was given added responsibility and a pay raise, Wendell was "demoted" from division manager in Maine to assistant division manager in Pennsylvania. This move nearly provoked a rebellion among his former subordinates in Maine, who felt their boss had been unfairly treated. It also turned out that almost half the American plant managers in Pennsylvania who now reported to Wendell were making more in salary than he was.

"It didn't bother me a damn bit," Wendell recalled. "I was interested in a job and bringing up a family. Salary didn't mean too much to me. It does to a lot of people, though. It means a lot to a lot of people."

[109]

Questions of salary and title were straightened out in time. But even as former Northeastern managers were given new authority, there continued to be tension between the operations people from Northeastern and what might be called the "engineering aristocracy" of American. A case in point was Tony Greco, the New Jersey division manager. In Ray Wendell's words, "Tony Greco was a guy that came out of a ditch, and I mean shoveling dirt out of a ditch. That guy, he could shovel more damn dirt than anybody else as a common laborer, and he became a very capable division manager."

Capable he might have been, but Tony Greco was not comfortable dealing with the American engineering aristocracy. His way of dealing with them was not to deal with them; he went around them. When he needed engineering support, Greco went to Tom Earl. Earl had joined the engineering staff in 1951, four years after John Ware took over and thus, in the eyes of the Northeastern people, was not "one of them."

Other former Northeastern managers also tended to deal with Earl, who recalled that "a lot of what I did was smoothing over the gaps in thinking between them and the American people." When Spike Aldrich retired as chief engineer in 1962, Tom Earl was chosen as his successor, no doubt in part because he had been successful in smoothing over gaps in thinking.

With the reorganization accomplished and relationships settling down, the next step was the move out of New York. One day in 1949, Jack Barr called Marshall Anderson, the treasurer of the company, into his office. "He said they were thinking about moving the company to Philadelphia," Anderson recalled, "and wanted to know what I thought of the idea. We were living in an apartment in Queens at the time and were planning to move anyway. So we didn't mind."

Howard Carlock, a native New Yorker, was not as happy. "My wife had never been to Philadelphia," he recalled. "She hadn't been out of New York City since we were married. If I had known about the move, I wouldn't have taken the job." However, the economy was a bit slack in 1950, and jobs were not plentiful, so Carlock went

The "Outcasts" Are In

Elwood H. "Spike" Aldrich, who became chief engineer at American after John Ware took control, had originally been chief engineer of the Community Water Service Company. After Community was acquired by American in 1936, Aldrich and the former president of Community, Reeves Newsome, left to form their own engineering consulting firm. A few years later, Newsome, not wishing to continue the travel involved in consulting, accepted a job as city manager of the town of Scarsdale, New York, leaving the consulting business to Spike Aldrich. Some time later, young Tom Earl went to work for Newsome as assistant city manager in Scarsdale. Meanwhile, Howard Carlock had been hired by Aldrich as an engineer in the consulting firm.

In early 1947 the old American Water Works & Electric invited Spike Aldrich to join the company (perhaps in an effort to ease relations between the old-timers on the American staff and the people from Community, who still felt they were treated as "outcasts"). Aldrich accepted and later brought Howard Carlock into the American organization as chief design engineer. In 1948, the year after John Ware took over, Spike Aldrich was named chief engineer. A few years later, in 1951, Tom Earl, looking for broader horizons, contacted Aldrich, whom he had met through his boss, Reeves Newsome, and Aldrich hired him as well. In 1961, when Aldrich retired, Tom Earl succeeded him as chief engineer.

So just as the outsiders from Northeastern now controlled the American company as a whole, the "outcasts" from Community emerged to dominate the engineering aristocracy of American.

along with the move—and remained with the company for the rest of his working life.

No Fixed Address

Keeping up with John Ware's deal making during the 1940s required Jack Barr to become, in the language of the police blotter, a man with "no fixed address." Shortly after he married in 1937, Barr had moved to Oxford, Pennsylvania, where John Ware lived. After the headquarters of Ware's water properties was moved from Philadelphia to Oxford, also in 1937, Barr enjoyed the luxury of living and working in the same town. When Ware bought Northeastern Water & Electric in 1942, however, Barr's office was shifted to the company's headquarters in New York. From 1942 until 1946, Barr and Reinicker shared a room at the Downtown Athletic Club in New York during the week, commuting home on the weekends. In 1946, having had enough of that, they arranged to move the headquarters of Northeastern to Camden, New Jersey, just across the river from Philadelphia. Barr then moved his family to nearby Haddon Heights. But he had barely got settled in the office in Camden when, in 1947, Ware took control of American Water Works, and suddenly the headquarters was in New York again. This time Barr shared a room with Reinicker at the Commodore Hotel, next to Grand Central Station, commuting to Haddon Heights on the weekends. In 1950, after three more years of commuting, the headquarters of American was moved to Philadelphia. Barr continued to live in Haddon Heights until his retirement in 1975.

Postwar Surge

While the new management of the company was taking care of such internal "housekeeping" matters as integrating people, decentralizing organization, and relocating the headquarters, powerful forces were at work in the world outside. In the final months of World War II, the "standard forecast," agreed to by most respectable economists, was that the end of the war would be followed by a serious recession, with demobilized troops unable to find jobs as industry converted to peacetime production. That was what had happened after World War I.

However, when most experts agree on anything, they often turn out to be wrong, especially when they see the future as a replay of the past. The end of the war was followed not by recession but by the greatest economic boom the world had ever seen. The boom itself got most of the headlines. Less noticed by the headline writers, and taken largely for granted by the public, was the need for "infrastructure": roads, sewers, streetlights, power lines, police stations, schools—and of course, water facilities—to support the surging growth. In the period 1954 through 1958, the American and Northeastern companies invested more money annually (measured in dollars of constant value) in expanding and improving their facilities than they had in any previous period.

Returning from the service, veterans found jobs. Having jobs, they got married. Being married, they started families. As families grew, they needed bigger houses. Building houses required labor, materials, furniture, appliances—all of which fed the boom—and water service as well. Meanwhile, most of the new housing was not located in the central cities, with their established water systems. Rather, it was built in the new suburbs, where the water system, if there was one, was often operated by a private company.

Not only were there more customers needing water, there was greater demand per customer. Automatic clothes washers were introduced. There was the second car to wash, big suburban lawns to water, backyard swimming pools. In addition, new industries emerged—aluminum, chemicals, plastics—requiring huge amounts of water, while existing companies built new plants, and developing communities wanted expanded water supplies in order to attract industry.

Beyond the surge of demand was another factor, less visible, less spectacular, requiring heavy investment. That was the deplor-

[113]

able condition of existing water facilities. During the speculative boom of the 1920s, the maintenance of physical facilities was the last thing on the minds of the promoters of many of the utility holding companies. As Ray Wendell would put it later, "You'd have your board of directors meetings every three months and you damn well declare dividends. That's about all you had on the agenda."

Then during the Depression years, with industrial activity down, the electric properties of the holding companies were hard hit. Although the revenues of water properties, with their largely residential business, held up better, managements used the water revenues not to maintain the water properties but to make up for losses on the electric side. Then came the war, with its shortages of manpower and material, and the water properties, already run down, were further neglected.

Another factor compounded the effect of all the others: Most of the local water systems had been inadequate in the first place. It had been a fact of life in the water business that new systems, public or private, had insufficient capacity almost from the moment they were built. With initial capital in short supply, too often they barely met the needs of existing customers and failed to make allowance for future growth—growth often made possible by the completion of the new water system. Through decades of neglect and growing demand, many of these inadequate systems were barely kept functioning. By the time of the economic surge of the early 1950s, they were fairly screaming for expansion and modernization.

According to Howard Carlock, "When I first came to the company I was shocked to see some of the junk we called water plants. Broken down old buildings, cracked walls. But John Ware kept 'em running. He replaced the equipment necessary to keep 'em running."

In Ray Wendell's words:

We all had run-down equipment from the prior owners. We had miles and miles of two-inch pipe trying to serve thou-

All Work and No Play . . .

Operating and expanding a water company under the demanding conditions of the early postwar years was serious business, and the people of American took it seriously. But boys will be boys, and engineers will be engineers, and the serious matter of running a major corporation did not preclude occasional horse-play. Tom Earl recalled one episode:

> We were at Tortella's restaurant one day with Bill Reinicker. Bill was a great friend of Roy Evans, who sold valves, fittings, and all, for Mueller Company. Roy and Bill were buddies from way back. Roy would come in once in a while and take a few of us to lunch. Roy had a gang over there one day. We always had the spaghetti, you know, and meatballs, and Bill hands me this thing—they had the grated cheese in this thing you shake—and he said, "Tommy, have some cheese." And I said, "OK," and I just grabbed this thing and shook it all over my spaghetti and it was sugar. So he loved a practical joke. That just knocked his socks off to see me spread sugar all over my spaghetti.

sands of people, and you could not serve them. If you had enough in source, which in a lot of places we didn't, or in the treatment plants, which were also lacking, you couldn't get enough through these damn two-inch pipes; some of which were galvanized and old and rusty.

One of the things we did through the years that I think is probably unrecognized by an awful lot of people, we improved those things. You can list some major projects which we had and they were wonderful. But year after year we worked at these things that people don't hardly recognize. Replacing two-inch pipe, improving filter plants, putting booster pumps in, putting all the storage tanks on the hills. That sort of thing we worked out, us guys, doing the best we could, getting the money out of the head office, and Jack Barr getting it out of the bankers. And we built what I think is a fine water system now all over the country. Through the years, in my thirty-odd years, I think we did a remarkable damn job.

EIGHT

"Howard, Can You Spare a Minute?"

Although dethroned from its former dominance and despite the problems of "interfacing" with the newcomers, the American engineering department—still the largest and best-qualified in the water utility industry—had a major role to play in bringing on stream the new or improved facilities of the postwar era. During that time no engineer was busier than Howard Carlock, the chief design engineer. Over the course of his career, by his estimate, Carlock designed a greater number of filter plants and other water facilities than any other engineer in the business. But no matter how busy he was, every now and then his telephone would ring and a gentle voice would inquire, "Howard, can you spare a minute?" Somehow, Carlock always found time for John Ware.

Ware had discovered that Carlock could get results in matters other than designing filter plants. And when John Ware came across anyone who could do things, he managed to find things for him to do. At one point, for example, Mrs. Ware noticed that the expensive silk drapes in the suite in the Ritz-Carlton did not hang *quite* straight. Ware turned to Carlock, who took care of the matter. On another occasion it turned out that the new wall-to-wall carpet in the living room in Florida was off a shade in color—just a shade—from that of the carpet in the dining room. Carlock saw that that issue was resolved.

Aside from regular briefings on the progress of the business from Jack Barr and Bill Reinicker, and calls to Carlock on such matters as carpets and drapes, Ware ordinarily had little contact with employees. Now and then, however, one would be summoned to his office. John Delaney, the company's public relations man during that period, recalls that on his occasional visits with the Boss, Ware, with his old-fashioned green eyeshade and sleeve garters, "seemed like a relic of another age, still surviving in that little suite of offices in Philadelphia."

On the Road Again

After his control of American was confirmed and the new management was in place, John Ware's interest continued to focus on Pennsylvania, particularly western Pennsylvania, where a number of water properties, both Northeastern and American, were clustered, and where the Municipal Authorities Act offered the prospect of additional sales of properties to generate cash to help pay the debt incurred in buying control of American. On his numerous trips in and around Pittsburgh, Ware would take an employee along to do the driving and to serve as a sounding board for an almost endless stream of ideas. In the early 1950s, Ware's companion on many of these trips was Ray Wendell, who was now in charge of American's regional office in Pittsburgh. Here are his recollections of his time spent with John Ware:

> We did a lot of traveling out in the country, and I mean *out in the country*. He delighted to drive around looking for places for pipeline extensions. He'd find out from me where does your pipeline end. Then he'd drive a mile or two or three down the road and he'd have this clicker counter and he'd count. Ostensibly he was counting houses so you could estimate the revenue from here to there. Actually, I'd hear the damn thing clicking and there wasn't a house in sight.
>
> We'd give Jack Barr these estimates—I'm the one that's giving them to Jack—of course I hadn't been counting, I was just driving the car. Jack would come back at me later when we got the bill for the customers connected and found out

[118]

how many they really were, and he'd give me hell. "I told the bankers we had so-and-so many customers," he'd say.

I told him it was the boss's count, not mine.

"That's all right," he would say. "But you're the guy who told me this stuff."

Come lunchtime and we were out in the country driving around, if he could find it, John Ware would go to a country grocery store and buy a box of crackers and maybe some cheese. And if he could find it we'd go to a local old-fashioned drug store where you could sit up to a soda counter and we'd eat crackers and cheese and a soda fountain Coke—in a tall glass with syrup, he didn't care for this bottled stuff—and that was our lunch. And he'd make me pay for it because I was on the expense account. Then he'd slip the clerk five bucks for a tip. Sometimes if it was real attractive young lad or young gal he'd give 'em ten dollars. And he'd make me pay the dollar and a half.

He was always asking for opinions. He would talk with you far into the night, asking your opinions of one thing or another, some of which you didn't know anything about. But he was interested in my reactions.

He would call me—my wife will tell you—he would call me away from the Christmas dinner table and talk for two, two and a half hours. Then, he'd realize later what he had done, and apologize and slip me ten dollars or fifty dollars. Once he slipped me a $500 bill, just feeling sorry for what he had done.

He was a very simple man. I don't remember three or four times we ate in a hotel dining room or restaurant. At his apartment in Pittsburgh, he'd order ground beef and some crackers sent up for our supper. The only time I ever had lunch with him was at these drug stores.

He used to talk an awful lot about his grandfather. More than he did about his father. In the quiet of the evening or past midnight, anecdotes about his grandfather. This advice that his grandfather would give him, principally about hard work and the desirability of hard work.

I don't know whether the Boss had anything to do with formal religion, but one thing about these foolish little lunches and hamburger dinners, he *never* sat down to eat one of those without asking a blessing. Never. I don't know what he said, but he would bow his head and he obviously

[119]

took the time to ask a rather simple blessing. I would judge he was thanking God and maybe asking for some help on whatever we were doing.

The largest public water system managed under contract by the company was the one in Westmoreland County, just east of Pittsburgh. In the early 1950s the Westmoreland system needed a new water treatment plant. Under the management contract it was Ware's responsibility to provide it, and he committed himself to build the plant at a cost of a million dollars. The anticipated volume of future sales would support no more than that amount. If the plant had cost more, the added interest on the funds required would have eaten into income to the point where, under the B bond agreement, some of the bonds Ware held would be canceled, and he would suffer a substantial loss.

Ware had hired an engineering firm to design the treatment plant. But the firm had "overdesigned" the project, so that when the plans were sent out for bid the cost proved to be not one million, but two and a half times that amount. However, since almost a year had already been lost, there was no time to follow normal procedures in having a new set of plans drawn up. At this point Ware turned to Spike Aldrich, his chief engineer, and Howard Carlock, his senior design engineer. This is what happened, as Carlock later recalled it:

> John Ware got ahold of my boss, Aldrich, and myself, and we had a meeting with him, and he told us the problem. He said to us, sitting in his office, "I've got a million dollars to invest. Can you design me a plant for like half of what the other guys were going to do—less than half? Do you think you can do it?" So we looked at each other and said, "Yeah, we think we can."
>
> Now keep in mind the design of a plant takes nine months to a year, routine design, drawings, specifications, you know. We get a plant and nine months later we're ready to go out for bid. That's typical, even today.
>
> So he said, "Okay, but do you think you can have the plans and specs all ready for bids in two weeks?" So with a deep

sigh, both knowing how long it takes to do these things, we say, "We'll try." What else could you say?

So I took six men and myself, worked eighty hours a week. We designed the plant in three weeks—which I could never do again. Everybody was dedicated. We didn't fool around, we didn't need approvals. I didn't have to go to my boss for approvals or anything. It was just *go.*

We finished in three weeks. We did 90 drawings in three weeks with six men. Now that probably means nothing to you. On a regular project, three weeks and you're just about thinking what you're going to do. But we jumped right in. I wrote the specifications and I had all these guys plugged right in. We'd answer questions—bang, bang—without interruption. How much is this? What are you gonna do here? How do you want that?

We got the job finished in three weeks. Ninety drawings went out for bid. I solicited bids from six or seven contractors. I had to put a bid in, too. I put a bid in under John Ware's window company, and I bid the amount we agreed to, a million dollars. The problem I didn't anticipate was the word got around the key water works builders that I was going out for bids, but I was just looking to see what it was likely to cost, that we weren't going to give it out, we were going to do it ourselves.

So when I went out for bids, only a couple of guys bid. We ended up as low bidder and had to take the job. All of a sudden the window company is in the construction business.

So I ended up with two hats. I end up representing the window company as the contractor and American Water Works as the owner. Now when I sat there and saw I had to make a change and add something, I had to say to myself, how much you going to charge us to add this pad of concrete and so on. You say you need that. How much you gonna charge? So then I had to put my other hat on and say, It's gonna cost you two thousand four hundred and seventy-six dollars.

What we did, we assigned a guy in the office, Bill Mac-Indoe, who did the window company work. He became the officer. He represented the window company. He was just down the hall. I'd write a letter to him, signed by me, requesting the change, always with the idea that I had to come in within the budget that Ware set up. Then I would write a letter from him to me agreeing to the change, take the letter down the hall, and he would sign it.

And, well, we got the job done. When you worked with John Ware you got the job done. But I only did that once. It's the kind of thing you couldn't psych people up to work on every few months. You did it once and everybody jumped in and made every effort to meet a timetable which was impossible, but we did get it done.

After we said we'd do it, John Ware never asked anything. He never asked about the budget, never asked anything. He just assumed everything was in order. You guys said you'd do it, get it done. Go get it done. He gave us two weeks, which was an absolute impossible thing, but it wasn't in the end. It was three weeks and we did do it.

But that's John Ware, and that's the way he could push you without demanding. He didn't demand. He just sort of laid it out for you. "If you say you can do it, all right. I need it in two weeks."

In 1948, the year after he acquired control of American, John Ware negotiated an agreement with the town of Bangor in eastern Pennsylvania to sell the local water company to a municipal authority. The following year he arranged to sell the Myerstown Water Company to another authority. The next year the Municipal Authority of Westmoreland County agreed to add the Vandergrift Water Company to its holdings. But now resistance to this type of transaction was beginning to grow. In 1949, a year after the sale of Bangor had been agreed to, one of the communities served by that company went to court to block the sale. Two years later the borough council of Bangor reversed itself and decided to oppose the sale as well. Later that same year the matter was put to a vote, and the electorate turned it down.

Bangor, Myerstown and Vandergrift were all relatively small transactions. But now Ware came up with a much bigger project. He proposed selling the South Pittsburgh Water Company, with 85,000 customers, to the Westmoreland Authority for $33 million, taking in return the usual 40 year management contract. As in the case of Bangor, the plan to sell South Pittsburgh was at first approved by local authorities. But then the proposal ran into heavy opposition. Critics pointed out that Ware would take a larger profit from managing the company after he sold it than he had been making while he still owned it. After a bitter exchange, in which Ware was accused of being a "business pirate," the proposal was defeated. That was the high water mark for transactions of this type. There were no more voluntary sales of water companies to municipal authorities in Pennsylvania. (This brought a sense of relief to the employees of American, among whom a rumor had begun to spread that Ware was planning to liquidate the company by selling it off in pieces.)

But the Boss was not yet finished. Now he had a far bigger project in mind. The city of Pittsburgh and its surrounding communities had traditionally drawn their water supply from the Monongahela and Allegheny rivers. With the tremendous amount of industrial activity along their banks, these rivers were among the most polluted in the United States. Heavy treatment made the water safe for drinking, but the cost of purification was high and there were chronic complaints about both taste and odor. In the cynical view of one visitor, "In Pittsburgh there's a full meal in every glass of water."

Forty-two miles southeast of the city, in the Laurel Mountains, was a plentiful supply of pure mountain water. And during the years of railroading, when steam locomotives were in use, the Pennsylvania Railroad had created a number of water systems in that area to provide the water needed to operate the locomotives. When diesel engines replaced steam, the railroad no longer needed the water systems.

In 1955, Ware bought the Mountain Water Company from the Pennsylvania Railroad. The system included a dam and reservoir on Indian Creek in the Laurel Mountains and 140 miles of pipeline extending along railroad tracks to a number of communities in the Pittsburgh area, including sections of the city itself. Ware paid $800,000 for the property, which was assessed for tax purposes at

$12 million. The local press considered this deal "one of the cagiest" of his career, "a bargain comparable to the purchase of Manhattan Island from the Indians."

Ware's plan was to build an enormous dam, half a mile across, on Indian Creek, creating a reservoir 12 miles long with a capacity of 154 billion gallons, enough to provide the entire Pittsburgh area with an ample supply of pure mountain water.

However, constructing the project was more easily said than done. The existing pipelines in the Mountain Water system ranged in size from 12 to 36 inches, too small to carry the volume required. And there was not enough room along the railroad right-of-way to enlarge them. Furthermore, the area between Indian Creek and Pittsburgh is mountainous, and the cost of pumping water over the mountains by some other route would have been prohibitive. The alternative was to bore tunnels through the mountains and build aqueducts across the valleys, so the water would move to the city by gravity flow, without the expense of pumping. That was what John Ware proposed to do. This approach would make the cost of getting water to the city affordable. However, the cost of drilling the tunnels and building the aqueducts would have been very high. Estimates ranged from $200 million to $300 million ($900 million to $1.4 billion in 1990 dollars). Raising that amount of capital from private sources would have meant prohibitive financing costs. But as usual Ware had an answer. Most of the money could be raised, as the money had been raised for the sale of his water companies, through the sale of tax-free bonds by a municipal authority. The balance of the financing could be provided by federal land reclamation or flood control funds. (The plan also included the usual 40-year contract under which American, for a fee, would manage the resulting system.)

This was the biggest dream of all, dwarfing the takeover of American, dwarfing anything else he had ever done, and John Ware threw himself into the effort to make the dream come true. Out of his own pocket he financed engineering studies on the feasibility of building the aqueducts and drilling the tunnels. He walked or drove every inch of the route himself. Ray Wendell accompanied Ware on many of these trips. Here is his account of one such excursion:

> One day in West Newton, Pennsylvania, the Boss wanted to see what it would be like to lay a pipeline to the south, down where he was going to come up with this big supply. We were on the railroad track, down on the bank of the Youghiogheny River. Well, to him the easiest way to get to Smithton, which was where he wanted to go, was right down those railroad tracks. Son of a bitch, we drove a Cadillac Coupe de Ville down the railroad tracks from West Newton to Smithton over my protests.
>
> "Jeez," I kept saying, "Boss, a train could come. Where in the hell we gonna go." Woods and a cliff on one side and the Youghiogheny River on the other. By God, we drove it. There were a couple of little towns on the way where he could get off the railroad tracks. No sir. We drove right through.

After the preliminary studies were complete, John Ware paid, again out of his own pocket, for the construction of an elaborate model of the Aqueduct Project, complete with running water, to demonstrate its feasibility to potential investors. When the model was finished, the Mellon Bank, which would presumably participate in the financing of the project, gave Ware the use of a conference room in Pittsburgh in which to set up his model. However, it turned out that the conference room was illuminated with incandescent lights, which cast undesirable shadows. Ware had a solution for that problem, too. He called Howard Carlock in Philadelphia. As Carlock recalls it, the conversation began in typical John Ware fashion.

"Hello, Howard," said the mild voice on the telephone. "Can you spare a few minutes?"

Carlock said he thought he could.

Ware explained his problem and wondered if Carlock could find some fluorescent light fixtures to replace the incandescent lights in the conference room in Pittsburgh.

"Sure," said Carlock. "I can get you some."

We talked it over and agreed that he would need six fixtures. When we finished the conversation—this was about ten o'clock in the morning—he said, "That's fine, Howard. There's an Allegheny flight leaving at 3 P.M. I'd like the fixtures to be on the plane."

Even at that point I wasn't worried. I thought there would be no trouble obtaining the fixtures. But I checked with the building superintendent, and he had no spare fixtures. I called the manufacturer, and he said there would be a six-month wait.

Time was clicking off. I knew John Ware would be waiting at the other end for these fixtures. So in desperation I got the electrician in the building to pull the fixtures out of Ware's office, and I sent them to the airport. They arrived on time and were there just as he expected them to be. He never knew where I got the fixtures. If he'd come home then, he'd have found six big holes in the ceiling of his office.*

In February 1956, when the news came out that Ware had purchased the Mountain Water Company, reactions were quite positive. The Pittsburgh *Sun-Telegraph* predicted that "within a few years thousands of families in Allegheny, Westmoreland, Washington, and Fayette Counties will be drinking some of the purest water in the country instead of the heavily-treated river water that now comes out of their spigots." The assumption was that the company's existing water mains would merely be enlarged and used to carry water to the city and some of its suburbs. A company spokesman predicted that when the system was fully developed it would be able to supply 80 million gallons of pure mountain water a day, double the amount of river water then being delivered by the company's South Pittsburgh water system.

*Ware was so concerned about the security of his model that he insisted that someone be there night and day to watch it. One morning three American employees were on the elevator at a hotel in Pittsburgh. One asked another, "Who slept with the model last night?" The other replied, "I think it was so-and-so." Two prim-looking ladies who were sharing the elevator left with shocked expressions on their faces. The people from American did not try to explain.

A year later, in March 1957, when Ware unveiled his plan for the Aqueduct Project, reactions were still mainly positive. The press called it a "fabulous project . . . a gigantic dream . . . the climax of a fantastic career." But now the goal was to supply not the 80 million gallons predicted earlier, but 650 million gallons a day, enough to meet the needs of the entire metropolitan area and to support future growth as well.

However, the papers noted that "property owners near the proposed dam site in Indian Creek Valley . . . have deluged the Greensburg office [of the Westmoreland Water Authority] with fears their land will be inundated."

At the time of the announcement, Ware conceded that, although his plan would improve the quality of the water delivered to the Pittsburgh area, it would not decrease its cost—in fact, it might even increase it. However, savings would come, he maintained, from the decreased need for soap and detergents and the elimination of water-softening units. Ware estimated these savings at $8.5 million per year, an average of $20.42 per family. He stated that there would be additional savings of $2.5 million a year for industrial plants as a result of using soft mountain water in place of hard river water.

According to Ware, the Pittsburgh municipal water system would be invited to join the project on a cost-sharing basis. He estimated that Pittsburgh would be the biggest user, consuming about 40 percent of the total supply. However, when asked whether Pittsburgh officials had been sounded out on joining the project, he declined to say. "In any event," the press reported, "Mr. Ware plans to push ahead with the project, terming it 'feasible' even without the city"—suggesting the customary John Ware refusal to be deterred by any obstacle, present or potential.

A short time after the Aqueduct Project was announced, an event occurred that in some ways was the high point of John Ware's career. He was chosen to receive the Horatio Alger Award, which is given each year to a small group of men who have risen to eminence from humble beginnings, like the fictional heroes of the Horatio Alger stories. Among those who had received the award were President Herbert Hoover, Captain Eddie Rickenbacker, and the financier Bernard Baruch. The award is still proudly displayed in the Ware home in Florida.

Later the same year, however, another event occurred. In Connellsville, near the site of the proposed Indian Creek Dam, John Ware was hanged in effigy by local citizens who were fearful that their homes would be flooded by the proposed dam. Ironically, Connellsville was the place where Kuhn Brothers & Company, predecessor to the original American Water Works & Guarantee, had been founded 75 years earlier, as well as the terminus of the railway company that had formed the nucleus of the utility empire of American Water Works & Electric.

But John Ware did not concern himself with hangings in effigy. He had other fish to fry. A few weeks before he went public with his plan, he had quietly arranged to have the Westmoreland County Commission pass a resolution enabling the Municipal Authority of Westmoreland County to participate in the Aqueduct Project by floating the bonds required to provide the financing. Several months later the state legislature, with very little debate, passed a bill providing the needed authorization at the state level. Meanwhile, Ware obtained a commitment of funds to seal off the numerous abandoned mine shafts in the Indian Creek area that might have jeopardized the purity of the supply by discharging polluted water, and he obtained tentative approval from Washington for the federal grant that would complete the financing package. All that remained now was to issue the bonds. What was now being called "Ware's Dream" was about to come true.

Then it became apparent that the opponents of the plan had been doing more than burn effigies. In September 1958, nineteen months after the Aqueduct Project was announced, a story appeared in the *Sun-Telegraph* under the headline "Is Ware Water Deal a Huge Public Sellout?" There followed a slashing attack on every aspect of the Aqueduct project:

Has a clever super-promoter sold a $200,000,000 needless water project which would drive an estimated 5,000 people from their homes and provide Pittsburgh with diluted mine drainage as their source of water?

Ware's representatives have told public officials that "only a few families" would be displaced. Leaders of the Indian Creek Valley said the "few" is roughly 1,500 families with a total population of 5,000.

Challenging the basic assumption of the project—the purity of the water it would provide—the story continued, "Opponents of the plan say Ware's water would be 18 times harder than Allegheny River water and much of it would be offensive mine drainage." Accompanying the story were pictures claiming to show that despite serious efforts to seal them off, abandoned coal mines were discharging large quantities of contaminated water into the Indian Creek watershed.

The story claimed that rates charged by John Ware's water companies were "excessively high," and went on to say,

There is little indication public officials who gave Ware a preliminary green light know much about Ware's project, except what he has seen fit to reveal to them. No unprejudiced, competent, municipally employed engineer has looked comprehensively into the merits—and demerits—of the project.

Every present Pittsburgh city councilman has said that Pittsburgh does not need the Ware water, but Ware and his associates go on merrily planning a new water supply for a city which has not asked for it. . . .

It is not too late to get full and complete engineering information from an unprejudiced source and to make it available to the actually millions of people whose lives and economic futures are involved and who will pay for "Ware's Dream" for the rest of their lives.

There was material available to answer most of the charges made by the opposition. John Ware had successfully sealed off mine drainage in other water systems in the past, and he contended that any remaining pollution problem would be solved as the water purified itself through a natural process of aeration as it flowed 42 miles to the city. Furthermore, many of the homes in the valley that would be flooded were not full-time residences but summer cottages. Presumably the shores of the newly created reservoir would provide attractive sites for many more homes than the ones eliminated; in fact, there had been predictions that the reservoir would create a major new recreation area, rivaling the Pocono Mountains of eastern Pennsylvania.

As for the statement that the rates charged by John Ware's water companies were excessive, these had been established by the State Public Utility Commission, as were the rates for any other private water company. The call for "full and complete engineering information" was not an unreasonable request. It should have been possible to meet it either with data from existing studies or with a newly commissioned analysis.

But John Ware, now almost 70 years old, was spending increasing time away from Pittsburgh at his homes in Oxford and Miami, and no one was empowered to speak in his absence. In any case, in the past he had not concerned himself with public opinion or public attacks. With engineering facts at his command, with financial arrangements under control, and with his singular knack for persuading key officials, he had not needed to. Furthermore, the arrangements were all but complete. The necessary legislative authority had been provided. Obtaining the remaining financing was familiar ground, and it seemed clear that the tax-exempt municipal bonds would find a ready market.

Despite its earlier commitment, however, the federal government now began to drag its feet, postponing a final decision on providing the funds required. Without a firm commitment of federal funds, the municipal bonds could not be sold. Without the bonds, construction could not begin. As a result, the project had to be put on hold.

Eventually, pressed for a decision, the Bureau of Reclamation in Washington reversed itself and decided the federal funds would not be forthcoming. The reason given was budget limitations.

However, it is a fact of life that officials at the national level tend to be sensitive to local sentiment, especially when it is expressed by a determined and articulate few—and some of those who owned summer homes on Indian Creek were influential people.

Time passed. Rumors flew. Doubts increased. In March 1959, six months after the broadside in the *Sun-Telegraph,* a story appeared reporting that there now seemed to be "an air of complacency" among people whose homes had previously appeared threatened by the Indian Creek Dam. "Reports have been getting around about this or that difficulty popping up," the story said, "There is an underlying feeling the whole big deal . . . has run into some kind of technical snag."

A full year later another story reported that the congregation of the Church of God in the town of Indian Head had announced that it would go ahead with plans to build a new church and school despite the fact that they would be located right at the center of John Ware's proposed reservoir.

"We're taking a calculated risk," a member of the congregation declared. "We've waited for two years but nothing seems to be done about the proposed dam and we decided to go ahead.

"We wrote to Mr. Ware on several occasions," the spokesman added, "trying to find out just what his plans were and whether he still intended to go ahead . . . but he never gave us the courtesy of a reply." Church officials also contacted a local attorney who had represented the Aqueduct Project in the past, but "he apparently didn't know any more than we did about Mr. Ware's plans."

Finally, at some point—the precise timing is unclear—the Aqueduct Project died. There was no public announcement, no obituary, no epitaph. It just faded away—its only monument the costly model, which gathers dust in the basement of the headquarters of the Westmoreland County Authority.

Hindsight suggests that there was much that was sound about Aqueduct. High-quality water has been a key to success in the water business since its earliest days. Furthermore, "regionalization," linking a number of local systems into an areawide network, has been a fact of life in the business from the start and has remained an important trend since. But Aqueduct ran afoul of the problem that has beset investor-owned utilities from the beginning—public ambivalence about private capital exercising a public function. (It did not help, of course, to have the press state, as it did more than once, that John Ware was worth half a billion dollars—which was not true—or to announce that "it's almost impossible to get a drink of water in Western Pennsylvania . . . without ringing John Ware's cash register." There is a saying that "Nobody loves his banker." Neither is there any general desire to make a rich man richer.)

In Davenport in the 1870s, or Lexington in the 1880s, there was no water system, and there was an urgent need for *some* water system, *any* water system, not only to prevent disease but to keep the town from burning down. In the Pittsburgh of the 1950s, they *did* have water. It might not have tasted good. It might have been expensive to purify. But hard water is just as effective as soft water for putting out fires, and it was not making anybody sick. So there was not the sense of urgency in providing a new supply that had prevailed at other times and places.

It is interesting and somewhat poignant to note that in the early days of his career Ware had been sensitive to and responsive to a remarkable range of opportunities, not only in providing water, but also in supplying electricity, building low-cost housing, experimenting with natural gas, devising creative financing techniques, and even producing optical lenses to meet wartime demand. In the postwar era the challenge of electricity was replaced by the electronics revolution; housing became a major boom; natural gas emerged as an important energy source; and discount stores, fast-food restaurants and motel chains proliferated, creating numberless millionaires in the process. A younger John Ware might have pursued any one or several of these opportunities. But the thinking of most people is shaped by their experience. As time passed, Ware had become more and more a water utility man, and a water utility man he remained. As his horizons narrowed, his dreams expanded. The Aqueduct Project was his last hurrah.

And it was not to be.

John Ware, Patriarch

Another factor was also at work in John Ware's life now. Acquiring control of American had not been his final dream, but it was a big dream, it did come true, and it projected him, as he had wanted it to, into the major leagues of the utility business. With American under his belt, he began to mellow. He spent more time in Florida and more time with his grandchildren, around whom his life increasingly revolved. There would be bursts of intense activity as he pursued the Aqueduct or some other project, then longer periods when he concerned himself with family matters.

Ware displayed a deep sense of obligation to be the head of the family, the patriarch, and he seemed well-cast for that role. At the time of the Horatio Alger Award, a reporter for the Philadelphia *Inquirer* wrote, "Your first impression of John Ware is that he'd make a fine grandfather. Not because he's wealthy, although in his case wealth would be no deterrent . . . but because he has a healthy, well-pressed look, a serenity of voice and manner, and, most important, because he has wonderful memories." Earlier, the Pittsburgh *Press* had described him as "a pink-faced little man who has the general appearance of a benign uncle, about to pass out dollar bills at Christmas."

In Ware's case, the bills were not just dollar bills, nor were they limited to Christmas. Nancy Ware Pascal, the daughter of Ware's younger son, Willard, recalls her grandfather taking her for long walks around the property in Oxford or Miami and then inquiring, "Nancy, is your heart happy?" then handing her a $100 bill.

Whether in Miami or Oxford—and there was frequent migration between—the life of the Wares centered on large family dinners. Everyone at the table would take turns telling what they were doing, what they had learned, what they had achieved. However, if someone said, "Guess what I figured out, Grandpa," or, "Look what I did, Grandpa," John would not respond "Congratulations," or, "Good for you." Rather he would say, "What's next? What else can you do?"

As Marilyn Ware Lewis, the daughter of John Ware 3rd, recalls it, "He kept urging us never to make the excuse you can't do it: 'Get out there and do it. Get moving. Get going, whatever it is you want to do with your life. And if one way doesn't work, try it another way.'"

A prime concern of Ware was to teach his grandchildren about the water business. This did not appear to be with the thought that they would necessarily enter the business, but simply to communicate his own enthusiasm, his love of the game. It may also have been that, recognizing his own mortality, he wanted to share the accumulated knowledge of his career, to pass on the torch. He would talk endlessly not only about the Aqueduct Project, but also about the problems the country would face in meeting its future water needs.

John Ware would sometimes invite one of the grandchildren to come with him on a business trip to Pittsburgh—usually on a last-minute basis. "Do you want to come and stay overnight? I'll buy you pajamas and a toothbrush." The grandchild in question would feel flattered by the invitation, but once there would become bored and sit under his desk and play, or be sent off with an employee to be entertained.

John Ware IV, one of the grandchildren, recalls going with his grandfather to check on progress in the construction of a dam. The only food available came from a little shack across the road from the construction site, where the entire menu consisted of canned tomato soup and toasted cheese sandwiches. The elder Ware ate his soup and sandwich without complaint, but then swore his grandson to secrecy about the meal. He did not like tomato soup, had issued orders that it *never* be served at his table, and did not want his wife Clara to know that he had broken his own rule.

The grandchildren recognized two sides to their grandfather's personality. One side was calm and imperturbable, in command of whatever business lay at hand, whether it be the purchase of a tube of toothpaste or the problems at an enormous construction project. The other side was volatile and impatient. When something triggered John Ware, he would "yell and stamp around." Then, "as fast as he would fire up, he'd get over it." Since they were not usually targets of his wrath, the grandchildren enjoyed these displays.

The impatient side of John Ware was never more vividly displayed than in periodic rides to the airport—and the grandchildren loved these. Ware was fascinated by air travel; he knew Eddie Rickenbacker personally; he loved to fly, bragged that he flew 10,000 to 20,000 miles a month, and was intrigued by the way flying saved time and allowed him to cram more business into a day. But he seemed incapable of getting to the airport on time. He always found something else to do until the last moment. Then would come the mad rush. The clock ticked away, Ware grew increasingly "rammy and obstreperous." The chauffeur would be ordered to run red lights and exceed the speed limit. Then came the screeching arrival at the terminal and the dash to the gate, with Ware often the last one on the plane.

He never stopped building, experimenting, trying new things. It was not unusual to arrive at one of his houses and find that he had decided to rewire part of the house, with the wires torn out of the walls and capped as he experimented with some improvement in the service.

He also built a miniature merry-go-round for his grandchildren at the house in Oxford. This was not a ready-made novelty from F.A.O. Schwartz. This was an honest-to-gosh authentic, old-time carousel. (As a boy John Ware had traveled to Cape May, New Jersey, in the summer to help his father run the merry-go-round in order to earn extra money to support the family. Now he was building a genuine merry-go-round for the entertainment of his grandchildren.)

Assembling an authentic merry-go-round was not an easy task. A young engineer from American was assigned to travel around the country, collecting the necessary parts from circus suppliers, secondhand stores and junkyards. When the time came to assemble the project, Ware, as usual, was personally involved. One day he fell from the scaffold and seriously cut his leg.

As the framework for the merry-go-round went up, there was

the usual curiosity in the town of Oxford about what John Ware was up to. At first Ware told the man in charge of the project to say nothing. Then, as curiosity reached a peak, he instructed him to tell questioners that Ware was building a spaceship. Given his record of behavior, there were those in the town who were prepared to believe that.

If there was any single activity that Ware enjoyed the most, it was buying toys for the grandchildren. Marilyn Lewis recalls:

> He *loved* to do that. We'd go to Wanamaker's in Philadelphia, where they had a train on the ceiling that you could ride. He'd ride it with me sometimes.
>
> I used to go with him almost every year. Then when I was 13 or 14 and thinking I was very sophisticated, I decided maybe I was too old to go. He said, "Don't *ever* get to the point where you're not fascinated by whatever there is in this world to play with, or to try, or to live in. Get out there and look at those toys. There's a new angle to every one of them."
>
> And he'd try out every toy that was there, especially anything mechanical or electrical. He'd go around and if there were smoke guns he'd fill 'em up and shoot 'em. Anything you could do with the toys, he would try.

Behind Every Great Man . . .

No account of Ware family dinners, or of the grandchildren, or of the life and career of John Ware himself, would be complete without taking note of the quietly influential role played by diminutive, gentle, soft-spoken Clara, his wife of more than 50 years. In the words of one family member, "She was the glue that held my grandfather together. She was a rock."

Clara Edwards Ware was born in 1888 in Lancaster, Pennsylvania, one of two girls in a family that included four brothers. Her father, Jesse Edwards, was a funeral director who was also a cabinet maker—cabinet making being a logical extension of the funeral-directing business. The cabinet-making led him into construction contracting. This in turn brought about the first meeting between the senior Edwards and young John Ware. As noted earlier, John, who was only 18 at the time, was bidding to supply the electrical work on a construction job on which Mr. Edwards was contractor. Concerned that Edwards might think he was too young to qualify, he is said to have lied about his age and got the job.

According to Ware family tradition, John first met Clara in New Providence, Pennsylvania, near Lancaster, perhaps in connection with a meeting between her father and John to discuss the construction project. It is said that John Ware took one look at Clara Edwards, then scrawled on a note pad which he showed to a friend or colleague who was there, "That's the girl I want to marry."

Not long after that, John, who was spending increasing time in and around Lancaster in connection with his business, began boarding at the Edwards house. Whether this arrangement was initiated by John or proposed by Clara's father is not recorded. Perhaps it was suggested by Clara herself. As Rhoda Ware Cobb puts it, "She had some good, womanly ways about her. She knew how to get things done." In any case, one thing led to another and the following year, when both were 19, the two were married.

In some ways, the marriage was a case of attraction between opposites. John could be impatient and stormy. Clara was patient and calm. John loved to travel by air. Clara preferred not to fly. (When the two traveled together, they took the train.) When John was on the road, he was unconcerned, not to say oblivious, to questions of amenity. He was content to eat crackers and cheese at a drug store lunch counter, ground beef in a hotel room or tomato soup at a construction site. Clara was the opposite. Whether organizing Sunday dinner, furnishing one of their homes or orchestrating a family celebration, she saw to it that everything was carefully, often exquisitely, arranged.

But if there were differences between the two, there were similarities. Like her husband, Clara remained modest and unassuming throughout life, retaining a quality of old-fashioned simplicity, despite the family's increasing affluence. Sunday meals were a case in point. The big family dinner at midday was prepared by the

[137]

cook with the help of an assistant, and served, course by formal course, by the butler (who doubled as chauffeur). On Sunday evening, Clara would take over. "She'd go into the kitchen," Marilyn Lewis recalls, "She knew where every pot and pan and spoon was—and turn out a meal that was just as good as what we had at noontime."

Clara made her own cheese, the kind known as cup cheese in Lancaster County; she saw to the preparation of homemade sauerkraut; her applesauce was legendary; and as her daughter-in-law, Rhoda Ware (mother of Rhoda Cobb), recalls, "She was the only person I ever knew who made her own crackers."

Like her husband, Clara was also thoughtful and considerate toward the people who worked for her. Marilyn Lewis recalled this incident:

> I remember a housekeeper who worked for them in Florida. She was raising her children by herself, and she had to take public transportation. My grandmother thought it would be easier for her if she didn't. So my grandfather and the chauffeur both jointly taught her to drive. It must have been a terrifying experience, because he couldn't drive very well himself. He was too impatient. But I remember this was my grandmother's idea. She sent them out and said, "Now let's do this."
>
> So they taught this woman to drive and then they bought her a car. And that solved a nagging problem for her.

Another trait John and Clara shared was deep concern for family. After their two sons were grown and married, Clara's attention, like John's, focused increasingly on the grandchildren. Like John, she left an indelible mark on each.

"She spent her life making us all feel loved and special," Nancy Ware Pascal recalls. "I don't know how she did that for so many of us."

"She never seemed to lump us together," in the words of Rhoda Cobb. "There were never any favorites."

John Ware, 3rd, and his wife Marian lived in Pennsylvania, so it was a treat for their children to visit Florida. Willard and Rhoda Ware lived in Miami, and it was exciting for the Florida Wares to experience winter in the north. "I remember going up at Christmas time," recalls their daughter, Rhoda Cobb. "She always arranged for it to snow." Clara would also arrange for an enormous Christmas tree, perhaps 20 feet tall, beautifully decorated and reaching to the ceiling of the "Crystal Room," a two-story, glass-enclosed space in the Oxford mansion. Around the tree would be gifts, chosen and wrapped by Clara herself, not only for the grandchildren, but for the children of friends and neighbors as well.

"Now, Jack . . ."

Clara was a tiny woman, delicate as a butterfly in her youth, plump and grandmotherly later. She was so small that visiting grandchildren, rushing into her arms, would almost knock her over, and more than once broke her glasses. Yet despite her small size and gentle nature, Clara was never intimidated by her formidable spouse. Marilyn Lewis explains:

> Having four brothers who were high-spirited—and all of them had a good sense of humor and did a lot of practical joking—she wasn't at all overwhelmed by John Ware. Her brothers were just full of it. Having helped to raise those four brothers, my guess is there wasn't much as far as being high-spirited that she hadn't seen.

Not only was Clara not intimidated by John, she had the capacity, when the need arose, to restrain him. According to Nancy Pascal:

> If he would get too demanding or drive too fast or something, she would say in a very quiet way, "Now, Jack, that's enough." And that's all she had to say. Right away he would

[139]

"To Grandmother's House We Go"

Nancy Ware Pascal, who in adult life was to become a member of the company's board of directors, recalls childhood visits to the house in Oxford:

> Everything was so beautiful in their home. . . . The other day I was thinking about her because they have these jugs of ice water on the table at board meetings. She had those in her house all the time.
>
> And she had flowers. When you walked into the house it was like walking into a garden. It always smelled wonderful; she always smelled wonderful. To me that house was like another world. She changed the sheets on the beds every single day. You got into that bed, and the sheets would be ironed. You'd sleep like on a cloud. It smelled so good, it was so smooth and so fresh. And when I would go there as a child, there would always be a new book on the nightstand, and a note would say, "Dear Nancy, enjoy this. Love, Babbie." We called her Babbie.
>
> And the meals. She grew her own vegetables. Corn and all kinds of vegetables they would grow right on the property. Every year they'd have a time when they'd put up the corn. They would scrape just the little nuggets of corn from the cobs, and freeze them in boxes with plastic lining. We would always hope that every meal included some of that corn. It was like gold to us. It tasted so good, it was so fresh. They would harvest it, and they would have just like a week of putting up this corn. My grandmother would be right there in the midst of it.
>
> Every meal was a production. We'd have homemade ice cream that would be made right there and frozen into molds of little rabbits or lambs. I mean, it was like heaven and it was all hers. She created an atmosphere and an environment. It was just like a dream.
>
> *(continued . . .)*

Even some great-grandchildren remember visits to Clara's house. Elizabeth Kuiper, daughter of Martha, Willard's eldest child, recalls

> toys, piles of toys . . . raisin cookies in a silver and blue dish . . . very formal dinners, always formal . . . finger bowls of beautiful china, with rose petals in them. . . .
> And the ice cream molds. The butler would come around with them on a silver tray and ask us which one we wanted. I always tried to get the biggest animal.

calm right down. She wasn't a nag. She never nagged. But if things got a little out of hand she would just very quietly say, "Now, Jack. . . ." And then he would try to please her. He adored her. He worshipped her. And she deserved it. She definitely was "the great woman behind the great man."

"I'm sure it wasn't easy all the time" adds Marilyn Lewis. "She was dealing with a very brilliant person who had these visions of what was going to be done and nothing was going to stop him. But it was a good lesson in what marriage can be."

One Final Deal

By the fall of 1960, John Ware was 72 years old. He had been in business of one sort or another for almost 60 years, and in the water business for more than 30. Through his ability not only to dream but to act on his dreams, he had bootstrapped himself out of poverty and obscurity to wealth and eminence. But now the dream of Aqueduct had faded, and his health was beginning to fail as well. It was time to go.

The arrangements for Ware's departure were, typically, both

decisive and complex. The first step came at the end of that year, when it was announced that John Ware would retire as chairman of the board of American Water Works, to be replaced by his older son, John 3rd. However, there was a difference. Though the senior Ware had carried the title of chief executive as well as chairman, now the job description of Jack Barr, who had been president of the company since 1955, was expanded to include the role of chief executive.

But John and Clara Ware remained sole owners of the Northeastern Water Company, which in turn controlled American. So the question was, who would control Northeastern? To resolve that issue, John Ware, deal maker par excellence, cut his last deal, demonstrating one more time the ingenuity that long had been his hallmark.

First he created an entirely new company, called the United Utilities Company. United Utilities then borrowed sufficient funds to purchase from John and Clara Ware all their stock in Northeastern. In the words of Kenneth Gemmill, Ware's attorney, who orchestrated the transaction, "Mr. Ware wanted cash. He wanted to be rid of the company and the responsibility of running it."

John Ware's will provided that the proceeds from the sale of Northeastern, something on the order of $15 million, be divided equally between his two sons. His other interests were also divided between them. John 3rd, who still lived in Oxford, Pennsylvania, was made the owner of his father's natural gas business, headquartered there. Willard Ware, who lived in Miami, received the aluminum window business, located there.

But now who was to control United Utilities? To take care of that problem, Ware created three classes of stock in the new company: 42,800 shares of Class A (voting) common, 385,000 shares of Class B (nonvoting) common, and 215,000 shares of nonvoting preferred. All of the preferred stock was given to the Ware Foundation, a charitable organization that has contributed to a variety of educational, religious and other causes. As for the rest of the shares, Ware proposed to divide the Class B (nonvoting) common, representing the bulk of ownership, between his two sons, his law-

John Haines Ware, 3rd (*left*), was a director of American Water Works Company from 1951 until 1985, and served as chairman of its board of directors from 1960 until he retired in 1984. A lifelong resident of Oxford, Pennsylvania, he headed the Penn Fuel Gas Company and the Oxford Publishing Company. From 1960 to 1970 he served in the Pennsylvania state senate, and from 1970 through 1975 was a member of the U.S. Congress, representing the Ninth District of Pennsylvania. He was also chairman of the Pennsylvania Republican Finance Committee, a district governor of Rotary International, a trustee of the University of Pennsylvania, and a director of the Pennsylvania Gas Association. In December 1984 the Pennsylvania Region Office of American Water Works Company was dedicated to John Ware, 3rd, in recognition of his contributions to the company.

Willard Myers Ware (*right*) was elected a director of American Water Works Company in 1953, and was vice chairman of its board from 1970 until 1982. After graduating from the Wharton School of the University of Pennsylvania, he established the Gas-Oil Products Company in Coral Gables, Florida. A founding director and later president of the Southern Industrial Savings Bank of Miami, during World War II he became president of the Delaware Optical Company, which made lenses for the war effort. Later he served as president of Ware Laboratories, Inc., a company that manufactured aluminum windows. He was also president and a long-time member of the Board of the Metropolitan YMCA of Dade County, Florida, and a director of a variety of other community services. After he died in 1984, the company's Southern Region Office in Charleston, West Virginia, was dedicated in honor of Willard Ware.

yer, Gemmill, and his chief lieutenants, Reinicker and Barr, with most of the shares going to the sons. The Class A (voting) shares, representing relatively little ownership but full control, were to be divided as follows: 11,984 shares, about 28 percent of the total, to each of the sons; an equal proportion, 28 percent, to lawyer Gemmill; and the balance, 16 percent, divided between Reinicker and Barr.

Jack Barr later recalled being informed of John Ware's plan:

> Mr. Ware called me to Ken Gemmill's office and told me what he had decided to do, and of course I was speechless. I remember going in and talking to Bill Reinicker about it. And to his credit he said, "Oh hell, we ought to share this. We shouldn't take it all for ourselves." So we went back to Mr. Ware and said we thought Marshall Anderson, Ray Wendell, Bill Gamble, Tony Greco and Ed Horner should also participate in whatever stock he saw fit to give us.*

Ware agreed to let the others have a portion of the nonvoting stock, but reserved the voting shares for Reinicker and Barr.

Ray Wendell remembers being told of his participation:

> You couldn't turn down the proposition. Bill Reinicker called me in and said, "If you will sign this agreement and write a check for so many dollars and give it to me, you will be the owner of so many shares of United Utilities Class B common stock."

---

*Marshall Anderson, who had joined American shortly before John Ware won control of the company in 1947, was at that time vice president and treasurer and a member of the board of directors. Ray Wendell, who had begun his career with the Northeastern Water Company and later became John Ware's traveling companion on his drives through western Pennsylvania, was also a vice president and a director. William B. Gamble was vice president and comptroller. Tony Greco, the son of Italian immigrants, had worked his way up from a common laborer to become, in Ray Wendell's words, "a very capable division manager." Edwin O. Horner was president of the Municipal Management Company, the subsidiary that managed the water properties in Pennsylvania that John Ware had sold to municipal authorities.

I didn't have the money in the bank to cover the check that he wanted me to write him, but he said, "No problem, no problem. Mellon Bank already has an account for you." And part of the papers I was signing was a note for $6,000 to Mellon Bank to cover the cost of the shares.

The net effect of all these arrangements was to perpetuate the status quo. The wealth John Ware had created during his lifetime would remain largely with his family. The businesses his two sons had been operating would continue to be run by them. And the management of the water company that Ware had put in place would remain in place—as in fact it did for another 15 years.*

With his responsibility to the business ended and his affairs now in order, John Ware did not linger on the scene. Ray Wendell recalled:

After he retired, he stayed in Florida. He had a home down there on Star Island near Miami. . . . We eventually closed his office in Philadelphia at Three Penn Center. . . . There was no sense in keeping it open. We did keep it open for quite a while, with a secretary there, just out of respect for the Boss.

He used to call me once in a while. We had these *long* conversations on the phone. He'd be asking questions about what we were doing and so on, and still asking my opinions on all sorts of various things, and principally just chatting. It was nothing to stay on the phone with him for a couple of hours at a stretch. My phone messages would pile up, and guys standing outside my door chewing their gums. I'd sit there, feet up on the desk, talking to the Boss. Well, that's what the old man wanted.

On March 24, 1962, John Ware's beloved Clara died. Not long after that, Ware's condition worsened, and he was confined to the hospital. Wendell remembers:

*United Utilities continued in existence until 1963, when its stockholders received shares of American in exchange for their holdings.

Up until the time he died he was still talking about this project or that. He wasn't able to do anything about it. He was really sick in fact. I didn't realize how sick he was, talking to him. His voice, you know, had changed a little bit, and his mind would wander. But not bad, not bad at all. I'd say up to the time he died I didn't realize how sick he was.

Finally on March 10, 1963, at age 75, the very full, very active life of John Ware came to an end.

About the time Ware was born, Rudyard Kipling wrote these words:

> I'd not give way for an Emperor,
> I'd hold my road for a King.
> To the Triple Crown I'd not bow down—
> But this is a different thing.
> I'll not fight with the Powers of Air—
> Sentries pass him through!
> Drawbridge let fall, 'tis the Lord of us all,
> The Dreamer whose dream came true!

Not all of John Ware's dreams came true. Nor did he become lord of everything he surveyed—although he did pretty well as far as the water business was concerned. But enough dreams did come true, and even the ones that failed were grand enough, to mark him as a remarkable individual and a significant if relatively unobtrusive contributor to the life of twentieth-century America.

Bill Reinicker and Jack Barr in the late 1950s.

The American management team from the late 1950s through the early 1970s included (*left to right*) Vice President Ray Wendell, Comptroller Bill Gamble, Vice President and Treasurer Marshall Anderson and President Jack Barr.

E. H. "Spike" Aldrich (*left*) and Jack Barr after dedication of the
Aldrich Water Treatment Station in Elrama, Pennsylvania, in 1961.
Aldrich retired in 1962.

The treatment basin developed by E. H. Aldrich combined a mixing and flocculation tank (center) and filters (perimeter) in one unit. Since 1960 the unit has been used widely in the American System to treat surface water supplies.

Engineers gathered at a construction site in 1955 with Service Company Vice President Ed Geehan (*right*) include (*from left*) Sam Bargh, Howard Carlock, "Spike" Aldrich, George Kaufman and George Paul.

His sons, friends and co-workers attended the ceremony the day John Ware received the Horatio Alger Award. From left are John Ware, 3rd; Bill Reinicker; John Ware with the award in his hand; Jack Barr; Willard Ware; George Sweeney, then chairman of the Westmoreland County Authority; and Ray Wendell.

Above: Using a scale model, John Ware explains his ambitious plan to create a reservoir in the mountains southeast of Pittsburgh, from which pure water would flow through an aqueduct to the city and its suburbs. *Below:* The aqueduct's proposed route.

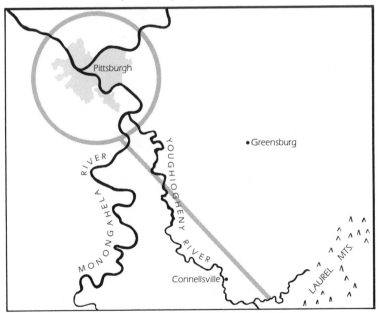

American Water Works managers and business associates got together for a fishing trip on Maryland's Eastern Shore in 1957. From left are Don Carpenter, a partner in Gannett, Fleming, Corddry & Carpenter, Engineers; Bill Reinicker; Tom Earl; Farley Gannett of Gannett, Fleming; Ralph Tyler, American's public relations manager; and Leroy Evans, a salesman with Mueller Company, a supplier of hydrants and valves.

John Ware built this merry-go-round in his yard in Oxford, Pennsylvania, in the 1950s to entertain his six grandchildren.

This was a favorite photo of John Ware, who enjoyed a reputation as an uncanny dowser. Dowsing is the ancient practice of searching for underground water with the aid of a forked stick or "witching rod."

A UNIQUE AND IMAGINATIVE LEADER RETIRES

Late in 1960, John Ware announced his retirement as Chairman and member of the Board of Directors of American Water Works Company.

With characteristic simplicity, Mr. Ware composed the following message for distribution to system employees:

"It is with great personal regret that I bring to an end my long years of association with these companies and my personal association and friendship with so many of you. However, I know that your friends and my friends will continue their excellent management of these combined Northeastern-American operations."

After 56 years as a unique and imaginative leader in the public utility field, Mr. Ware thus severed his connection with the system companies he had guided to their present stature in the water works industry.

Although he has retired to enjoy the relaxation and relief from the daily turmoil of business he so justly deserves, we know he will continue to use his soaring imagination in ways that will be of benefit to the nation.

What John Ware created—trained management with a depth of knowledge and experience unmatched in the water works field—will keep the Company on course as we face the challenging years ahead.

This tribute to John Ware appeared in both the American and Northeastern annual reports for 1960.

III

THE ENTERPRISE EVOLVES

NINE

"By God, Jack, We'll Find the Money"

Although John Ware was now physically removed from the scene, his legacy remained. It remained in the enterprise he had created, in the group of managers he had developed, and in the tales told and retold of his adventures and achievements. It also remained in the level of debt he left behind and the continuing need for cash.

In its massive "white paper" of 1935, the management of the old American Water Works & Electric claimed to have an advantage in raising funds by virtue of its location "in the principal national financial market in the City of New York." However, after the operating headquarters of the new American company relocated to Philadelphia, there is no evidence that Jack Barr had any difficulty making contact with investors. For one thing, most of the major sources of funds—the insurance companies that were in the habit of buying the company's bonds—were located not in New York, but in places like Boston, Hartford, Newark and Philadelphia. (The principal buyer of American's bonds for many years was the John Hancock Life Insurance Company of Boston.) Furthermore, through the use of such devices as the train, the airplane, the automobile, the telephone and the U.S. mails, Barr was able to communicate more than adequately, face-to-face or otherwise, with potential investors.

Having access to investors is one thing, however. Obtaining funds at the time, in the amount and on the terms desired is another. The difficulty was that for much of John Ware's working life his various enterprises had existed on the edge financially. American Water Works was no exception. Ware's imagination, his energy, his ambition, nearly always outran the prosaic and inconvenient question of where to get the money. In their late-night talks in Oxford, as Jack Barr later recalled, "Some of his ideas, I had to say, 'Oh God, you can't do that. We can't afford that.'"

"By God, Jack," Ware would respond, "we'll find the money."

According to one account, Ware bought the old flour mill he used to generate power for his first electric company with a down payment of $100, borrowed from a druggist. His first water company very nearly failed during the 1930s, and Ware was reduced to exchanging ten-cent Christmas gifts from Woolworth's with his managers and distributing shares of nearly worthless stock (which later became valuable). In the case of the sale of the Greensburg and Apollo water companies to municipal authorities in Pennsylvania, it is said that it became necessary for Ware to finance their operations out of his own pocket to the tune of several hundred thousand dollars before they turned the corner. The Northeastern Water & Electric Company was bought in 1942 with a small down payment and a large amount of faith, and was held together largely by Barr's ability to say no—witness Ray Wendell's difficulty in obtaining a new fire hydrant for Caribou, Maine—while Ware sold off properties to raise cash. When Ware bought control of American, again he stretched his credit to the limit. The assumption, at least implicitly, was that there would be a grace period of a few years in which to reduce the debt. But there was no grace period, as the company was immediately overtaken by the postwar surge of construction, whose pressures in turn were compounded by the inflation in costs and rise in interest rates resulting from the Korean War.

However, where there's a will there's a way, particularly with John Ware providing the will and Jack Barr to find the way. In addition to such borrowing as the existing level of debt permitted, the Ware/Barr approach to financing was two-pronged. The first avenue of attack was a matter not of borrowing money but of hanging on to it: of being very careful—not to say stingy—in paying out earnings in the form of dividends. As Barr recalled:

> During the early years, the fact that American was a family-controlled company was almost essential to the way we developed. We were criticized rather broadly for not paying out a sufficient part of earnings as dividends. The thing that wasn't recognized was that we had to use those earnings to liquidate the debt and get established. A great part of the earnings of the company went to meet sinking fund payments on bonds, and into construction.

Of course, the fact that Ware and Barr said that "We need the money to pay off the debt" did little to mollify the 6,000 or more owners of the other 40 percent of American's stock, who were not receiving the level of income they had expected in return for their investment. They might have been inclined, as were the old-time employees of American, to say to the newcomers, "Who needed you?" But the reality was that John Ware, in the Great American Free Enterprise Tradition, had gone into the market and purchased control, and he now was in position to call the shots, including the use of earnings as he saw fit. (The same complaint was made in the 1980s about the corporate "raiders," who borrowed heavily through the use of high-yielding "junk bonds" to purchase control of a company, then used the company's excess cash, or sold off other assets, to pay off the bonds. In this, as in other ways, John Ware was ahead of his time.)

"A Routine Revision—What's That?"

Even with the heavy use of retained earnings, however, the financial demands on the company could not be met without gaining control of the cost of the huge amount of construction that had to be done. At Northeastern, after Ware took over, control of capital spending was crude but effective. Jack Barr said no. At American, the situation was different. Not only was most of the construction impossible to postpone, but since the days of H. Hobart Porter, starting in 1914, the engineering aristocracy had been in control of the company, and its habits of working and thinking had been shaped during the freewheeling days before the crash of 1929. Normally, the engineers would simply decide what they wanted to do, then tell the financial people to go to the market and obtain the money to do it; if the original amount requested did not cover the cost, there was always more where it came from. During the 1930s and early 1940s, for all practical purposes, construction stopped, so there was no occasion to challenge the old ways of doing things. Then in the postwar years, as the construction surge began, the American-bred engineers went back to business as usual. As Jack Barr recalled it:

> Well, you know, in those days we grew almost like Topsy. Budgeting was something, hell, we didn't have. We had construction budgets, and God you did argue, and you'd want to shoot some of the engineers at times. You wind up finding that they gave you an estimate of $50,000 to build something, and you didn't know till it was done three years later that it cost you $250,000.

Not only did a $250,000 final cost for a project budgeted at $50,000 put a strain on scarce resources and play hob with financial planning; in addition, if the regulatory authorities—newly diligent in the aftermath of the abuses disclosed in the 1930s—concluded that the facility was not worth $250,000 in terms of meeting the needs of the customer, they would not allow the company to include the entire amount in its rate base, which was used to determine what could be charged for water. Instead the overrun had to be deducted from earnings, which were already under strain.

The first step in correcting this situation was simply to put teeth—real teeth—into the existing system of work orders. If a project was approved by the board of directors of one of the operating companies (each subsidiary company had its own board, which approved its own projects) with a price tag of $50,000, a work order would be authorized by the board for that amount, and the engineer in charge of the project was required to come back to the board for authority to spend beyond that $50,000 limit; with Barr in attendance, that was not always an easy or a gentle process. In the early 1950s, when Ken Earnhardt was assistant manager of the water company at Alexandria, Virginia, perhaps the fastest-growing company in the system, he once appeared before his board and announced that he needed "a routine budget revision."

"A *routine budget revision*!!" came the voice of Jack Barr. "What's *that*?!!"

Never again did Ken Earnhardt regard any budget revision as routine, nor did he casually request a revision of any sort—which is no doubt the result Barr had in mind.

Intimidation has its limits, however, as a technique of budget control, particularly when the budgets in question are of uncertain merit in the first place. What was needed was a more orderly, disciplined process. As it turned out, improvement came from within the engineering department, although not from the old-timers from American. Tom Earl, who in 1961 succeeded Spike Aldrich as chief engineer, described the effort:

> One of our problems was communication. Each engineer, if he thought something was needed in the way of a capital improvement, would write whatever he felt necessary and submit it as a report, and that would sort of get bounced up through channels and would get reviewed as to whether it had merit, and it was so chaotic, we had such a volume of things to sort through, that we just had to develop some uniformity. So we developed a formal memorandum system where, when you looked at a capital improvement, you defined what the problem was, what you were talking about, the dollars involved, the capital cost, the operating cost, and so on. We would take that memorandum, review it, check the figures, hone it over, make sure it made reasonable sense. Then you could take it to the board of directors and they had a realistic picture of what the story was.

Along with that came the need to more accurately account for our time, which had been sort of loosely done in the past. On some projects, after they were finished, the engineers would go back and make a real neat record, based on after-the-fact recollection, of how they had spent their time, which isn't exactly the way you are supposed to do it.

Not surprisingly, a more formal, structured system for developing proposals, and the requirement for real rather than imaginative recording of engineering time, did not sit well with everyone. "Some of the older engineers weren't too pleased," according to Earl. "In fact, I think one of them might have retired over it."

The need for more realistic budgeting and stricter financial control, combined with the unprecedented number and size of rate increases required to cover the cost of new construction, meant that over the course of the 1950s and 1960s the relative importance of the financial function within the company steadily increased, while that of the engineering department continued to decline.

"What Did He Do for the Dollar and a Half?"

The requirements of financing and the demands of the regulatory process have resulted in an unusual structure for public utility holding companies. Investors who lend money to build facilities or refinance debt want the loans to be secured, not by the high hopes and good intentions of management, but by "real property": bricks and mortar, pipes and pumps, dams and filter plants. Furthermore, they want the "income stream" that will service the debt to come not from some undifferentiated slush fund at a distant corporate headquarters, but from specific payments for actual water service provided to the customers of the system in question. By the same token, when regulators are considering whether to grant a rate increase to the water company in a town, let us say, in New Jersey, they are not interested in hearing what the cost of providing water might be in Pennsylvania or Kentucky (except perhaps for comparative purposes). They want to know the actual cost for the company in question in the locality in question.

This reality is the basis for the holding company structure. A local water company is not simply a branch, department or division of the parent company. In legal terms, at least, it is a separate corporation, with its own charter, its own officers and directors, and the power to borrow money secured by its own assets. It also applies to the regulatory authorities of its own state for its own rate increases, based on its own cost of doing business.

Meanwhile, the engineering or other services provided by the parent company have to be paid for by the operating subsidiaries if they are to show up on the books as their costs and thus be considered by the regulators in setting rates. This requirement is taken care of by the device of the "service company." A service company, also a separate corporation, is also owned by the parent company. But its only "customers" are the operating subsidiaries, to which it provides services. (In the freewheeling 1920s, holding company managers used the service company as a device to exploit the operating subsidiaries, charging inflated fees for services rendered. Today that practice is not tolerated by the regulators. At American, the service company shows neither a profit nor a loss. All of its costs, meticulously recorded, are billed to the operating companies.)

The result is a rather curious structure, compared to that of most other business organizations. In the case of American, the parent company, which is called simply the American Water Works Company, has almost no employees: a president, a corporate secretary and a handful of staff. There are several dozen other employees sitting in the same building as the president (and inclined to do what he tells them to), and a few thousand more in other locations, but all are on the payroll of one or another of the subsidiaries.

As already noted, the parent company owns or controls all of the subsidiaries, usually holding 100 percent of their common stock, and virtually all of the directors of the subsidiaries are connected with the company in some way. The result is a curious ritual. Every three months, a meeting of the board of directors of each operating subsidiary is called to order. General operating conditions are reviewed, budgets are approved, dividends are declared—to be paid to the parent company—and the meeting is adjourned. Then a meeting of the board of directors of another subsidiary—usually consisting of the same people—is called to order. In the course of a single day, as many as five quarterly meetings for as many subsidiaries will be held, for the most part by the same people, sitting in the same room.

As for the service company, which in the case of American is called, not surprisingly, "the American Water Works Service Company": The president of the service company also functions as the number two man for the enterprise as a whole, equivalent to a chief operating officer in another kind of corporation. (Most of the officers and directors of the operating subsidiaries are in fact employees of the service company.)

If a chemist employed by the service company makes a trip to a subsidiary to help it solve a problem, he charges that subsidiary for his time. If an engineer or executive goes out to testify in a rate case, he does the same. Meanwhile, there are overhead costs: the operation of the mail room at headquarters, for example, or the time a lawyer or an engineer spends reading professional journals. Since *all* costs of the service company are required to be charged either to the parent or to one subsidiary or another, at the end of each month the overhead costs are divided among the subsidiaries, using a formula based on size. As a result, when a local company goes before its state public utility commission, the commissioners, in reviewing expenses, may discover that the vice president for communications of the service company had charged that operating company for $1.50 worth of his time. Predictably, such an item can cause amazement and amusement. "And what," a commissioner will inquire, perhaps with an eye on any reporters present, "did he do for the dollar and a half?"

Despite the comic opera quality of episodes like this, the service company serves a useful purpose—indeed an essential one: No one has thought of a better way of doing the job. In fact regulators have come down strongly in the past in favor of the service company setup as a valid means of providing services and allocating cost in the public utility business. So after a certain amount of joking on the part of the commissioners, the $1.50 item is nearly always approved, along with a number of more substantial ones.

Looking After the Relations

The rising volume of applications for rate increases during the postwar period had an impact on external as well as internal relationships, particularly on relations with the regulatory authorities, who now more than ever held the fortunes of the company, not to say its survival, in their hands.

In the early days of the water utility business, relations between the struggling young companies and regulatory bodies were chaotic, to say the least. The manager of a local water company was more concerned with getting water to the hydrants and collecting past-due bills than with the subtle, often delicate business of cultivating public and political relationships. The regulatory authorities—normally local city councils—were more responsive to the shifting tides of opinion and the pressures of bureaucratic jealousy than to the financial and engineering realities of providing an efficient and reliable water supply. The long-running battles between the water company and the local establishment in places like Pekin or Cairo, Illinois, created a regulatory situation that was not so much chaos as anarchy.

This situation served nobody well, so pressure accumulated for reform in the shape of "preemptive legislation" that would take the regulatory function out of the hands of short-sighted and contentious local jurisdictions and put it in the presumably more responsible hands of regulators at the state level.*

---

*Regulatory reform actually started with the railroads, as a result of widespread protests against excessive or discriminatory freight charges. But once the pattern of state-level regulation was established, it spread to other utilities as well.

The first legislation creating a state public utility commission was passed in Wisconsin in 1906. Other states soon followed. The new mechanism was greeted with enthusiasm by reformers and defenders of consumer interests, who believed the creation of these impartial, quasi-judicial bodies marked the beginning of an era of fair and responsible regulation of public utility rates. These hopes were quickly disappointed, because just at the moment when the state regulatory commissions were created, the giant public utility holding companies were beginning to emerge, and they could afford to treat the new regulatory bodies as at best a necessary evil and at worst a minor inconvenience. Those regulators who could not be bought could be overwhelmed or intimidated by the enormous wealth and platoons of legal talent the utilities could deploy. As the Roosevelt brain-truster Thomas Corcoran would put it later: "It is a sheer problem of arithmetic. How much money have you against how much money? How many good lawyers have you against how many good lawyers? These are the actualities of the regulatory process—the drip, drip, drip of pleasure and influence; the out-maneuvering, the out-braining, which . . . simply make it impossible to handle these aggregations of power."

During the depression, public anger at these abuses culminated not only in the eventual breakup of the holding companies but also in a much tougher, more professional approach to regulation itself. The Public Utilities Holding Company Act of 1935 gave the newly created Securities and Exchange Commission a major role in regulating holding company affairs. When the state regulators saw the sophistication, professionalism and concern for the consumer the SEC was bringing to bear, not to be outdone, they upgraded the level of their own staffs and the objectivity of their approach. Thus in the early 1950s the increasingly professional utility representatives and the newly professional regulators eyed each other across a chasm of suspicion, resentment and ideological difference left behind by the trauma of the 1930s. This was not a healthy situation at a time when frequent and adequate rate increases were essential to the companies' survival.

"They Lifted Their Eyebrows at Us"

The first step in bridging the gap between the regulators and the regulated was to attempt to put the relationship on a more informal basis than was possible during a rate hearing. With this objective in mind the senior people of American Water Works, along with their counterparts from other utilities, began to attend meetings of the National Association of Regulatory Utility Commissioners, to which state regulators belong.

"We got into that to improve our relations with the commissioners," Ray Wendell recalled. "To get so that we can go into their office and talk with them and know each other. At first some of them lifted their eyebrows at us, but the electric utilities and the gas utilities were all doing it, so we got into it, and we became known among the commissioners personally."

Any activity involving the intangibles of "relations" and relationships—public relations, community relations, government relations—can be difficult for a hardheaded, financially oriented manager to evaluate, because it is seldom possible to trace its contributions to specific numbers on the bottom line. "To tell the truth," Jack Barr observed later, "I don't know a single instance where all these relations meant a buck to us, unless you'd say they avoided misunderstandings." Nonetheless, over the years the spending by the company on improving and maintaining relations with its various "publics"—customers, regulators, legislators—has increased steadily, suggesting that it does perceive a contribution there.

However, better relations did not by themselves provide the company with the rate increases needed to maintain a satisfactory level of profitability; the machinery of regulation itself was too cumbersome and slow. The result was a "regulatory lag," in which the revenue provided by the increases was always a year or more behind the rise in costs resulting from inflation and spending for new construction. What was needed was action to streamline the regulatory process itself, and this was a task not just for one company, but for all companies in the industry, mobilizing whatever political clout they could muster.

The investor-owned water companies had no national organization at that time, but American Water Works had long been a member of the Pennsylvania Water Works Association, of which John Murdoch, the company's chief counsel, was president. So beginning in 1959, under the leadership of Murdoch and Jack Barr, the membership of the Pennsylvania association was gradually broadened to include companies from other parts of the country, and the name of the organization in time was changed to the National Association of Water Companies. In the years since then, NAWC, as it is known, has worked patiently with state regulatory commissions and the regulators' national organization in the effort to find ways to make the rate-making process more efficient. As environmental issues came to the fore, NAWC also became active in working toward regulation that would assure the quality of the water supply without burdening the water companies with unnecessary costs. Then in the late 1980s it joined forces with the regulators in opposing provisions of the tax code that were considered unfair to investor-owned water suppliers and their customers.

Buying and Selling Companies: Two Opposing Trends

As the postwar construction effort surged ahead and the American organization shifted from a primarily engineering orientation to a more financial one, and while the company paid closer attention to regulatory matters, two other trends that had been a part of the water business from the start—in fact part of the entire public utility business—were continuing. One was the steady increase in customers, assets and volume of water sold as American purchased smaller properties whose owners were either unable or unwilling to continue on their own. The second was the periodic loss of customers, assets and income as a result of the sale of water properties, sometimes voluntarily, sometimes under the pressure of individuals or groups who felt that providing water to a community was more appropriately handled by public than by private hands.

The purchase of water systems is a fairly straightforward matter. If a property comes on the market, if the company is interested and if the price is right, the company buys. The properties most likely to come on the market are systems too small to be economically viable or those whose owners have grown tired of raising money, fixing pipes and listening to customer complaints. American has historically been most likely to buy properties adjacent to its existing holdings, properties that can be added to those systems, increasing sales, spreading costs and enhancing profitability. Over the years, American has bought a number of smaller companies and consolidated them with its existing holdings.

Occasionally a larger company will come on the market also, one capable of operating on a stand-alone basis; now and then an entire group of companies becomes available. But the yardstick is always the same: Will it make an attractive and profitable addition to the system? If the answer is yes, the company buys. If the answer is no, it passes.

The sale of water properties is a much more complex affair. As we have seen, in the days before he bought American, and for a time afterward, John Ware was more than happy to sell water companies to municipal authorities in Pennsylvania, taking in return not only attractive prices made possible by low-interest, tax-exempt bonds, but also potentially lucrative holdings of B bonds, along with profitable long-term management contracts. From time to time, also, the company will sell a property because it is simply unable to operate it profitably, either because it is too small, because its source of supply is inadequate and no suitable alternative can be found, or because a hostile regulatory environment will not permit it to earn an acceptable rate of return. In most cases, however, when American has parted with one of its properties, it has been because of a takeover, or threatened takeover, by local government authorities.

Sometimes the municipal takeover of a private utility will occur as a result of public outrage on account of poor service. At other times, the service as such may be acceptable but the takeover effort will be a reaction to bad relations between the management of the company and local officials to clumsiness in dealing with customers. However, the management of American is well aware that if service deteriorates or local relationships go sour, its ability to survive in a given community will be in doubt. Thus, not surprisingly, it has worked hard over the years to see that its standards of performance in both respects are high. To do otherwise would be to invite the forced liquidation of the company.

A high proportion of attempts by public officials to take over a private water company are not the product of any groundswell of public sentiment—although public opinion usually becomes involved before the matter is decided—but are simply a matter of bureaucratic "turfing" or empire building, as one local power center seeks to take possession of the jobs, the assets and the influence controlled by the other.

The trigger for a takeover attempt will often be a rate increase (despite the fact that the water bill, with or without the increase, usually comprises a negligible part of a family budget). Particularly in a time of inflation, an increase in the cost of any service gives a local official an occasion to view with alarm the rising cost of living, to commiserate with the plight of the poor and the elderly, to excoriate the greed of the profit-seeking company and its presumably bloated capitalist stockholders, to play on the public ambivalence that has historically existed over whether the provision of such a fundamental resource should be in public or private hands, and to raise the time-honored cry of "throw the rascals out."

Often after the leaders of a smaller community have declared their intent to acquire the local water system, they will take a closer look at the figures, realize the cost in money and management for purchasing and operating such a capital intensive, technically demanding business, change their minds and back away. Larger communities can be another story, since they are more likely to have access to the funds required to buy the local system and the system itself is likely to be large enough to support the level of technical and managerial expertise required to run it. Thus over the years some of the largest and most profitable companies in the American system have become targets of municipal takeover attempts—companies American least wanted to give up.

The Gentlemen from Birmingham

The first major challenge to American's jurisdiction over one of its properties came less than a year after John Ware acquired control of the company. In 1948 the city commission of Birmingham, Alabama, proposed that the city buy the Birmingham Water Works Compány. With 90,000 customers and 10 percent of the company's assets, Birmingham was second largest in the American system at that time, exceeded in size only by the South Pittsburgh Water Company.

The Birmingham company had been acquired by the old American Water Works & Guarantee in 1899. In 1921 the system needed a major overhaul, requiring a large investment. To assure the stability of income needed to recover the cost of the improvements, the company (by now it had become the American Water Works & Electric Company) asked the city for a 30-year contract to supply water. The city granted the contract, but in return required that the city have the right to buy out the company at any time during the life of the contract.

With the contract due to expire in January 1951, it appears that some sharp-eyed lawyer or civil servant read the contract, came across the buy-out provision, thought, "Well now, that's an interesting concept," and brought it to the attention of the town fathers, who obviously agreed that it was an interesting concept and initiated discussions aimed at buying out the company.

At first the local management of the Birmingham company resisted vigorously. They conducted a publicity campaign urging that the property remain in private hands. Thousands of postcards were mailed out to customers, asking them to participate in a straw poll on whether or not the company should be sold. According to William H. H. "Put" Putnam, who was manager of the company at the time, the response was "tremendous," with 20 or 30 percent returns, and a vote of 19 to one against selling.

Despite that result, however, John Ware abruptly decided to sell. The local employees were mystified. Some were bitter. No clear explanation was given. "I never did know how he felt," observed Putnam.

A factor in the decision was no doubt the fact that the price proposed was $5 million and at that point in its history the company had use for the money. As a further inducement, the city agreed to give American a contract to continue to manage the Birmingham operation for five years, until 1956.

The management of American obviously hoped the management contract would be renewed. However, when it was due to expire, the members of the Birmingham Water Commission called Jack Barr to Alabama and informed him that "The general public will not accept that we continue to pay damyankees" to run their water company. (The good people of Birmingham may in fact have been unwilling to continue to pay "damyankees." Or it may have been that the shrewd horsetraders of Birmingham had merely dangled the five-year contract, and the possibility of renewal, as a sweetener to persuade John Ware to do the deal in the first place.)

Despite the parting of the ways, however, the relationship with the town fathers of Birmingham remained harmonious to the end, in distinct contrast to the situation in later acquisition attempts. As Barr recalled, the members of the board were "high-caliber people, gentlemen to the core." In Ray Wendell's words, "The guys down in Birmingham were all very friendly, but they decided that they didn't need us anymore, so with no trouble, no fuss, we left."

The Maine Chance

While the Birmingham situation was sorting itself out, John Ware and Jack Barr had another problem on their minds. The 15 water properties in the state of Maine—where Ray Wendell had started his career—were only marginally profitable, and they tended to give the management headaches. (Technically, the Maine properties were not a part of American Water Works. They were still held by Northeastern, owned by John and Clara Ware, which in turn owned 60 percent of American. But, since both companies were headed by the same people, a headache for the management of Northeastern was no less of a headache for the management of American.)

The Maine companies had several problems. In the first place, they were small and isolated, and thus could not support the management and technical skills required to run them efficiently. Also, the winters in Maine are long and hard, as Ray Wendell knew well, so the problems of maintaining service were severe, and the cost was high. Furthermore, the Maine companies, which had been starved for maintenance before Ware took over—"everything run down to hell and gone," in Wendell's words—did not fare much better in the hands of Barr. Thus, by the early 1950s, with inflation heating up, their need for upgrading was acute.

But when it came to obtaining the rate increases needed to finance the improvements, the companies in Maine were in a peculiar situation. Most of them had been built in the late nineteenth century by an entrepreneur named John Moore. Moore would go into a community and make a contract with the town fathers to install a certain number of fire hydrants in return for annual "hydrant fees." He would then risk his own money in building a water system in the hope that enough customers would be found to make the system profitable, taking shares of stock in the company in return for his investment.

The rates that can be charged for water (or electricity or gas) by a public utility depend on the "rate base," the value of the facilities that provide the service. If, for example, the facilities of a given water system represent a value of $10 million, and under the law the company is allowed to earn 12 percent on those assets, the regulatory authorities will authorize rates for water service that provide the opportunity to earn a profit of up to $1.2 million a year.

There are three methods of determining the rate base: "original cost," what it cost to build the system in the first place; "replacement value," what it would cost to build the system today; and "fair value," which is some combination of the two.

However, back in the late nineteenth century, when the companies in Maine were established, there was not much concern with formal methods of valuation. The companies simply entered on the books the value of the stock—as they saw it—that had been issued to John Moore in return for building the systems. Since the size of the rate base determines the rates that can be charged, the companies tended to value the stock rather generously.

This method of valuation posed no problem so long as water rates were set by local municipal authorities. Later, however, when the legislature put the regulation of rates in the hands of a state public utility commission, it ordained that thenceforth original cost and only original cost would be used in determining utility rates. This decision created problems for the Maine properties, particularly in the early 1950s, when rising inflation demanded frequent increases.

As Ray Wendell recalled it:

> Part of the trouble we had with rates up there was to justify what the hell was the original cost. Maine was a strict original cost state. I mean you couldn't get a dime for valuation. And part of our problem was to come up with records that would justify what we would claim as original cost, because that's what the companies originally set up on the books.
>
> Well the commission would *scoff* at us. "Well, hell, that stock that you set up there on the books, why that's *good for nothing . . . good for nothing.* What did you do for it?"
>
> "Well, the guy who owned it built a water system."
>
> "Well, okay, but it didn't cost anything like *this!*"

Wendell was transferred to western Pennsylvania in 1949, and left the problems of the Maine companies behind, but they did not go away, and as time passed the pressure on their profits became increasingly severe.

Meanwhile, John Ware had another headache. Howard Butcher, a leading figure in the Philadelphia business community, was an investment banker who was also head of a utility system called the General Waterworks Company. As Ware emerged in the major leagues of the water utility business, Howard Butcher decided they should go into business together and proposed that they merge their two companies. Ware had never liked the idea of going into partnership with anybody. However, Butcher was determined, and he continued to press Ware to do a deal.

As Jack Barr worried about the profitability of the companies in Maine and as John Ware fussed about the importunings of Howard Butcher, Barr had a happy thought. Why not sell the Maine properties to Butcher, thereby satisfying his desire to do a deal and at the same time unloading a problem operation? In 1955 the properties were offered to Butcher. He quickly accepted and the deal was done.

The whole matter was settled before Wendell got wind of it:

> Jack Barr did that to me while I was out in western Pennsylvania. He never told me a damn thing about it.
>
> Once I got to Philadelphia, I found out—for God sake, the Maine properties were gone!
>
> So I stomped into his office and asked him about it.
>
> "Oh, yeah," he said. "We sold 'em."
>
> "By God, you didn't ask me."
>
> Pretty sneaky, I thought. But it was too late. They were gone.

Some time later, after Butcher had gone through one or two winters with his new acquisition and had learned about the problems of dealing with the Maine Public Utility Commission, he ran into Barr in Philadelphia. As Barr later recalled with a twinkle, "That was some bargain you sold me," Butcher growled.

[167]

Wichita Split

In 1956, the same year in which the city of Birmingham decided not to renew its management contract with American, and the year after the Maine companies were sold, another challenge to the company's ownership of a major property began. This involved the water company in Wichita, Kansas, which had 63,000 customers at that time, about 8 percent of American's total.

The key fact about Wichita was that it was what could be called a hybrid situation. The company owned the distribution system but purchased its water from the city, which owned well fields and a filter plant outside of town.

Experience has shown that a situation like that tends to be unstable. With joint jurisdiction, the public partner often decides it no longer wants to settle for half. It is equivalent to letting the camel get his nose under the tent. Sooner or later the entire camel wants to come in, leaving no room for the original occupant.

Niccolò Machiavelli, the sixteenth-century writer on politics, had some words of advice on precisely that situation. In his classic work *The Prince,* Machiavelli argued that a ruler should never invite a stronger outsider into his domain to help him solve a problem, because once the immediate crisis is past, the outsider may decide not to go home, and the prince who invited him will find himself out of his castle and out of a job. Machiavelli cited as an example the Venetians, who in 1499 asked the king of France to come into their territory to help them conquer two towns in neighboring Lombardy. The king obliged, but then instead of going back to France, proceeded to take over two-thirds of Italy, including the domain of the Venetians—hardly the outcome they had in mind.

To the eye of the casual observer, the Wichita, Kansas, of 1956 would not have borne a very close resemblance to the Italy of 1499, nor would Mayor A. E. Howse of Wichita necessarily have reminded one of King Louis XII of France. But the essentials were the same. When the Wichita water system was established in 1911, allowing the city to install the well fields and build the filter plant obviously saved the company considerable investment. But that gave the city both the position and the temptation to expand its holding at a later date. Furthermore, in any showdown between the public and the private side in such a partnership, the public side normally holds an advantage. Under what is called the law of eminent domain, a unit of government has the right to take private property for public use.

For many years, however, nothing was done. Then in the time after World War II, as the city grew rapidly and demand for water increased, the water table beneath the city's well fields began to fall. Some action was required, and the city fathers concluded that the best first step would be to consolidate the entire operation into a single system under municipal control.

Although Mayor Howse was by no means a Renaissance man, he was nonetheless an interesting character. The owner of a local furniture store—an unlikely power base for a prince—he claimed a close association with General Eisenhower during World War II. Perhaps because of some cloak-and-dagger aspect of his wartime experience, he had an unusual arrangement for his office. When Jack Barr would pay a visit to the mayor, he would be ushered through a door on the first floor of the furniture store where he faced a blank wall. After he had satisfactorily identified himself, a button would be pushed, and the wall would mysteriously draw aside, revealing a staircase that led to the mayor's office on the second floor. Once in the office, a visitor would find the mayor seated on an elevated platform, while the caller sat humbly below, a situation with which King Louis of France would undoubtedly have found himself at home.

The mayor was a hands-on type. Once, after the city had purchased a new fire engine, the mayor decided he would be the first to drive it. The task proved more than he could handle. In short order the fire engine had demolished a parked car and broken off a fire hydrant. Regardless of his skill, or lack thereof, in driving fire engines, however, the mayor knew what he wanted so far as the water system was concerned, and he notified American that the city intended to take over the holdings of the Wichita Water Company.

[169]

In 1956, five years after it had surrendered its property in Birmingham, with its financial situation now improving, the company had changed its mind about disposing of water properties. It concluded that henceforth its business would be operating companies, not selling them. So it initially resisted even discussing the sale of Wichita. But the mayor was insistent and, with the power of condemnation at his disposal, knew he held the stronger hand.

"At first we refused to talk," Barr recalled, "but then we had to go out and talk."

They not only had to talk, but with the virtual certainty of condemnation hanging over their heads, they decided to deal. The pain of parting with a major property was no doubt assuaged somewhat by the handsome price—$30 million. Furthermore, as in Birmingham, it appeared that all was not lost. The annual report for 1956 announced, "Subject to adoption of certain enabling legislation the integrated system will be managed for the City by an affiliate of the Company under a management contract."

However, there's many a slip . . . The report for the following year noted cryptically, "Negotiations for management of the integrated system by an affiliate of the Company were terminated by mutual consent." Perhaps there had been a glitch in obtaining the enabling legislation. Or maybe the prince of Wichita had simply changed his mind.

Summing up the transaction, the report for 1957 declared that the sale of the Wichita property relieved the company of "supplying substantial capital funds to enlarge a system in a community with a promising but uncertain economy dependent to a significant degree upon one principal industry"—a statement about which there was perhaps a whiff of sour grapes.

TEN

You Lose a Few,
You Win a Few

In the months after the resolution at Wichita, the company agreed to sell two other properties: the Winchester Water Company, with 3,000 customers, to the city of Cambridge, Maryland; and the North Little Rock Water Company in Arkansas, with 18,000 customers, to that city. But now it appeared that an ominous trend was under way. In 1959 efforts were mounted to take over the company's properties in a number of communities. These included the water companies in Lexington, Kentucky, with 55,000 customers; Peoria, Illinois, with 45,000 customers; and Ashtabula, Ohio, with 10,000. It began to seem that what had begun as a trickle might become a flood, and unless the company took a stand, all of its more profitable subsidiaries could be nipped off, one by one, by opportunistic political attack.

Take a stand it did. The annual report for 1959 declared:

> The company has advised the governing bodies [of the cities in question] that we are unwilling to agree to the disposition of the subsidiaries or their properties. . . . It has been our firm policy [this was perhaps stretching the truth a little, considering the surrender at Birmingham] to resist these efforts by all legally proper means. We consider it our prime responsibility to maintain the integrity of the company's investment in the water works field.

Easy to say. Not so easy to do. In most states the right of eminent domain is absolute, the reasoning being that the citizens of a community, through their elected representatives, are entitled to take any property if just compensation is provided. Furthermore, in many cases, as in Birmingham, there is no need to invoke eminent domain. The franchise contract, agreed to by the company, gives the city the right to take over the property—again with compensation—whenever it sees fit.

But the language of contracts and the processes of the law are not the only pieces on the board in the game of local politics. There is also public opinion and the institutions through which public opinion finds its voice. In some cases the franchise contract provides that a referendum be held before the water company can be purchased by the city, to determine whether, in fact, the public wants to buy the property. In other cases, if a referendum is not specifically provided for in the contract, any individual or group can compel one by collecting enough names on a petition. And where that avenue is not open, mayors, city councilmen and county commissioners are keenly sensitive to the public mood—at least if they want to be reelected they are. If public sentiment is opposed, or can be caused to become opposed, to the public takeover of a private business, the powers-that-be will be very slow to go ahead, even though they might have nominal authority to do so.

Therefore, if the primary avenue of attack on a privately owned public utility is legal, the principal line of defense, and the obvious point of counterattack, is political. (Machiavelli recognized the power of public opinion, even in the despotic city-states of the sixteenth century, and counseled the prince on the importance of winning and holding public support. The difference then, of course, was that if the public attitude turned sour, it expressed itself not merely in a painful defeat at the polls, but in riots and rebellions, conspiracies and assassinations.)

In Lexington, Kentucky, the struggle came to a head quickly, as described in the American Water Works annual report for 1960:

> The City of Lexington moved early in the year to acquire the Lexington Water Company under the terms of its franchise. Because we were convinced that the best interest of the company would not be served by the sale of this subsidiary, and that it would not benefit the public served, we advised the City that we would be unwilling

sellers, and we were prepared to conduct a vigorous campaign to gain support of Lexington citizens in opposition to the acquisition.

The campaign was successful. "Late in the year," the report went on, "the City abandoned its proposed acquisition . . . when incomplete valuations indicated the extent of the undertaking and it was realized that public opinion was opposed."

The effort in Ashtabula reached a climax the same year, this time by means of a referendum. The annual report almost gloated over the company's victory: "The citizens voted almost 4 to 1 against municipal ownership. The voters were convinced that city ownership would mean higher water rates, higher taxes, and politics in the operation of the water system."

In Peoria the city went to court in its effort to take over the water system. However, in the company's view, "This action is considered of doubtful validity and we will continue to resist." Whether by virtue of the strength of its legal position or the vigor of its political resistance, the following year the company was able to announce, "On November 14, 1961, the City Council of Peoria, Illinois, voted to abandon its effort to purchase the Peoria Water Company."

That was the last of the takeover efforts in Lexington and Peoria, at least as reflected in the company's annual reports. In Ashtabula the opposition apparently did not know when it was licked. Three years later, in 1964, another referendum was held. This time the takeover effort was defeated by a vote of 2 to 1, a narrower, but still healthy, margin.

That's What Friends Are For

The year 1960 taught—or rather reinforced—another important lesson about what it takes to succeed in the water business. As Jack Barr noted afterward, "Part of the success of Lexington and the like has to be assigned to the manager's local position." In other words, if the manager of the local water company has been active in community affairs and has established himself as a meaningful presence in the community, when the time comes to decide the fate of the company, it is perceived not simply as a faceless entity, a puppet whose strings are pulled and whose profits are siphoned off by some remote, impersonal corporation. Rather, the manager is accepted as "Mr. Water Company," a real human being, a neighbor and a friend. (He also has the benefit of lines of communication that provide early warning of impending trouble, as well as IOUs, social and political, to be cashed in time of need.)

Not surprisingly, as time passed and challenges continued, the company put increasing emphasis on encouraging all employees— not just managers—to participate in local affairs, and on promoting to managerial positions those who showed a talent for developing and maintaining harmonious local relations.*

The Magic Money Machine

In addition to encouraging employees to participate in local affairs, the company began devoting increasing attention to formal programs of public and community relations.

The public relations efforts of utility companies have a checkered history. In the period after World War I, as the growth of the giant utility pyramids of the 1920s gathered momentum, the holding companies mounted a vast "educational" campaign to persuade the voters that existing mechanisms for regulating public utilities

---

*The "flip side" of a policy of promoting those who show an aptitude for community relations is finding a means to dispense with the services of those who do not. Ray Wendell describes an example of the latter:

"I had to fire a guy once for being too much of a company guy. My God, he got us in more trouble with city officials and contractors by pounding the table for the company's rights. And usually he was right, too. But dammit, you don't go around telling mayors where to get off because the company's right and the mayor's wrong, and he insisted on doing that. So finally I had to fire him."

But if Wendell was tough, he was also compassionate. "It was about a year," he added, "before that fellow got another job. I told him we'd keep him on the payroll till he got another job, you know, figuring it's going to be a few weeks or maybe a few months. But it was a year."

(which the companies could easily control) were adequate and that any increase in the public ownership of private utilities would be dangerous. The cost of the campaign ranged between $25 and $30 million a year (equal to $150 to $200 million in 1990 dollars), all of it charged to the customers through their utility bills. The leaders of the industry urged executives not to spare their "educational" budgets. "All the money being spent is worthwhile," declared the managing director of the National Electric Light Association. "Don't be afraid of the expense. The public pays the expense."

A vigorous effort was made to persuade customers to buy utility stocks and bonds, on the ground that this was "the best kind of public ownership." Manuals were prepared and study courses and meetings held to equip employees to serve as "missionaries for private ownership." Even the educational system was employed, using every means from picture books for kindergartners to retainers for college professors, "to fix the truth about the utilities in the young person's mind before incorrect notions become fixed there."

In the words of one observer, "They made state regulation satisfactory to themselves, because they largely succeeded in regulating the sources of public opinion from which regulation springs." The utilities had, in effect, created a kind of "magic money machine" that spent the customers' money to persuade the customers that it was all right to charge the customers still more money. It seemed almost too good to be true.

It was. In the aftermath of the crash of 1929, the stocks that had been sold to customers as "the best kind of public ownership" proved to be an excellent way for people to lose their money, and the power to control state regulatory commissions, which had been so carefully cultivated, was abused in an effort to protect the companies' earnings. In a drama that might be compared to an old-time morality play, the backlash of public anger at the companies' abuses brought the very increase in regulation they opposed, as well as the expansion of public ownership—the Tennessee Valley Authority, the Rural Electrification Administration—they most feared.

Forty-three Bulletin Boards

Although American Water Works & Electric was not accused of the excesses of a Samuel Insull or an Electric Bond & Share, it did support the idea that a vigorous program of customer and community relations was essential to the success of a public utility company. Early issues of the employee magazine *Water,* published by the Water Works Division (which in 1947 became the new American Water Works Company), make that clear.

In October 1925 the magazine observed, "If a public utility employee can help out in a civic enterprise, he not only benefits himself in the eyes of his fellow citizens, but also improves the public standing of his company." It went on to report admiringly the example of W. H. Hulsey, a young engineer at the Birmingham Water Company, who during his lunch hours sold no fewer than 43 bulletin boards to local businessmen as part of a Junior Chamber of Commerce campaign to cut down the number of accidents and thereby reduce insurance rates in the city.

In January 1927 the magazine reported at length on a speech by Warren R. Voorhees, a vice president of AWW&E, who told an audience at Indiana State University that "the public has been the great gainer from the policy of grouping public utility companies under a central management and control."

In August of the same year the magazine featured the results of a high school essay contest, sponsored by the water company in Joplin, Missouri, on the subject of "The Water Supply of Joplin":

> The prizes were awarded at the graduation exercises, attended by six thousand parents, other relatives and friends. The Water Company throughout received much favorable and deserved publicity while the people of the city obtained a more intimate knowledge of their most necessary public service company.

A featured editorial in May 1928 made clear that public relations was everybody's business:

> Some very modern public utilities . . . have a Department of Public Relations with a Director, who has a mahogany desk and his own

stationery. But no Department of Public Relations is worth organizing unless every member of the organization from the manager
to the assistant janitor is a full-fledged member three hundred and
sixty-five days in the year. The Director of Public Relations may
belong to every lodge in town, and he may play golf with the Mayor
every Sunday morning, but he cannot make friends as fast as a
cashier with a snippy tongue and a wintry eye can make enemies.

The Old Order Passeth

The positive, not to say aggressive, attitude toward public and community relations of utility companies in general, and of the old
American Water Works & Electric in particular, was not shared by
John Ware. Although he had a singular talent for motivating and
inspiring the loyalty of subordinates and a compelling persuasiveness in dealing one on one, Ware displayed neither a talent for nor
an interest in developing a positive public image or cultivating people in groups. A diligent search of public records in Lancaster,
Pennsylvania, where he built the electric company that laid the basis of his fortune, turned up not a single reference to John Ware,
aside from his telephone number, two listings in business directo-
ries and a brief announcement of his wedding in 1907. Later, after
Ware moved to Oxford, Pennsylvania, he did not exactly go out of
his way to cultivate local relationships. When he discovered that
some of his neighbors were cheating on the meter readings for
steam heat from his gas company, Ware abruptly closed the service
down. When he decided to move his house, he simply and spectac-
ularly picked it up and moved it, while gleefully feeding the local
rumor mill with wild stories about what he was up to, challenging
the city council to declare him insane if they saw fit, and throwing
a party in the house while it was en route. It is also said that when
he drove downtown to get a haircut, if there was no parking space
available in the street, he would park in the middle of the sidewalk.

None of this behavior in any way impeded Ware's progress in
building his fortune. Perhaps it helped, causing potential oppo-

nents to underestimate this quiet, determined man. However, when near the end of his career Ware was ready to proceed with his dream of the Aqueduct Project in western Pennsylvania, he simply announced it, laid it abruptly on the public through the press, and that was that, making no provision to answer criticism nor any effort to shape opinion in advance. At least in part as a result, the project failed.

In the First Battle of Ashtabula, John Delaney, the recently hired public relations man for American Water Works, organized the publicity campaign that opposed the takeover, was credited with the victory, and came home expecting to be congratulated. Instead, he encountered a John Ware still smarting from the failure of Aqueduct, and was told sourly that the battle could have been won "without all that public relations nonsense." Delaney was crushed.

But the hour was late for Ware. Aqueduct was in fact his last hurrah; he retired a few months later. In the years that followed, the company not only continued but expanded "all that public relations nonsense" whenever and wherever the situation required.

Reinventing the Wheel

During the first 10 years after John Ware took control of American, while the management was preoccupied with paying off the debt and meeting the demands for new construction, there was only one passing mention in an annual report of anything having to do with public or community relations. The first example of a formal effort at press or public relations involved, ironically, Ware himself—although it was his subordinates who took the initiative and made the arrangements. In 1957, when Ware was about to receive the Horatio Alger Award, honoring his rags-to-riches story, the management retained John Delaney, then a writer-editor for *Iron Age* magazine, to prepare a package of biographical material on Ware to be given to the press. The results were positive. The coverage was excellent. Ware was delighted. Recognizing the need to cultivate better local relationships, the management decided to put Delaney on the payroll full-time.

The very next year the new approach began to show. Photographs and drawings were used for the first time to illustrate the annual report, and the graphics were more dramatic than before. The report also included an essay entitled "Community and Public Relations," which declared: "An informed public is an understanding public.... During 1957 we intensified our program of advertisements, letters, and leaflets informing customers of our operations, improvement programs, and financial problems."

In 1960, the year the challenges in Lexington and Ashtabula were dealt with successfully, the company announced a program of granting college scholarships to promising high school students, describing it as "an important element in our growing emphasis on public relations in the communities we serve." The first college scholarships were awarded in 1961. (Interestingly, one of those scholarships was awarded to a student in Peoria, where the battle for control of the local water company was even at that moment coming to a head.) The company also initiated a new management newsletter that served as "a forum through which subsidiary managers and other personnel exchange ideas on public relations and other management problems."

The report for the following year closed with a statement that could serve as the charter for the public relations efforts of any utility company:

> The principal objectives of the public relations programs of our subsidiaries are to emphasize their positions as good citizens in their respective communities, to create and develop a greater awareness of the many contributions a sound investor-owned utility makes toward the economy and welfare of the community, and to generate a deeper appreciation of the importance and value of a high standard of water service. These programs are conducted through all the various media available, but the most effective work is performed by our own personnel through their memberships on various public-spirited committees and their participation in campaigns for community betterment.

The Quick Brown Deer

The intangible arts and stratagems lumped together under the heading of public relations were, and to a considerable extent still are, somewhat of a mystery to line managers, particularly those schooled in the quantifiable certitudes of the financial discipline. A case in point occurred in connection with the making of a movie about the water utility industry. The film crew that had been hired to do the job wanted to take a trip to see the company's properties in California, in the hope that they might find some interesting footage there. They were well aware that, given the uncertainties of the movie-making process, they might come back empty-handed. That was a perfectly acceptable risk—indeed a necessary risk—so far as they were concerned. By contrast, Marshall Anderson, whose background is financial, was reluctant to see them go unless there was reasonable assurance there would be a payback for the trip.

This is the story as Anderson tells it:

At one point John Delaney talked us into making a movie. "The Joy of Water," I think it was called. So he hired this outfit in Philadelphia to make the movie, and one day he came in and he said, "They want to send a crew out to California to work on this movie."

I said, "What can they do out there that they can't do in Pennsylvania?"

He said, "Well, they want to go out there . . ." and so forth and so on.

I said, "All they want to do is go out and have a free trip on us."

Well, they were pretty insistent on it. I don't know that I gave 'em an okay on it. Somebody else must have okayed it. I don't think I did.

Anyhow, they went out there, and when they came back we saw the movie, and I said to John, "What is there in that movie that was taken in California?"

And he said, "You remember that little section

(continued . . .)

(. . . continued)

    where that pipeline comes down over the hill, and
there's a little deer that comes along and hops over
the pipeline?"
    I said, "Yeah."
    And he said, "Well, that's it."

    "And that," concluded Anderson, "is what we paid for
them to go to California for."

The Tide Turns

Hindsight reveals that the period 1960–61 was the high-water mark
for attempts to take over the company's properties. In a curious
turnabout, the trend that appeared so threatening one year had
largely faded by the next. Over the next dozen years there were
periodic mentions in annual reports that discussions were being
held with the authorities of one city or another regarding a possible
takeover. But most of the discussions came to nothing. In the time
between 1962 and 1973 only a few companies were sold and, with
two noteworthy exceptions, these were very small properties.

    However, the posture of the company during this time was by
no means entirely defensive. During the 1960s and early 1970s, at
the same time that it was giving up a handful of properties, the
company or its subsidiaries acquired no fewer than four dozen.
Once their tenure had been reaffirmed, the Lexington, Ashtabula
and Peoria companies all acquired adjacent water systems. In 1966
the East St. Louis and Interurban Water Company purchased the
Stookey Township Water Works, one of the first acquisitions, as the
annual report noted happily, of a municipal system by an investor-
owned company.

    In general the acquisitions were small ones. However, in Janu-
ary 1962, American bought six water systems with a total of 20,000
customers in the rapidly growing suburbs of Philadelphia and

merged them together under the name of the Norristown Water Company. Three years later, in 1965, in an exchange valued at almost $23 million, the company bought the water properties of the Southern Gas & Water Company, with a total of 77,000 customers served by 16 separate systems in 56 communities of West Virginia.

Transactions of considerable magnitude are sometimes arranged in remarkably casual ways. Marshall Anderson, a vice president at the time, recalls the encounter that led to the purchase of Southern Gas & Water:

> Some of us were down at the meeting of NARUC [the National Association of Regulatory Utility Commissioners] at the Greenbrier. One afternoon Rusty Renick, who was the Charleston manager for Southern Gas & Water, was talking to me. We each had a drink in our hand. He said, "These guys are trying to sell that property and can't sell it. Why don't you talk to them about it. Would you be interested?"
>
> I said, "Well, I don't know. We'd be interested in talking about it."
>
> His ears perked up just like that, and the next morning I had a telephone call from him in the hotel, and he said, "These guys want to talk to you about this thing."
>
> And I said, "Well, okay, we'll talk about it."
>
> Within a week or so we were back in the shop and we were talking with them, and one thing led to another and first thing you know we were going over indentures and papers of one sort or another, and we ended up buying the property.
>
> One of their guys told me afterward that he thought they got a little better of the deal than we did. I said, "Well, as long as we're both happy, why, that's just fine."

California Dreaming

The following year the company made an acquisition that dwarfed even Southern Gas & Water. For a price of $47 million it bought the water utility assets of the California Water & Telephone Company, with 84,000 customers. That was the largest acquisition since

John Ware had gained control of American in 1947, and it was exceeded in size only by the purchase in 1936, by the old American Water Works & Electric, of the Community Water Service Company, which at the time had more than 200,000 customers.

California Water & Telephone had been acquired earlier by the General Telephone & Electronics Company, which kept the telephone properties but decided to sell off the water holdings. Marshall Anderson was involved in that transaction as well. This is his recollection:

> We had a lot of fun with the acquisition of that thing, Jack Barr, Ray Wendell, Tom Earl and I. They were taking sealed bids on the deal, and the bids had to be in on a given date. We decided that we'd make a bid on it, but we were going to be damn sure we wouldn't give them our bid until the last minute, because we weren't going to have anybody open our bid and see what was in it and have something go wrong.
>
> There was a question in our minds as to where the bid had to be submitted. One was to be delivered in California, and one was to be delivered in New York at the same time. So we got these two sets of bids made out. Jack said he'd take the bid to California, because he was going out there for some reason anyway, and he said to me, "You take the bid to New York."
>
> So at ten minutes to three on this given afternoon—the bids were due in at three o'clock—I walked in to the New York office, and he walked into wherever the office was in California and said we'd like to give you our bids. I sat there with the bid in my hand, looking at my watch, making pleasantries with the guy sitting across the desk. He was a nice fellow. And finally I looked at my watch, and I said, "Well, I guess it's about two minutes to three; here's the bid." And he said thanks, and he said, "Are you staying over in New York?"
>
> I said, "Yeah, my wife came with me and we are staying."
>
> About five o'clock I happened to be in the hotel room. The telephone rang.
>
> "Mr. Anderson?"
>
> "Yeah."
>
> "This is Jim Jones," or whatever his name was.
>
> "Yes sir."

He says, "We've looked at your bid. You're the high bidder, but we'd like to talk to you about it. Would it be possible to talk to you folks tomorrow?"

And I said, "You can talk to me, but only with Jack Barr being present."

Jack was coming back that night. So I said, "I think you can safely make the date for after lunch tomorrow."

Well, I was able to reach Jack before he left California, and I said, "We've got a date over here tomorrow, because they told me that we had the high bid but they wanted to talk about it."

In a way it was kind of ridiculous to expect that we were going to make the bid higher when they already told us that it was the high bid. I think he slipped a little bit on that.

So Jack and I went in the next day and met with him after lunch, and that's what the guy said, "Well, we'd like to see whether we can't push you on this a little."

And Jack said, "No, you can't. That's our bid. We will not move. We will not increase the bid at all."

So they finally said, "Well, thanks. We got a deal."

The California acquisition was greeted with great optimism by the management of American. It held the prospect of opening a new chapter in the history of the company. In the words of the 1966 annual report, "The acquisition established the company on the West Coast and places us in an excellent position to acquire additional properties in the nation's fastest-growing state."

In December of that year American also acquired the Pollock Water Service, Inc., a small company serving territory adjacent to that of California-American, and the following year purchased the nearby Village Water Company. As though to celebrate this trend of events, in 1966 American Water Works was for the first time listed by *Fortune* magazine among the 50 largest public utility companies in the United States.

The American Water Works Service Company offices
were on the fourteenth floor of 3 Penn Center Plaza
(*right*) in downtown Philadelphia in the 1960s and
early 1970s.

American Water Works Company President Jack Barr (*center*) steered the company from 1960 to 1975 with the counsel of Vice Chairman Willard M. Ware (*left*) and Chairman John H. Ware, 3rd.

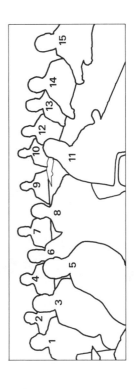

The 1966 officers and directors of American included: (1) Marshall A. Anderson, (2) Lawrence T. (Bill) Reinicker, (3) Robert W. Kean, Jr., (4) John H. Ware, 3rd, (5) John L. Plummer, (6) Raymond T. Wendell, (7) John J. (Jack) Barr, (8) Homer Reed, (9) Willard M. Ware, (10) William B. MacIndoe, (11) Howard H. Briggs, (12) Kenneth W. Gemmill, (13) William B. Gamble, (14) W. James MacIntosh and (15) Charles A. Briggs.

Jack Barr at about the time he retired as president in 1975.

ELEVEN

Alexandria, Jewel in the Crown

The decade of the 1960s was a busy one for the company, as it defended its properties in Lexington, Peoria and Ashtabula and acquired major holdings in West Virginia and California, along with a number of smaller properties in other locations. All other events of that period were overshadowed, however, in the drama of the confrontation, in the stature of the participants and in the memories of those who took part, by the challenge to the company's ownership of the Alexandria Water Company in northern Virginia, just across the Potomac River from Washington, D.C. For James V. LaFrankie, who was then assistant manager of the Alexandria company and eventually became president of the American system, the events of Alexandria were not only the landmark experience of his early career, but also a decisive influence on his future thinking about the water business.

The Alexandria Water Company, founded in 1850, was the second oldest in the system, exceeded in age only by the Berwick Water Company in eastern Pennsylvania, which was started in 1818. The original reservoir in Alexandria was built by slave labor. As noted earlier, unlike the situation in many other systems, the founders of the Alexandria company made prudent allowance for future growth. Its first annual report stated that although the population of the city was only 10,000 at the time, the reservoir was designed to serve a population of 20,000.

The city of Alexandria is, as the saying goes, "steeped in history." Young George Washington helped lay out the original plan of the city in 1748. Washington's residence, Mount Vernon, lies a few miles downstream on the Potomac shore. Washington was also a vestryman of Christ Church in Alexandria, steward of the Alexandria Jockey Club—he owned his own race horses—and Worshipful Master of the local Masonic lodge.

When the U.S. Congress, after protracted bickering, was unable to agree on a site for the new national capital, it passed a law in 1790 decreeing that the capital be located somewhere along the Potomac River between Maryland and Virginia, but left it to the new president, George Washington, to pick the site and acquire the land. After considering a site a bit upstream and another somewhat downstream, Washington selected a quadrangle of land that included Georgetown, Maryland; Arlington, Virginia; and, perhaps not surprisingly, Alexandria.

According to tradition, Washington originally selected a parcel of land at the southern end of the city as the site of the new Capitol building itself. (This would have been an easy ride from his home at Mount Vernon.) However, Washington's critics charged that he was trying to increase the wealth of his family by putting the Capitol in Alexandria, where they owned considerable property. When he heard these rumors, Washington decreed that the Capitol would be across the river on the Maryland side, and hired Major Pierre Charles L'Enfant to design the new city.

As a result of that decision, all the major buildings of the government, along with the business district and the fashionable residential neighborhoods, developed on the Maryland side of the river, while Alexandria, along with Arlington to the north, remained sleepy southern cities, little changed in any fundamental way from the days of George Washington. After a few years, the citizens of Arlington and Alexandria, disappointed at having been left out of the good fortune, petitioned the Congress to allow them to become a part of the state of Virginia again. This the Congress agreed to do in 1846. But curiously, although Alexandria had previously been the seat of neighboring Fairfax County, the Congress made it a separate city, independent of any county government. This quirk of jurisdiction was to have an impact on later events.

Over time, the only significant developments on the Virginia side of the river were such low-density facilities as Arlington National Cemetery, originally created for the burial of Union casualties during the Civil War; the National Airport; and the Washington Masonic National Memorial, located on the site Washington had originally chosen for the Capitol—which, as it turned out, was right next to the original reservoir of the Alexandria Water Company.

Alexandria remained largely unchanged until the beginning of World War II, when, with space running out in downtown Washington, it was decided to build what was then the largest office building in the world, the Pentagon, on the Virginia side of the river. In the aftermath of the war, with the military and intelligence organizations demanded by the cold war, with the new economic agencies resulting from the Marshall Plan, and with the civil bureaucracy required by expanding domestic programs, what was a surge of growth in the rest of the United States became a virtual explosion of growth in northern Virginia. New highways were built, spawning new housing developments, which in turn generated new shopping centers and satellite communities. In a short time the northern Virginia area became the fastest growing metropolitan region of the country. And there, as everywhere, new houses, offices and businesses required an expanded water supply.

It was impossible for the original Alexandria reservoir, built by the founders in 1850, along with additions that had been made since, to handle this explosion of demand. So the company purchased an old dam and reservoir on the Occoquan Creek, 20 miles to the south, and made plans to expand it. (History is inescapable in that part of the world. One of the tributaries of the Occoquan is Bull Run, where two of the greatest battles of the Civil War were fought. The course of events that led to the Second Battle of Bull Run began when General "Stonewall" Jackson seized the Union supply depot at Manassas Junction, a short distance from the point where Bull Run joins Cedar Run to form the Occoquan.)

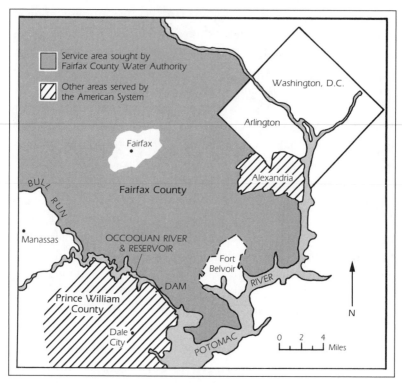

This map of Alexandria, Virginia, and its environs shows the Alexandria Water Company service area, the objective of a takeover attempt by the Fairfax County Water Authority.

The American Water Works annual report for 1948 stated:

> The largest single project contemplated for 1949 is the construction of a complete new source of supply [on Occoquan Creek] with related pumping, filtration and transmission facilities for the Alexandria Water Company. . . . As designed, the new system will be sufficient to meet the present and anticipated demand for service throughout the entire area, and the Alexandria Water Company's operations and revenue should be substantially increased.

The forecast that the Alexandria company's operations and revenues would be substantially increased by the new development was right on target. The prediction that the new facilities would be

No Thanks to Uncle George

One of the most elegant sections of prewar Alexandria was a group of estates along Seminary Road, named for the Virginia Theological Seminary nearby. In the mid-1950s, while the city and its environs were exploding in suburban growth, a group of nine young bachelors, including Gilbert Cross, the author of this book, rented one of the estates on Seminary Road. There, in a handsome country house furnished with authentic antiques from George Washington's time, they lived in quiet elegance, sheltered from the ferment of growth around them by 78 acres of beautifully landscaped grounds, woods and bridle trails.

They could afford to live this way because the landlady, the widow of an admiral, wanted to keep the place occupied until she could sell off the land for development. She charged them a rent of $350 a month, which came out to $38.89 per man. The landlady also offered to sell some of her land to any bachelor who might be interested, at a price of $7,500 an acre. None took her up on the offer, which is unfortunate, since the same land today, if any were available, would go for no less than $300,000 an acre.

The estate was ideal for entertaining, so a lot of entertaining was done. A guest at a party one Saturday night was a young gentleman named John Washington, a direct descendant of George Washington's half-brother Lawrence—George and Martha had had no children. Tall and athletic, young John looked as though he might well have been capable of throwing a silver dollar across the Potomac. And if his handsome features had been framed with a powdered wig and ruffled shirt, he could even have been mistaken for the subject of the well-known portrait by Gilbert Stuart.

It did not occur to Cross at the time to inquire whether the Washingtons still had landholdings in Alexandria. If they did, which seems likely, the increase in family wealth, so long postponed by the rather arbitrary decision of Great, Great, Great, Great, Great, Great Uncle George, was even then in process of occurring.

"sufficient to meet the present and anticipated demand for service throughout the entire area" was considerably off the mark. Within a few years another expansion of the Occoquan facility was required, and again in 1962 the company reported, "The largest single project planned for 1963 is that programmed by the Alexandria Water Company to keep pace with the growth of its service area."

During that period Jack Barr inquired of Spike Aldrich, the company's chief engineer, why the company was always behind in providing facilities to supply the needs of Alexandria. "Because," replied Aldrich, "we don't believe our own estimates."

As fast as it might attempt to expand its supply of water, there was no way the Alexandria Water Company could stay abreast of the pell-mell growth of demand. A developer would acquire a tract of land, lay out roads and proceed to build houses and sell them. If water was not available, as often it was not, he would simply drill a well or dam a nearby stream and install a water system. Then, as complaints about unreliable service or poor quality of water began to come in—as they have for every carelessly constructed water system since the beginning of time—the the builder, who had already taken his profit, would be anxious to unload the property. In some cases he would even be willing to give it away, in order to be free of the headaches. There was one particularly attractive property which came on the market at that time. This was the Annandale Water Company, which supplied a number of developments in Fairfax County. The company was for sale, the price was a fair one, and American was more than willing to buy. However, there was a problem. Most of the assets of the Annandale Company were "contributed" assets: property that a developer had been so eager to get rid of that he had given it away, or land or facilities donated by towns that were anxious to have better water service. And under Virginia law, a public utility company's rate base, the assets on which it can earn, could only include those in which it had actually invested money. It could not include "contributed" assets.

The law had every good intention. It was meant to prevent an abuse common in the 1920s: a holding company promoter would contribute property to an operating utility he controlled, then include an inflated valuation of the property in the rate base. However, the effect of the law in this case was to prevent any private company that might purchase the Annandale property from charging rates adequate to provide a decent return on the purchase price. That was not the intent of the law, but it was the effect. It was unrealistic. It was unfair. But the law was the law.

The Alexandria Water Company appealed to the Virginia Corporation Commission for an exception to the law based on the special circumstances. The commission refused. Contributed assets could not be included in the rate base.

So the company faced a problem. It could buy the Annandale property with the purpose of protecting its opportunity to benefit from the growth of its service area, knowing that its investment in *future* development could be added to the rate base, but accepting that it would not be allowed to charge enough to recover its original purchase price. Or it could pass up the opportunity to buy the company, recognizing that the company was on the market and sooner or later someone else might find a way to buy it.

At another time, the decision might have been made to buy the Annandale property, regardless of the immediate economic impact. But things were moving too fast, and there was continuing preoccupation with the near-term bottom line. So before anyone had really focussed on the broader implications, a public body had been created, the Fairfax County Water Authority, which in 1959 bought the Annandale Water Company. (Under the law, a public body has no problem buying contributed property. Being itself an arm of government, it sets its own rates, and is not subject to regulation by any other arm of government.)

Thus the company was confronted with a replay of the infamous "Wichita Split," against which Machiavelli had warned so long ago. The camel of public ownership had once again worked its nose under the tent of private enterprise. It remained to be seen whether—or in this case, when—the entire camel would attempt to take possession of the premises.

The wait was not long. In Wichita the situation had rocked along for a number of years before the pace of postwar growth drew down the city's water supply, triggering the takeover effort. In northern Virginia in the 1950s, nothing was rocking, everything was rolling. In 1959, the same year that challenges were issued to the company's properties in Lexington, Ashtabula and Peoria, the Fairfax County Water Authority notified American Water Works of its intention to take over its property there, including its reservoir and treatment facility on the Occoquan. Because of the jurisdictional quirk created by the act of Congress a century earlier, making Alexandria a city without a county, Fairfax County did not have jurisdiction over, nor power to condemn, the property within the city itself. And because the company had enjoyed a close and cordial relationship with city officials for more than a century, no serious effort was made to take over the original reservoir and distribution system there.

As far as the management of American Water Works was concerned, the Alexandria situation was not going to go the way of Wichita if it had anything to say about it. When the annual report of 1959 declared that "the company has advised the governing bodies that we are unwilling to agree to the disposition of the subsidiaries or their properties," it was referring not alone to Lexington, Peoria and Ashtabula. It was referring above all to Alexandria.

After the Fairfax Authority issued its challenge, Jack Barr moved almost full-time to northern Virginia to supervise the campaign of opposition. Young Assistant Manager Jim LaFrankie was assigned to assist Barr. And just as Jack Barr, thirty years before, had been thrilled at his first encounter with John Ware, so now LaFrankie was not unaware of the implications of an opportunity to work closely with Barr. "My participation in that case was a growing experience," he recalled, "not only to take part, but also for a chance to be associated on a daily basis with the president of the company."

It was not actually LaFrankie's first meeting with Barr:

I remember the first time I ever met him. A division manager named Jerry Powers had died. Jerry Powers had been a military officer in the war, and he was going to be buried in Arlington National Cemetery. Jack Barr called and said, "Can someone pick me up at the National Airport and take me to Arlington Cemetery?" So here was an opportunity to meet the president of the company and drive him over to Arlington.

I had an old blue Lincoln. I'll never forget it. It was a 1956 Lincoln Capri, with a fancy ornamental exhaust in the back. So I took that old blue Lincoln and I was going to impress the hell out of Jack. I made contact with him at the airport, and he said hello and got in.

I had been there about five years in Virginia, but like any city you can get lost pretty easily. So I drove around like I knew where the hell I was going, and I'll be damned if I didn't end up in the Pentagon parking lot.

The pair made it to the funeral in time, and Barr forgave the early misstep. But according to LaFrankie, "I don't think Jack ever forgot that I landed him in the Pentagon parking lot."

A Game of Chess

The first step for the opposing sides in the Battle of Alexandria was to retain counsel. According to Jim LaFrankie:

We already had counsel in Alexandria, a jovial fellow who was a former state senator named Armistead Boothe. Army Boothe, as we called him, was a colorful individual who would stand in the courtroom with his eyes closed and go through all the beautiful southern discussion of legalese and so forth. He was just a beautiful person.

In addition to Army Boothe, we hired a law firm out of Richmond, Virginia—Hunton, Williams, Gay, Powell & Gibson, a big, well-known firm that represented the Virginia Electric Power Company and a lot of other utilities. We were represented by two members of the firm, John W. Riley and Milton Farley.

What followed can be compared to a chess game, with a move by Black (the Fairfax County Water Authority, the "Bad Guys," as far as the company was concerned) countered by one by White (Barr, LaFrankie and company—the "Good Guys").

Black obviously had the first move. Otherwise there would have been no game. The water authority did not have statutory power to condemn the property without first obtaining the permission of the State Corporation Commission. Although the commission had ruled against the Alexandria company in the matter of "contributed" property, the water authority apparently did not want to risk a turndown by going that route. So the authority went to the Fairfax County supervisors. Under the law, the supervisors did have the power to condemn a property, so the water authority asked the supervisors to do the job on their behalf. The supervisors obliged, and filed suit to condemn the Fairfax County property of the Alexandria Water Company.

Now it was White's move. The company cried foul and appealed the supervisors' action to the State Corporation Commission, claiming that the suit was nothing but a subterfuge: that since the suit was being made on behalf of the water authority, it needed the approval of the corporation commission. This time the corporation commission ruled for the company, declaring, with perhaps a touch of bureaucratic pique, that it should not have been bypassed, and that the condemnation proceeding could not go ahead without its approval.

Black countered. The Fairfax County supervisors appealed the ruling of the corporation commission to the Virginia Superior Court. The court backed the supervisors, ruling that they did indeed have the right to condemn the property without the permission of the corporation commission.

This ended the opening stage of the contest. The way was now clear for the supervisors to condemn the property. There was nothing the company could do to stop or even delay that process. Under Virginia law no referendum is allowed on a decision by county supervisors. (Perhaps the old Virginia aristocracy had not liked the notion of submitting a decision to a direct, *popular* vote.)

However, the game was by no means over. Once a property is condemned, which was now a foregone conclusion, a trial is held before a jury (called a commission in this sort of case) to determine how much the owner of the property should be paid. Once that decision has been handed down, the actual money to complete the purchase must then be appropriated by the county supervisors.

The company adopted a two-pronged strategy: First, it would extract the highest possible price from the jury trial—in Jack Barr's words, "we're going to inventory every nut and bolt"—so that if ultimately the property had to be sold, the company at least would be well compensated. And then, who could know? If the purchase price turned out to be high enough, perhaps the taxpayers of Fairfax County could be persuaded, through a vigorous publicity campaign, that it was a higher price than the supervisors should, in fact, be allowed to pay.

During the whole course of the controversy, even after the property had been formally condemned, the company continued to invest heavily in water facilities in Fairfax County. This was no doubt in part because continuing growth of demand required continued expansion of supply. Also, the company obviously wanted to demonstrate that it was capable of continuing to meet the needs of its customers—and doubtless wanted to make clear to its opponents that it had no intention of backing away. But it may also have reflected a determination to raise the ante. The purpose may have been not only to "inventory every nut and bolt," but to make sure there were just as many nuts and bolts as possible there to be inventoried, along with pipes and pumps, dams and reservoirs, offices and filter plants.

As already noted, there are two basic methods of evaluating a utility property: original cost and replacement cost. History shows that if a property had been built at a time when costs were high, as in the 1920s, and later was being evaluated when costs had dropped, as in the depression, the company would argue that the higher of the two, original cost, should be the basis for valuation, while its opponents would take the opposite view. On the other hand, if a property had been built when costs were low, and then was being evaluated when costs were high, the company would argue that replacement cost was the proper basis. Its opponents again would take the opposite view.

At the time of the challenge to the Alexandria property, prices were not only high but rising. As a consequence, the company argued that replacement cost was the proper basis for valuation, and its opponents took the opposite view. The difficulty with using replacement cost, however, is that the process of determining the cost of replacing a utility property is very complex and extremely expensive, potentially running into millions of dollars. Thus when Jack Barr opted for the replacement approach, he gambled. If the court accepted it and therefore set a high price on the property, the expense of valuation would be more than justified. On the other hand, if the court rejected it, and opted instead for original cost, a substantial amount of money would have been wasted.

"Every Nut and Bolt"

The first step in the evaluation process is to establish an inventory. On this matter the two sides are required to agree, and in time they do agree. If the engineers representing the company say there were 283 of a certain kind of valve in the system and the engineers for the county say there were only 273, somebody has to go out and count again until an agreed-upon number is arrived at.

Once the inventory has been established, it is necessary to place a value on it. On this matter the two sides will obviously disagree, for that is the name of the game. If the company paid $40 for a particular valve in 1947 the engineers for the county, who are operating on the basis of original cost, will write down $40 as the starting point for their evaluation. However, if the same valve or the equivalent had been purchased in 1966, it would have cost $150, so the engineer for the company writes down $150, the replacement cost, as his starting point.

Then there is the matter of condition. To a significant extent, to paraphrase a well-known saying, in evaluations of this sort, "Depreciation is in the eye of the beholder." An engineer for the county looks at the valve in question, shakes his head and concludes that its useful life is very nearly spent. The company was lucky that it lasted this long. He cannot in good conscience assume that it will last much beyond another year or so. Taking an original cost of $40, and assuming a useful life for the valve of 20 years (and even that is being generous) and amortizing the cost over those years, the value of that item today would *at most* be $4, not a penny more.

By contrast the engineer for the company inspects the same valve, marvels at its excellent workmanship ("They don't hardly make 'em like that any more"), admires the maintenance conscientiously provided by the employees of the company over the years, and concludes that the valve is, if not as good as new, then something close to it. Taking an assumed useful life of *not less* than 40 years, and deducting *at most* $50 in depreciation from the current replacement cost of $150, the value of that valve today would be $100, not a penny less.

There clearly is a discrepancy.

Not only did valves have to be inspected, but pipes had to be dug up in a number of places and sections cut out and analyzed to determine how much useful life might remain in a main that was installed many years ago. (A cast iron water main might in some conditions last 200 years or more.) Motors and pumps also had to be tested for efficiency and wear, to see what value remained.

In determining reproduction cost, the engineers for the company employed the "single-impulse" method of evaluation. This meant that the assumption would be, in Jim LaFrankie's words, that "we're going to build it all today. Not over 15 years, but today." LaFrankie explained it this way:

> When you build it all today, you're going to have to borrow tremendous amounts of money to start contractors everywhere putting in all this pipeline. And you're entitled to payment of interest on this money during the construction period.
>
> In addition, we're going to assume we install these pipelines under paved streets today, whereas they were built in

dirt streets when we built them. So we have a tremendous cost in repaving all these streets. We also have interference from other utilities to contend with, gas lines crossing water lines and so forth, and have to allow for the cost of that.

Another element involved in evaluation is compensation for so-called severance damages. The county had condemned the Occo-quan supply, but the company was to keep the distribution system in the city of Alexandria itself. Therefore, the city system was losing its source of supply.

LaFrankie continues the story:

We took the position that no one ever told us they were going to sell us water after the condemnation. Maybe we don't want to buy our water from you. We're going to build a pipeline to Alexandria from the District of Columbia. In fact, we had our engineering firms develop a pipeline route past National Airport and across the Potomac to the District of Columbia, and we had an acknowledgement from the District Corps of Engineers that yes, the District would be willing to sell water to Alexandria. So we were claiming severance damages of $7 to $10 million, the cost of building a new pipeline because we were losing our source.

When the judge was presented with the claim for severance damages, he made short work of it. The law in Virginia provides that in a condemnation case the condemner is required to continue service to the entity that remains in private hands—in this case the Alexandria city system. Therefore, the judge ruled, since there was no severance—the city was not going to lose its source—there was no damage, and this part of the claim was disallowed.

Another element in valuation is the matter of "going-concern value." This is the difference between a "live plant" and a "dead plant." A dead plant is merely a collection of facilities. A live plant, in LaFrankie's words, is "an assembled, established plant, serving a developed area, connected with its customers, doing business and earning money and rendering an adequate and efficient service." Since the county was proposing to buy a live plant, not a dead one, the company argued, quite legitimately, that it should be compensated for the difference.

While the evaluations were being prepared, LaFrankie, who had been studying business administration at night at Georgetown University, prepared organization charts of the Alexandria Water Company. When Jack Barr saw the charts, he dismissed them. Like John Ware, he had no use for this nonsense of putting people into little boxes, thereby limiting their initiative and cramping their style. Later, one of the attorneys saw the charts and said, as LaFrankie recalls, "Oh hell, that has value. That's going-concern value." So during the trial, young LaFrankie was called to the stand to show the jury his charts and discuss "all the finite details that go into operating a water system."

Shortly before the trial began, the judge who was to preside, a seasoned, older man, died suddenly, to be replaced by Albert Bryant, a much younger judge. At first the company side was worried that Judge Bryant was too young for that level of responsibility. However, as the trial continued, both sides were impressed with his intelligence and obvious knowledge of the law.

With a new judge on the bench and the jury chosen, the time had come for each side to present its estimate of the value of the property. The county figure, based on original cost, less depreciation, came to $28 million. The figure offered by the engineering firms hired by the company, based on reproduction cost, less depreciation, came in at $55 million. Jack Barr then took the stand and testified that, based on his long experience in buying and selling water companies, the property was worth no less than $65 million. As the trial progressed the jury was not only presented with copies of the inventory and heard the testimony of experts on each side as to its value, they were also loaded on a bus and driven out to take a look at the actual facilities they were buying. LaFrankie recalls:

Knowing that you're going to take the jury out to view your property, of course you want to spend some time getting it fixed up. So it isn't any secret that you would buy paint and paint everything you could see—pumps, motors, booster stations, all those kinds of things.

Well, the jury did go on a bus with us and I did the commentary, telling them what they were looking at—no dollar figures, but these are the facilities. Down in the booster stations there were comments about, "Gee, you can smell the fresh paint." But we overlooked these comments and the jury understood that, sure, we're going to make it look as nice as possible.

During the trial the engineers for the company made detailed presentations about the equipment, its age and origin, and statistical analyses of its efficiency. As for the other side, as Jim La-Frankie recalls it:

Their engineers took a sort of nonchalant attitude: "Yes, they're pumps, and they're running."

I remember one particular day, John Riley, the lawyer for our side, was trying to reduce the value of the testimony of one of the engineers for the other side. John Riley would ask questions like, "Did you ever run any tests on these motors?" and their engineer would say, "Naah, we didn't run any tests."

And Riley says, "You mean to say you didn't even put your hand on a pump to check the vibration?" And the engineer answers, "Yes, I put my hand on a pump." John Riley says, "What happened?" The engineer says, "I got paint on my hand."

Well, the courtroom broke out into laughter.

During the entire course of the trial, which took about six weeks, "Jack Barr sat there in a front seat and twisted a piece of string and played with it as all the evidence was presented." Toward the end of the trial, as the proceedings were winding down, young Judge Bryant, who had wit as well as wisdom, took amused judicial notice of the time Barr had spent playing with a piece of string.

With the differing valuations before the court and the supporting evidence presented, nothing remained except for the judge to deliver his instructions to the jury. First, he informed the jury that their task was to evaluate the property as of the "date certain," March 31, 1966. Any investments the company had made after that date were to be evaluated in a separate proceeding. The judge then proceeded to explain the law as it applied to the evaluation of condemned property:

> The value of the property is the market value. The market value is the price it will bring when offered for sale by one who desires but is not obliged to sell and is bought by one who desires but is under no necessity to purchase. [It is] the price which a hypothetically willing buyer would pay to a hypothetically willing seller in an assumed free and open market.

The language was elegant and the reasoning precise. But in this case the seller was anything but willing, and a condemnation proceeding is by no means a free and open market.

> In determining the fair market value you are to take into consideration the adaptability of the plant, property and equipment for any legitimate purpose. . . . Compensation must be awarded on the basis of the property's most advantageous and valuable use, provided such use is so reasonable and probable as to have an effect on the market value on March 31.

Presumably, if a diamond mine had been discovered on the property on March 29, the county could not have gone ahead and purchased it two days later for the price of a water system, but instead would have had to pay the going rate for diamond mines. However, no diamond mine was discovered, and in general the assets of a water system are most useful and therefore most valuable if they continue to be used as a water system. The judge continued:

> The value of the property is an indivisible gross amount. Value is not to be determined by adding up the value of each of the separate items. It shall be determined by considering them all as inseparable parts of an entity.

Thus allowance was made for the element of going-concern value, which tended to work to the company's advantage.

"While the evidence of original cost has been presented to you . . .," the judge continued. "Original cost." Those hated words. The words the company most wanted to avoid. The words the county was most hoping to hear. One can imagine Jack Barr stiffening, his fingers pulling his piece of string to the breaking point, while the county supervisors leaned forward expectantly.

> . . . such evidence of original cost is not the equivalent of fair market value and should *not* be considered by you as such, although you may consider it as a factor in arriving at fair market value. . . .

Now the moment of truth:

> The Court instructs the Commission [jury] that *the law favors reproduction cost new, less depreciation*, as the sounder basis for the ascertainment of the fair market value of the plant, property and equipment of the water system as of March 31, 1966.

Bingo! Jack Barr had won his gamble. The jury was to determine the price by the higher of the two standards. But reproduction cost is merely a concept; it establishes a range. It now fell to the jury to fix the actual purchase price within the range the judge had specified.

The jury retired. The hours passed. The tension grew. Jack Barr's piece of string no doubt got a further vigorous workout. Finally the jury returned. Had the jury reached a verdict? "We have, Your Honor." A paper was passed to the judge, who scanned it, then handed it to the bailiff to read aloud. The price was—Jim LaFrankie can still recite the numbers from memory—45 million, 231 thousand, 182 dollars. Taken together with approximately $3 million later awarded for improvements after the "date certain," the total came to nearly $50 million, a very generous settlement indeed.

(The company team had set up a pool on what the amount of the award would be. The winner, with a guess of $45 million, was a young assistant to Armistead Boothe, Hugo Blankenship, who in 1990 was still counsel to the company.)

Down to the Wire

So far so good. If the company were finally forced to sell, the price would be a handsome one. But the company had no desire to sell. It wanted to keep the property and the opportunity for future growth it represented, and there was only one remaining opportunity to do so. With no referendum permitted under the law, the company would have to persuade the people of Fairfax County to put enough pressure on their county supervisors to cause them to reject the bond issue required to raise the funds to meet the purchase price.

From the moment it became clear that the challenge at Alexandria was serious, the company had responded with a barrage of publicity. As soon as Jim LaFrankie was assigned to assist with the defense, that became his primary activity. LaFrankie and John Delaney, the public relations man from headquarters, organized a campaign around the theme "We Oppose." Bumper stickers were printed and distributed, brochures were circulated, advertisements run, interviews arranged, press conferences organized. "I wouldn't guess how many times we talked on radio," LaFrankie recalled. (Television was not a major factor locally at that time.)

The company argued that supplying water was a task best left to private enterprise and that it had been doing and would continue to do a more than competent job. The opposition countered with the argument that if the authority took over, the public would get its water at substantially lower rates.

The condemnation award was handed down on April 18, 1967. The meeting to vote on the bonds required to pay that price was scheduled for June 1, six weeks later. As the day approached, the publicity reached a crescendo, while private lobbying to influence the supervisors became even more intense.

There were seven supervisors. A majority of four would decide. The company was confident of three votes. One additional vote was needed to defeat the bond issue. The meeting began at 6 P.M.

in a jammed and stuffy hearing room. Witness after tiresome witness appeared, supporting first one side, then the other. Finally, at 5:30 A.M., after eleven and a half hours of emotional argument, the weary supervisors voted. The count was 4 to 3 in favor of the bonds. The county had prevailed. The Fairfax County property was lost.

"A lot of us thought they voted the bond issue just so they could go home and go to bed," Jack Barr observed later.

As recalled by LaFrankie, after the bonds were approved,

> We then had the determination to make whether we wanted to appeal the decision to the State Supreme Court, or did we want to accept it and get out. It wasn't a bad award. In fact it was a pretty good award. After a long period of consultation, we decided it was in the best interest of everyone to take the $50 million and let Fairfax County go ahead and have the property.

At 12 noon on October 10, 1967, the transfer took place. Jack Barr accepted a check for $48,231,182. The company withdrew its supervisory personnel—they had all been offered jobs elsewhere in the company—and the authority took over. "We walked out; they walked in," in the words of Jim LaFrankie.

After the transfer was complete, one of the authority people asked Barr where to go to buy supplies: "Where do you get your lime and so forth?"

"The first place to look would be the Yellow Pages," Barr growled.

"It was not," said LaFrankie, "what you would call a friendly acquisition."

The maintenance parts for the equipment on the condemned property had not been included in the sale, so the company carted them off to Alexandria. (The authority accused the company of having also taken the toilet paper and light bulbs.) "A year or so later," according to LaFrankie, "we sold the maintenance parts to the authority for $25,000."

A few months later, in a curious footnote, several Fairfax County supervisors were sent to jail for accepting bribes from real estate developers in return for their votes on zoning matters. Over the course of the Alexandria contest, Jim LaFrankie recalls, "A number of feelers were extended to us as to whether we would be interested in striking some sort of deal if we wanted to stay in business there."

In the bad old days of Samuel Insull, such a suggestion might well have been pursued. However, for better or worse, that was not the way American was in the habit of doing business.

In its campaign to take over the property, the Fairfax County Authority had promised consumers a reduction in rates. This they delivered through the expedient of increasing the "connection charges" made to real estate developers. In the years that followed, however, as the cost of providing water continued to rise, the charges to consumers increased.*

With the Fairfax property gone, there was no longer enough work in Alexandria for Jim LaFrankie, so he accepted a transfer back to home ground in Pittsburgh, where he became assistant division manager.

---

*In 1988, 21 years after the Alexandria case was settled, a movement arose in Dale City in neighboring Prince William County to take over the American Water Works property there. Assisting in the defense was the same Milton Farley who had helped with the original Alexandria case. This time, the Prince William County board of supervisors ruled against the takeover attempt on the ground that the cost—based on the precedent of Alexandria—would be too high.

TWELVE

Bitter Water

The Alexandria controversy began in 1959 and was not settled until 1967, eight years later. As noted earlier, during that period, despite the energy and attention devoted to that case, the overall trend was positive. Even allowing for the loss of the property in Virginia, the company gained far more customers and assets through acquisition than it lost through condemnation. In 1968, the year after the Alexandria case was concluded, this positive trend continued. The company acquired properties serving a total of more than 8,000 customers and signed contracts to acquire properties serving 6,000 more. During the same period, it agreed to give up only the St. Mary's Water Company in northwest Pennsylvania, with 3,500 customers.

But that was not the whole story for 1968. In the annual report for that year, tucked away after the announcement of the good news, was a final item:

> On May 10, 1968, South Bay Irrigation District, an agency formed in 1956 to purchase water from the San Diego County Water Authority for resale to the predecessor of California-American Water Company, filed a petition with the San Diego Superior Court seeking to acquire by eminent domain all the facilities of the Sweetwater District of the California-American Water Company.

Here once again, a public authority, sharing jurisdiction over a water system with the company, was challenging its ownership of its facilities—and challenging in California, where the property had been acquired with such bright hopes only two years earlier.

As has occurred in more than one marriage, the union had

looked far better during the courtship than it did after the honeymoon—and the honeymoon was brief. At that time California was not only a strict original-cost state so far as rate setting was concerned, but its regulators had historically been more concerned with maintaining low rates for consumers than with looking after the interests of investors. In its eagerness to acquire a position in the California market, the company had paid substantially more than original cost. In addition, as Marshall Anderson, the company treasurer, recalled, "We were aware of the fact that regulation out there might be a little bit tough—we'd been told there were some negatives. Nevertheless, we thought we would give it a try."

Once the company took possession of the California properties, however, and went to the regulators to ask for what it regarded as a legitimate and necessary rate increase, it found the regulation to be not merely "a little bit tough," but in Jack Barr's words, "a horrible experience, a more demanding approach than we had ever seen before." What followed was a vicious circle.

Because it was unable to earn what it felt was a reasonable return on its investment, the company was reluctant to put additional money into expanding capacity to meet the rapidly growing demand. Without the needed expansion, service deteriorated: There were shortages of water during dry spells. Inadequate service triggered public protests. Word of these reached the ears of regulators, who in turn became even more reluctant to grant increases. Angry exchanges between company representatives and the public utility commission followed, and relationships deteriorated further. The result, inevitably, was a movement to "throw the rascals out," culminating in the condemnation proceeding of 1968.

The reaction of the company was predictable. As it had in Ashtabula, Lexington, Peoria and Alexandria, it vowed to fight the takeover with all its resources. Once again, Jack Barr took up residence almost full-time at the scene of battle, in order to direct the defense. (His colleagues at headquarters were not unanimous in the view that extended stays in California were the most efficient use of Barr's time. As one of them put it, "I think he liked it out there.")

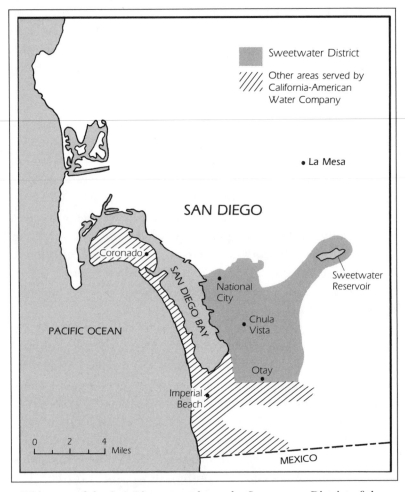

This map of the San Diego area shows the Sweetwater District of the California-American Water Company, the object of a takeover attempt by a public authority there.

The strategy in California was the same as that in Alexandria: to try establish the largest possible value in the condemnation proceeding, hoping that the cost, along with the vigor of the company's resistance, would then discourage the water authority from completing the purchase—but assuring a very good profit in the event the case was lost. (Although California was an original-cost state in rate-setting terms, in a condemnation proceeding the courts would not necessarily be bound by the original-cost principle, so the settlement could be generous.) In addition, because California, unlike Virginia, permitted a referendum in a condemnation case, the company had the option of appealing to the voters.

In California as in Alexandria an evaluation process began. But here it was a massive undertaking, costing an estimated $4 million, in contrast to the approximately $2 million spent in Alexandria. An earthen dam, said to be the oldest in the state, had been built with the labor of Chinese coolies. A calculation had to be made of how much it would cost, using modern bulldozers, to duplicate the efforts of nineteenth-century Cantonese peasants. Some of the 75-year-old water mains had been created by riveting sheet iron, a technique that had not been used for years; estimates had to be developed as to what it would cost to duplicate a riveted pipe in 1969.

The company had assumed at the outset that, as in Alexandria, the value of the California property would be set by jury trial. However, at pretrial conference it was pointed out that the entire proceeding might take several years. Since holding a jury together for that time would have been difficult at best, the court recommended that the matter be decided by a judge alone, and with great reluctance the company and its lawyers agreed. Long experience has shown that a jury tends to produce a more generous price than a judge alone.*

The litigants were provided with a list of three judges from which to choose. One was agreed on. When the judge and the representatives of the two sides were taken on a bus to view the property being condemned, the lawyers rode in the back of the bus in wary silence, while Barr sat beside the judge and chatted, perhaps

---

*In the case of Alexandria, the company's success in obtaining a generous price for the property was attributed not merely to the fact that a jury was used in the proceeding, but also to the composition of the jury. They were, in Jim LaFrankie's words, "business people who wouldn't be frightened by numbers like $45 or $50 million."

hoping to exercise a bit of charm. The judge was friendly. He inquired where Barr was from, and when he was told it was Haddon Heights, New Jersey, he remarked that he had an aunt who lived there. Then for some reason the conversation turned to clothes. The judge informed Barr with some satisfaction that he had found a store where he could buy shirts for $4.50 each. The lawyers in the back turned pale. "A judge who pays $4.50 for his shirts," one commented later, "is too cheap to give a decent settlement."

The trial began on November 1, 1971. The company's annual report for 1972 brought the news. The lawyers had been right. The company had asked $60 million for the Sweetwater property. The judge awarded $14,485,000. "Appeals from the trial court finding are planned," the report went on, adding pointedly, "The ultimate taking of the property is subject to approval by the electorate in the service area." Jack Barr was serving notice that if he lost the appeal in the courts he might take his case to the people. But now came an admission that the strategy might have backfired, that instead of the handsome profit anticipated there could even be a loss. "Should the trial court's award be sustained and the electorate's approval [of the verdict] obtained," the report went on, "there could result an extraordinary charge to income in the approximate amount of $2 million."

The company filed a notice of appeal in the Fourth Appellate District Court in San Diego on May 14, 1973. But by the end of the following year, 1974, five years after the condemnation proceeding had begun, a hearing date for the appeal had not been set. However, the company now raised its estimate of the potential loss to $2.7 million.

A World They Never Made

While the Sweetwater case dragged on, events were occurring in far away places that seemed at the time to have little bearing on the management of a water company. On one side of the world the United States had become increasingly entangled in an ancient quarrel in a place called Vietnam. Young men were being drafted for the conflict, including employees of American Water Works and their sons and brothers, and some were being killed. But aside from an occasional note in the company newspaper, the war did not otherwise seem to have an impact on the conduct of the business. However, President Lyndon Johnson wanted both "guns and butter"; he attempted to finance both the war and the programs of his Great Society without raising taxes. The result was a steady rise in the cost of everything the company bought, of the money that it borrowed, of the people that it paid.

Meanwhile, on the other side of the world in the Middle East, another ancient conflict seemed, if anything, less relevant to the water business than the troubles in Vietnam. But in 1973 (the year the appeal of the Sweetwater verdict was filed) came the Yom Kippur War and the Arab oil embargo. The resulting "oil shock" compounded the already serious problem of inflation. In 10 years consumer prices doubled, interest rates trebled and more, pressure for wage increases rose, and strikes were common. Rate relief became mandatory, but despite continuing efforts to improve it, the regulatory process continued slow, squeezing profits. And as rate increases were eventually granted, one upon the other, there were frequent demands for municipal takeover of local water companies.

It was now more than a quarter century since John Ware and his crew of outsiders had taken command of American Water Works. But now, inevitably, the aggressive young managers of 1947 were older by that span of time. They all had had long and full careers, and some had become well-to-do on the basis of the stock John Ware had given them. This harsh new environment was a world they did not welcome, a world they never made. The time had come for change.

The first to go was Ray Wendell. As was nearly always the case with anything involving Wendell, there was a story attached:

> I had bought a fishing boat, a yacht really, with the stock the
> Boss had thrown at me, and I had enough money from stock
> dividends or whatever, and I wanted to retire and go fishing.

[211]

Well, I wrote this letter of retirement. I was resigning from the company on a certain date and had already talked to Jack several times and told him I was thinking about it, and I knew that he was even beginning to think something about it, too.

Well, finally I gave this letter to his secretary and it came to be about one month away from the time I had said I would retire. I went in and asked him about it. He pulled out the middle drawer of his desk and the letter was lying there. He said that is where it had been since I wrote it. He said, "I'm not ready to let you go." I said "Please, Jack, I want to go." So we arranged for this to take place about a year later.

Wendell took early retirement at the end of 1973. Six months later, on June 30, 1974, Marshall Anderson, who had known no career other than American Water Works since he left the Navy in 1946, also took early retirement. He was followed a year later by another key member of the team, William B. Gamble, vice president and comptroller. At the end of 1975, with the Sweetwater case still dragging on, Jack Barr himself, at age 61, after 43 years in the business and 20 as president of the company, took early retirement as well, although he continued as a member of the board. (At Barr's retirement party, Jim LaFrankie presented him with a copy imbedded in plastic of the check for $48,231,182 that had settled the Alexandria case.)

The same annual report that recorded Barr's retirement announced that a hearing had been set on June 10, 1976, for the company's appeal of the Sweetwater verdict. The annual report for the next year brought the unhappy news. The Court of Appeals had sustained the finding of the lower court, and in December 1976 the Supreme Court of the State of California denied a petition for a further appeal.

The last avenue of legal remedy had been exhausted, but there was still the option of taking the matter to the voters. However, the contest was now entering its ninth year, millions of dollars had been spent, a referendum would mean another costly and distracting ordeal, and a new management was struggling to keep the company profitable in the face of escalating inflation. Prudence argued that it was time to cut their losses. The report for 1976 concluded, "In on-going negotiations for a settlement . . . in lieu of further litigation, the company anticipates an award which will substantially reduce the potential loss." The next year's report announced the outcome:

> On August 30, 1977 the company accepted $19,000,000 for the property. . . . The amount received was $1,444,000 less than the aggregate of the net book value of the property transferred and condemnation expenses. A federal income tax credit of $1,132,000 reduced the loss to $312,000.

IV

A NEW ERA

THIRTEEN

A Big Pair of Shoes

Like many strong leaders, Jack Barr had not precisely gone out of his way to groom a successor. In fact, if economic conditions had not been so difficult, he might not have chosen to retire when he did. In any case, many people resent and resist the idea of retirement, and assume, at least subconsciously, that if they prepare no one to fill their shoes, they will somehow manage to wear those shoes indefinitely. However, when Barr informed his board that he planned to retire at the end of 1975, they were obviously going to have to find someone to take over his title and responsibilities, if not his shoes.

As noted earlier, there have traditionally been two kinds of people in the water business—operations people and financial people. Bill Reinicker, who in 1947 was named the first president of the newly constituted American Water Works Company, was an operations man, trained as an engineer. Reinicker shared authority with Barr, a financial man. After Reinicker retired, Ray Wendell, also an operations man, also trained as an engineer, took his place as the operations member of the management team.

When the search for a successor to Barr began, the senior operations man in the company was Jim LaFrankie. After returning to Pittsburgh from Alexandria in 1967, LaFrankie in 1970 had risen from assistant manager to manager of the Central Division (including, at that time, western Pennsylvania, Virginia and part of West Virginia), replacing "Put" Putnam, who had retired. Six months before Wendell retired in mid-1973, LaFrankie was transferred to headquarters in Philadelphia to take over Wendell's responsibilities. A hearty, convivial individual, LaFrankie had come to know virtually every supervisor in the organization on a first-name basis during his 25 years with the company. It is a fair assumption that if the matter had been put to a vote, the choice of the rank and file for the next president of American Water Works would have been Jim LaFrankie.

The senior financial man at the time was John A. Gubanich. In contrast to LaFrankie, Gubanich was a relative newcomer to an organization which had not always looked kindly on newcomers. As far back as 1936, the old-line American Water Works & Electric people had not been eager to accept the outsiders from the Community Water Service Company; they were even more reluctant to welcome the rough-and-ready characters who arrived with John Ware. In the time since, only a relative trickle of management-level people had been hired from the outside. The majority had come up from the ranks of the old American organization, the old Community organization or Ware's Northeastern Water Company.

John Gubanich had joined the company in 1967, only eight years earlier, as corporate treasurer, replacing Howard Briggs, who retired. Thus, in the view of many in the rank and file, Gubanich was still, relatively speaking, a newcomer. He did have one thing going for him, however, and it was no small matter. During the years when Jack Barr was spending much of his time in California, it had fallen to Gubanich to begin developing the programs and applying the disciplines needed to restrain pyramiding costs, to win the rate increases necessary to recover those costs and to attract the funds required to support construction programs. At this point, his efforts were clearly showing results.

With Barr's retirement approaching, with inflation mounting and with regulatory delays continuing to put a drag on earnings, the board of directors met to choose a successor to Barr. It did not take long for a consensus to form. Newcomer or no, John Gubanich appeared to be the man with the right skills at the right time to cope with the mounting financial pressures. In December 1975, the month Barr retired, Gubanich was elected president of American Water Works. Balancing the team, Jim LaFrankie, the operations man, who had been named president of the Service Company a year earlier, became his second-in-command.

In a curious parallel, just as in 1947 the financial skills of Jack Barr had been indispensable for reining in spending and conserving cash in order to pay off the debt John Ware had incurred in buying control, so now, almost three decades later, the financial skills of John Gubanich seemed no less essential for coping with the challenge of inflation and all that that entailed. In the words of lawyer Kenneth Gemmill, who was a director at the time, "John was always pushing for more rate increases, for more net, for more bottom line. He'd been successful. He'd done a great job. So the thinking was, Why shouldn't he continue?"

As there had been a clear contrast between the genial, pipe-smoking Bill Reinicker and the strong-willed, decisive Jack Barr, and later between Barr and the gregarious, story-telling Ray Wendell, so now there was a marked contrast between the styles of John Gubanich and Jim LaFrankie. Commenting on the differences, one observer puts it this way:

> They both are very likeable people. But John Gubanich was—I want to say more autocratic; maybe that's not right. He would tend to be more argumentative. He would get into arguments over something, and be very competitive to make his point, and technically he would know and be very good.
>
> Jim LaFrankie, on the other hand, was equally knowledgeable, but with a quite different, relaxed personality, more inclined to slap somebody on the back and say, "Well now, look, Joe, this is what you think, and this is what I think. Now let's look at it together and work it out."
>
> Jim has an Italian background, outgoing, one of the boys, could always have a beer with somebody. John Gubanich just wasn't that kind of person.

"So I Just Stepped In"

John A. Gubanich was born in 1919 in Phoenixville, Pennsylvania, a suburb of Philadelphia. He attended Notre Dame, where he majored in accounting. (He also lettered in varsity football—a fact he more than once found a way to mention when appearing before a regulatory body.) Gubanich chose a career in accounting ("I earned my CPA certificate on the first try") and in 1941 went to work in the Philadelphia office of the accounting firm of Peat Marwick, Mitchell & Company. During World War II he spent 30 months in the 32nd Finance Disbursing Section of the U.S. Army in the Pacific ("I paid all the GI's on time."), then went back to work for Peat Marwick. One of his clients was the General Waterworks Corporation—headed by the same Howard Butcher to whom Ware and Barr had sold the Maine water properties in 1955. In 1956, Butcher wanted to replace his retiring secretary-treasurer. In Gubanich's words, "He called me, and I talked to him; and before I got back to my office I was hired."

In 1967, General Waterworks agreed to merge with a company called International Utilities—later known as IU International. International Utilities was headed by John M. "Jack" Seabrook—of the family that founded the Seabrook Farms frozen food company. As Gubanich tells it:

> Jack Seabrook was the dominating factor in the merger. He had First Boston [his investment banker] prepare a report indicating that IU should exchange 1½ shares of its stock for each share of General Waterworks. Our investment banker, Blyth & Company, came up with a similar report. At that point I prepared a report where I pointed out to Blyth and First Boston the mistakes they had made. I came up with an exchange rate of 2¼ shares of IU stock for each share of General Waterworks, and I persuaded Blyth & Company to accept my findings.
>
> The day when the boards of the two companies met, one consultant says an exchange rate of 1½ and the other says 2¼. So they compromised and split the difference. We

ended up getting 1⅞ shares of IU for each share of General Waterworks instead of the 1½ First Boston recommended.

Jack Seabrook did not particularly care for my insistence that 2¼ would be better than 1½. As a matter of fact, for a couple of years in his report to the stockholders he kept insisting that the reason why IU's performance was below par was because they had issued too many shares in exchange for General Waterworks. . . .

In any case, my philosophy did not conform with Jack's. Jack was a high-flying individual. He was known to say, "I'm looking for men whose wives like to wear mink coats and drive sporty cars. They will drive the men."

My wife was not of that nature and I didn't want to be involved with that kind of thing, so I let it be known that I had no particular interest in continuing after the merger. Then I had an opportunity. Howard Briggs, who was Treasurer of American Water Works, was approaching retirement. American was looking for his replacement, so I just stepped in.

End of an Era

When Gubanich and LaFrankie took over at American, it was more than merely a shift in management, a changing of the guard. In a real sense, it marked the end of an era. The era was ending not simply because the key players had changed, but because the game itself had changed. And the game had changed not for water companies alone, but for all companies, for all institutions, for the great majority of individuals. The "oil shock" brought about by the Arab embargo, along with the Vietnam War and the inflation that accompanied them both, were not so much causes of the change as symptoms. A time of casual, often careless use of seemingly unlimited resources—the so-called "cowboy economy"—had ended, to be replaced by an era of clearly limited, increasingly expensive and difficult-to-manage resources.

In the words of John Gubanich, "I characterize the years of my tenure as a period of profit motivation." Jim LaFrankie, on the other hand, describes the post-Barr era as "a time of professional management." Both descriptions are correct. Both approaches were essential. In a time of rampant inflation and record interest rates, attention to the bottom line was required as never before. But to generate the revenues and apply the disciplines required to deliver the profits to the bottom line, new organization structures and management techniques were no less necessary.

However, while history-by-hindsight can be divided into neat packages, life as it is lived is not as tidy. Well before the formal end of the Jack Barr era, Gubanich and LaFrankie had begun introducing modern management techniques and developing programs and strategies for dealing with the new financial realities. Furthermore, although Barr surrendered the title and responsibilities of the presidency at the end of 1975, he did not go gentle into that good night. By no means. He remained a visible and vocal member of the Board of Directors, a board he had dominated for 20 years, of which he had been a member for almost 30, over an organization in which he had played a significant role for more than 40.

Thus, while strong-minded and sometimes argumentative John Gubanich was attempting to lead the company into the new era, he found it necessary to do so under the scrutiny and frequent close questioning of a strong-willed—not to say stubborn—representative of the old. It was a reasonable assumption that the experience would not prove as relaxing as a day at the beach.

From the start, the primary focus of the new management team was on facing the challenges of the new era. But a necessary first step, and a symbolic one, was to liquidate a legacy from the old. During his extended stays in California, Barr had put the day-to-day management of the company into the hands of a kind of regency. Rather than surrendering control to a single deputy, he had divided the service organization into three parts, placing one of the three senior vice presidents in charge of each. Ray Wendell was given charge of the Central Region—Pennsylvania, Maryland, Virginia and West Virginia; Marshall Anderson, the Plains Region—

the Midwestern states; and Bill Gamble, the Coastal Region—the East and West coasts.

As a result, in Gubanich's words, "We had a system where Marshall Anderson was operating his group of companies one way, Bill Gamble another, and Ray Wendell another. There wasn't really a centralized organization." Compounding the problem was the fact that the company continued to reflect the old John Ware management approach: "Just stick your nose in anywhere and see if you can find a way to make yourself useful."

"If you tell three guys that," Jim LaFrankie observes, "you have real turmoil. Individuals floundered because they didn't know what their jobs were."

Clearly there was a need to define roles and responsibilities and clarify channels of command. John Gubanich, no less than Jim LaFrankie, was a believer in using organization charts for that purpose. But Gubanich, like LaFrankie, had encountered Jack Barr's distaste for the business of "putting people into little boxes." Shortly after he joined the company as treasurer in 1967, Gubanich had become involved in preparing an "offering brochure," a document used in selling an issue of bonds. In the section of the brochure describing the company's management, he inserted, as a matter of course, an organization chart. When Barr saw the chart, he not only reprimanded Gubanich for including it, but ordered the brochure revised to eliminate it.

Now that he was president, Gubanich ordered charts drawn and job descriptions prepared for the entire American system. And in time even Barr acknowledged the need. In the old days in Alexandria, LaFrankie recalled, "Jack Barr was furious because I put people in squares and boxes. But finally he came around to accepting that."

However, if clearer organization was vital, the need for cash—cash flowing into the till, cash dropping to the bottom line—was critical. In 1975, the year Gubanich was named president, the rate of inflation passed the 10 percent mark and the prime interest rate reached 22 percent. To increase income at a rate even approaching the spiralling costs, it was necessary to obtain rate increases at a faster pace than ever before.

For much of the history of the water utility industry, it had not been necessary for most operating companies to ask for a rate increase more than once every ten or fifteen years. This was particularly true during the 1930s, when the Depression kept cost increases low, and during World War II, when wages and prices were controlled. Even in the early postwar years, although inflation was a problem, it was a manageable one, and the rapid growth in sales kept profits increasing at a satisfactory rate.

Until about 1977, all rate matters for the company had been handled by about a dozen people. Now, with subsidiaries requesting increases yearly, and some more often than that, in the next eight years the rate staff increased to around 40, who worked with the local managers in the almost continuous process of preparing rate increase applications.

But solving one problem created another. As had often been the case, frequent requests for rate increases, particularly large ones, provoked an outcry in the community affected, along with a call for a government takeover of the local water system. To counteract this rising level of resistance, it was obviously necessary to strengthen local relationships. By now John Delaney was approaching retirement, so T. Ward Welsh, another former journalist, was hired by Gubanich as coordinator of community relations. Welsh's assignment was not so much to travel to subsidiaries when they needed assistance in communicating, as Delaney had done, but rather to hire and coordinate the activities of full-time community relations people in each regional office and in the larger operating companies as well. These people continued to promote the traditional activities: joining the Rotary Club, leading the Boy Scouts, contributing to the building fund for the YMCA. In addition, when a rate increase application was being prepared, even before it had been submitted, it was the job of the community relations person to help the local manager make contact with opinion leaders in his community—the mayor, the newspaper editor, prominent businessmen—

to explain the realities of the situation: the trend of costs and the importance of increased revenues to maintaining quality service.

Neither Gubanich nor LaFrankie would ordinarily appear before the regulatory authorities when an application for a rate increase was being considered. The demands on their time would have been inordinate; in any case, the local managers and rate staffs, with the help of expert witnesses, were competent to make the case. Furthermore, the appearance at a rate hearing of a senior executive from the parent company was an invitation for a fishing trip by an inquisitive regulator—"What is your salary? How much do you pay directors? What was your profit last year?"—or an attempt to regulate the parent company, over which the regulators in fact have no jurisdiction.

But in particularly difficult situations Gubanich would sometimes testify. One such instance involved a subsidiary in New England. Over several years, each time the local company had applied for a rate increase, the town government had protested so vigorously that the state public utility commission had turned the application down. Finally, Gubanich decided to make a personal appeal.

A point of contention at the rate hearing was the method used for calculating the company's provision for federal income tax. The town had hired a local attorney to represent it. Local attorneys do not ordinarily have a thorough understanding of the intricacies of public utility law, and it soon became apparent that the town attorney was beyond his depth.

At one point, Gubanich recalled, "The counsel for the city asked me, 'Mr. Gubanich, what is your effective tax rate?'

"I said, 'I don't know what you mean by effective tax rate. Can you give me a definition of what you mean?'

"Obviously he couldn't. He was embarrassed."

The hearing examiner, wanting to spare the attorney's feelings, jumped in. "Well, you know what he means."

Not wanting to irritate the examiner, Gubanich uttered a few general words on the subject of effective tax rates, thus getting the town attorney off the hook.

Later, despite the rocky start, Gubanich was able to persuade the town attorney to arrange a meeting with the mayor:

> We had a meeting with her, and we explained our situation: what we were willing to provide in the way of additional facilities if she would take the pressure off the regulators. She agreed to that, and we promised certain things in return.
>
> After I left the city hall, the local manager was driving me to the railroad station. He said, "John, I'm going to turn the radio on. This is the time of the day the mayor gets on the radio." So he turned the radio on, and sure as the dickens, the mayor was reporting that she had just had the most wonderful meeting with the president of American Water Works. He had come to town to meet with her, and she promised to do this and he promised to do that and so forth.

With town opposition removed, it was still necessary to persuade the state public utility commission to grant the increase. Gubanich describes the hearing this way:

> The only person who gave us any problem was the consumer counsel for the state. He was just rough. I got to a point where I was so frustrated I said, "It is obvious that no one here understands the principles of consolidation."
>
> At that point the commissioner hearing the case began to chew me out for making comments of that nature. No sooner had he finished than I spent about five minutes telling him and everybody what I thought the situation was, and I wasn't going to let the company suffer because of a lack of knowledge on the part of certain individuals.
>
> The entire room was silent. The commissioner was stunned. He recessed the hearing, called a side conference, and admonished me for, in effect, contempt of court.

The hearing continued. Despite Gubanich's straight talk—or perhaps in part because of it—a substantial increase was granted at last. Moreover, the log jam now seemed broken. Gubanich sums up, "After that I think we had the best returns there of any company in the system. And that commissioner became one of the best friends the company had."

As the spiral of costs continued and regulatory delays persisted, it was clear that merely filing a continuous stream of rate applications and having occasional collisions with individual regulators was not going to keep revenues increasing at a satisfactory pace. A major difficulty was the fact that state regulatory commissions and their staffs were primarily concerned with electric power and telephone utilities, whose revenues were many times those of the water companies. Water was a step child, an afterthought. Compounding this problem was the fact that the water business is by no means the same as the other two. In John Gubanich's words, "The aspects of the water business are so different. Water is more capital-intensive. It takes more dollars of plant to generate a dollar of revenue in the water business than in any other industry—mining might be an exception."

In addition, there were matters of qualification and turnover. People are sometimes named to regulatory bodies for reasons having little to do with effective regulation. Membership can be used as a stepping stone to higher office. It can be the reward for long and faithful service to an outgoing official. In any case, the terms of regulators are limited, usually no more than four years, and reappointment is not automatic. Therefore, if someone who lacks the necessary background accepts appointment to a regulatory commission, by the time that person gains the necessary expertise, his or her term may be over.

Further compounding the other problems is the fact that politicians do not ordinarily run for office on a platform of raising utility rates. Nor do consumer activists gain political clout by promoting the interests of private, profit-making companies, and in too many cases the members of either group know little and care less about the economics of the industry in question. Thus, if a regulator, having finally come to understand the industry he regulates, votes in favor of what he sees as an appropriate and necessary increase, he may well be rewarded by being turned out of office.

It was to deal with these problems that Jim Kelly—a man John Gubanich describes as "my best hire"—was brought into the picture. James McGirr Kelly—he is today addressed as the Honorable James McGirr Kelly, Judge of the U.S. District Court in Philadelphia—was born and raised in that city, graduated from the Wharton School at the University of Pennsylvania with a degree in economics, then took a law degree at Temple University. After stints in the district attorney's and U.S. attorney's offices in Philadelphia and as assistant state attorney general, he was appointed to the Pennsylvania Public Utility Commission. During his ten years in that capacity, Kelly became president of the Great Lakes Section of the National Association of Regulatory Utility Commissioners, then, in 1976, was elected president of the national organization. In that role he became known to, accepted by—and in many cases good friends with—most of the public utility commissioners in the United States.

Kelly's term on the Pennsylvania commission expired in 1977, and he set about establishing a private law practice. John Gubanich picks up the story:

> Because we had regulatory problems, I was looking for an individual who could sort of act as liaison between the regulators and the company people. At a discussion at a dinner with one of the Pennsylvania commissioners, we got to talking about Kelly, and this commissioner said, "Well, gee, John. I hear Jim's law business is a little slow getting started. If you talk to him you might be able to persuade him to join your organization." The next morning when I got back to the office, I called Jim Kelly, and he showed interest."

A series of discussions followed, and it was agreed that Kelly would join the company as director of regulatory relations.

It was fortunate that Kelly and his wife enjoyed traveling, since maintaining contact with regulators is not exactly a desk-bound job. Each year the members of NARUC would hold regional meetings in various parts of the country. Kelly's responsibility was "to be present at those meetings, to make his presence known and with whom he was associated, to introduce regulators to company personnel."

Despite the fact that he was now on a corporate payroll, Kelly continued to be accepted by the regulators as one of their own. At the final dinner of each section meeting, "invariably he sat at the head table as past president of NARUC." Over time, according to Gubanich, the regulators came to accept that "we were not carpet baggers or green monsters with horns."

Jim Kelly recalls: "One thing I tried to do was help the regulators recognize the high degree of professionalism there is in the water utility business." Too often, in Kelly's view, the regulators tended to dismiss water utility people as "plumbers with neckties."

In addition to attending commissioners' meetings, Kelly was able to set up lines of communication that could bring about a solution when a particularly difficult problem arose. A case in point was the situation in one midwestern state. For many years, public utility regulation in that state had been carried on at the local level. Then a state regulatory commission was created and charged with processing all rate applications. Shortly after the commission was established, a disagreement arose between the commission staff and American Water Works over whether its rate base should be based on fair value or original cost. The company carried the dispute to the State Supreme Court. As a result, the commission staff was resentful, and that resentment tended to surface each time the company filed a rate request. In the face of that situation, Jim Kelly made arrangements for Gubanich to meet informally with members of the commission. Gubanich recalls the meeting:

> We were not talking about rate of return. We were not talking about what we needed or anything. We wanted to explain our situation.
>
> I identified to those present that we are in the business of investing in the common stock of operating water properties. That was our business. And we were willing to make investments in the common stock of our companies in that state, except for the fact that there wasn't any return. We couldn't even sell securities to bondholders, who had prior-

ity over everyone. If you could not even sell a first mortgage bond with a lien on the property, how could you expect someone to buy the common stock?

I also identified one of the unusual requirements they had at that time, that if you made an investment in the common equity of a utility company, you had to wait six months before you could get a return on it. "How many of you individuals would like to invest a million dollars in your local savings and loan and wait six months before you could get any interest on it?"

They were all shocked.

In the aftermath of that meeting, as Gubanich tells it, "we did not get a full, complete treatment, but we did get some concessions to where the investments that were being made would be getting returns commensurate with returns we were getting in other states." In that case as in the earlier one, there was longer-term improvement as well. "Over time, as the staff changed and as a result of the meeting with the commissioners," the hostile attitude gradually faded away.

Jim Kelly's bridge building at the meetings of NARUC and his good offices in touchy situations were clearly paying dividends. But the fact remained that a great many utility commissioners continued to be largely uninformed about the practicalities of running a water company. In an effort to remedy that situation, Kelly established what he called American's "Water College." Gubanich describes it this way:

> Jim would set up a two-day seminar on water operations, say, in Illinois. We would invite our people to come to it, maybe eight or ten of them. Then we would invite regulators and staff from that state to join us. "We're having a seminar for our people on water operations. Would you be interested in coming down and joining us for a day or two?"

The regulators and their staffs were usually interested. Their minds were not closed to learning about the water business; they simply had not had a previous opportunity. Regulators were not the only ones invited. Consumer advocates—traditional adversaries of the utilities in rate cases—were also asked. In some cases they also chose to attend. In Jim Kelly's words:

> We really gave them a primer on the water utility business. How we acquired water. How we cleaned up water. How we delivered water. How we planned these things. It wasn't the economics of water as much as it was the operation of water utilities.
>
> Also, inferentially, of course, what we needed to do the job: filter plants, pumps, pipelines, the mammoth undertaking of building dams.
>
> Most unsophisticated people can't understand why you charge for water, "Water is free," they say, "Why do you charge for it?"
>
> You don't pay for the water. You pay for the service. Can you imagine what it costs to pump tons of water up a hill, across a dale, around a corner, and put it in your bathroom at 40 or 50 pounds pressure so it doesn't blow the spigot right off your sink? So that when you feel like it, at 2:00 A.M., you can grope your way to the bathroom and help yourself to a glass of water, and you are so confident that it is pure that you don't even bother to turn on the light?
>
> That is what you are paying for. You are not paying for the water that is in the river, or the water in some well, but to get that water into a treatment plant, and to have the reserve capacity to fight a fire while you are getting your drink of water or your wife is doing her laundry. That is what you are paying for. That is what you have to understand. That is what those seminars were designed to do.

At the end of the two-day meeting, the regulators and others present might or might not have bought entirely into the company's point of view. But they would go home with a significantly better understanding of the business they were regulating, and having spent two days rubbing elbows and talking shop with the people who actually operate water companies, they would have learned firsthand that these people were in fact something more than "plumbers with neckties."

Kelly is well-remembered in the company for the contribution he made in explaining the water business to the regulators. Interestingly, when he himself describes his role, he puts as much emphasis on the part he played in explaining the regulators to the water people:

> I think what I brought to American was a sort of devil's advocate. Most people at American, as with most utilities, they walk in the door at age 21, somewhere around that age. They work there for 40 years, and they retire. Most utility people believe that if they do a good job with what they have, that's enough. But it's not only what you do, it's what you're perceived as doing. That's very, very important.
>
> In the time I was at American, I believe I was of assistance in helping them understand another point of view. Understanding what utility commissioners and staff look at. Understanding what the public looks at. In other words, seeing across the table.

As the company's rate staffs grew in size and competence, and as, with Jim Kelly's help, communication with the regulators improved, there was steady progress on the regulatory front. But regardless of how many applications might be filed and how skillfully they might be presented, and no matter how many individual log jams might be broken, or how many meetings of NARUC Jim Kelly might attend, there was no realistic prospect in that political and economic climate that revenues would increase at a rate to keep pace with the onrush of inflation.

One obstacle continued to be procedural—the regulatory lag. Despite continuing efforts to improve it, the machinery of regulation still had so many delays built into it that in a time of rapid inflation, before a given application could be approved and put in force, the cost data on which it was based would have become obsolete. The other obstacle was political. As inflation surged ahead there was intense pressure on regulators, from politicians and consumer activists alike, to hold down rates, regardless of the merits of a particular case. So paralleling the effort to increase rates there was no less a need for an intensive program to control costs.

John Gubanich,
president of American
Water Works Company
from 1976 to 1983.

Jim Kelly, a lawyer,
utility regulator and
later U.S. District Court
judge, helped American
tell its story to regulators
in the late 1970s
and 1980s.

Jim LaFrankie (*right*), then vice president of American Water Works Service Company, and John Murphy, president of the West Virginia operating companies, visit a construction site in 1973.

When John Gubanich retired in 1983, Jim LaFrankie and company managers presented him with a videotape on Notre Dame football and a blow-up of a 1940s photo of Gubanich in his Notre Dame uniform.

This elevated tank in the Richmond District of Indiana-American Water Company is characteristic of hundreds that mark cities and towns served by American subsidiaries.

Downtown offices with drive-up service like this one in Pekin, Illinois, were almost universal in the American System by the 1980s.

Two water treatment plants that typified smaller facilities in the American System in the 1980s. *Left,* Illinois-American Water Company's plant on the Mississippi River at Alton, Illinois; *below,* the modern facility in the Moshannon Valley District of Pennsylvania-American Water Company.

American System managers—Keith Bossung in this photo—sometimes set up displays at public meetings to demonstrate the amount of drinking water customers can get for the price of a soda.

Management development workshops, like this one in New Jersey in 1987, have been central to American System operations since the 1970s.

Third-generation Wares who became American directors in the late 1970s and 1980s include (*clockwise from top left*): John H. Ware, IV, Vice President, Penn Fuel Gas Company; Rhoda Ware Cobb, financial advisor; Marilyn Ware Lewis, educator and editor; Paul W. Ware, President, Penn Fuel Gas Company; and Nancy Ware Pascal, Vice President, United Propane, Inc., a Maryland gas distributor.

There was a significant difference, however, between Jack Barr's struggle to control spending in the 1940s and early 1950s, and the task confronting John Gubanich in the mid-1970s. Barr's concern had been almost entirely with construction costs. John Ware had borrowed so heavily, first to buy Northeastern and then to buy control of American, that there was a limit to how much more the company could afford to borrow—even if the banks had been willing to lend it—to meet the surging demand for new construction. So it fell to Barr to say no to any capital spending that was not absolutely, unquestionably, incontrovertibly essential.

As for operating costs—payroll, chemicals, insurance, energy to run the plants—they were less a problem. As long as these costs were reasonably in line with those of the industry as a whole and with what the company had asked for last time, the regulators were inclined to authorize a level of rates sufficient to cover them. Gubanich recalled one conversation:

> When I first came with the company in 1967, the only discussion we had with the operating companies had to do with construction. I remember asking Bill Gamble [the comptroller at the time], "Bill, when do we look at the income statements?" "Oh, John," he said, "we don't look at those."

But now, in the late 1970s, not only had the regulators become very stingy in approving the cost of new construction, they were no less grudging in approving increases to cover rising operating expenses. Furthermore, even if the regulators had been willing to pass through to water users the full cost of inflation, the larger the increase, the greater was the likelihood of a political reaction and a movement for municipal takeover. Thus the company had a compelling motive to do everything possible to restrain operating as well as construction costs. Gubanich explained the process this way:

> We had strict budget controls. We were very careful. Once a year for every operating company we had a meeting on the establishment of the budget for the following year. Everything had to be justified. Increases in personnel had to be

[233]

justified, with the understanding that there wasn't going to be any impact on the bottom line. To the extent that there was an impact on the bottom line, preparations for a rate application got under way immediately, and a date was set for that case to be filed. . . . If additions to the staff were going to made, they were going to be made only after the receipt of the rate order that would pay for them.

As far as construction was concerned, construction was classified into two categories, mandatory and optional. Mandatory were those matters that were prescribed by regulation. The Safe Drinking Water Act came into effect during this period, and we had to make certain changes in our processing. Questions about dam safety also arose during this period. There were a couple of big dam failures in the country during the 1970s. None were ours, but that brought about legislation that required the reinforcement of a lot of our dams.

Optional was to improve the system where we had small-diameter pipes, or expansion to meet increases in demand. Once the individual items were classified, we put a limit on the construction budget as a whole. We had what we called the 80 percent rule. This meant that construction expenditures could be incurred to the extent of the cash flow of the company plus interest costs on the borrowing of new money, provided that the interest costs did not reduce the return on equity below 80 percent of that allowed by the current rate structure.

In the matter of operating costs, regulators tended to make a distinction between normal year-to-year expenses and abnormal or extraordinary ones. If, for example, last year a given company spent $50,000 for chemicals to purify the water, and this year wanted $55,000, and next year asked for $60,000, the regulators were reasonably comfortable with those figures. Depending on the political climate, they might or might not go along with the full amount of the increase, but they would accept most of it. The same would be true of interest expense, payroll expense, energy and so on.

Problems arose with what were considered extraordinary expenses. If an expense showed up this year that could not be found in last year's budget, the consumer advocates were likely to complain that it was unnecessary and argue that a rate increase to cover it should be denied. One major expense that fell into that category was the cost of repainting storage tanks. The cost of painting a tank was substantial, running from $50,000 to $150,000, depending on the size of the tank. But it is not an expense that occurs every year. Historically, a tank had to be painted about once every five years. With improvements in coatings, the interval could be stretched to seven years. If a company filed an application for a rate increase, and it contained an item to cover the cost of painting a storage tank, the consumer activists were likely to declare that it was an abnormal expense and urge the regulators to deny it.

Abnormal as it might seem to an outsider, the fact was, of course, that the expense was not only legitimate but essential. If a storage tank is not repainted, it will eventually rust out and require repair or replacement at many times the cost of a new paint job. So, from the standpoint of the water companies, or indeed of the customers who would pay the bill in the long run, this situation was neither logical nor fair. But nobody said rate regulation was always logical or fair. In the real world of politics, when extraordinary items popped up in a rate application, like ducks in a shooting gallery, the activists would draw a bead on them and make every effort to shoot them down.

The company reviewed the problem with the accounting section of the regulators' national association, and was able to persuade the regulators that tank painting, instead of being considered an expense, could fairly be regarded as an addition to plant—a capital cost—and as such could be added to the rate base, to be amortized over the life of the paint job in question. Suddenly, as if by magic, an extraordinary expense had become an ordinary investment, and that regulatory problem disappeared.

FOURTEEN

Darwin Would Have Understood

As it struggled to cope with the pressure of inflation, the company's approach to rate increases assumed a higher priority and became more aggressive, and its system of financial controls became tougher and more finely tuned. But these were not the only changes. Under the impact of the newly demanding environment, the organization as a whole and all its ways of doing things were reshaped and brought to a keener edge.

From the standpoint of old-timers in the organization, the degree of change that occurred during this period was no doubt considered radical. From the longer view, it was no novelty. Over the past century, with a survival reflex Charles Darwin would have understood, the company in its various incarnations had periodically reinvented itself in response to the imperatives of economic change. As the poet Goethe put it, "A man must earn again his father's heritage before he truly owns it."

Although John Gubanich's financial disciplines were effective in restraining construction spending, its growth nonetheless continued. When the cost of complying with new water quality and environmental regulations was added to the demands of modernization and growth, and the whole was compounded by the rising cost of everything, including money, the construction budget continued to set records.

The traditional method of financing construction was for an operating company to obtain a short-term construction loan from a bank at the prime interest rate. After the project had been completed and the new facilities were on line, the company would then apply to the regulators for the rate increase that would pay for the new facilities. Only after the increase had been granted and the added cash flow thereby assured, could the company sell bonds to investors—usually insurance companies—refinancing the project at a lower rate.

As the volume of construction increased and the cost of the money needed to finance it escalated, there was an obvious need on the part of the operating companies to sell their bonds as quickly as possible in order to pay off the bank loans and reduce their interest costs. But just at the moment when the need to sell bonds became acute, the market for those bonds dried up. Responding to the same pressures the water companies were feeling, the insurance companies were working to control their own costs. Once upon a time it had been possible for Jack Barr to travel to the state of Maine and peddle $50,000 in water company bonds to a local broker. No more. The larger insurance companies were no longer willing to invest the time of expensive staff in investigating a $50,000 or even a $500,000 issue. Now they would not consider an issue of less than $5 million to $10 million. And even the smaller companies had given up looking into smaller financings. It was easier and cheaper for them to "piggyback" on the research of the giants. They would wait until a large company had approved an issue, then step in and bid for their share. As a result, the $50,000 or $500,000 bond issue the typical American subsidiary so urgently needed to sell was effectively shut out of the market.

But every action invites reaction. The obvious answer to consolidation on the part of buyers was consolidation on the part of sellers. The need was to combine the financing needs of a number of individual companies into one large package the insurance companies would be willing to consider. In an enterprise as far-flung as American Water Works, with its large number of subsidiaries, finding a number of loans to consolidate was not a problem. Furthermore, the company had a financial subsidiary, called the American Commonwealth Company, that could serve as the inter-

All Boats Rise with the Tide

The primary responsibility of a corporate treasurer, the job John Gubanich accepted in 1967, is to obtain the financing the company needs on the best terms possible—issuing bonds at the lowest interest rate he can find, selling stock at the highest price the market will bear. But Gubanich discovered that, just as ten years earlier the company had had no organized program of community relations, so in 1967 it had no effective program for communicating with investors who might be interested in purchasing its securities; there was no way to provide them with information on the progress of the company, along with an understanding of the economics of the water utility industry as a whole. And just as a lack of effective communication in a local community invites the growth of problems there, so the lack of an adequate program of investor relations is bound to make the raising of money more costly and difficult than it would otherwise be. Financial markets are competitive. A company that wants to borrow money or sell stock is competing against other borrowers for the attention of investors and the security analysts who advise investors on what to buy. Yet despite the fact that the stock of American Water Works had long been listed on the New York Stock Exchange, many investors and analysts were barely aware of its existence; certainly they did not understand the company or the water utility industry. And people are not usually eager to put money into something they do not understand.

John Gubanich set about to correct that situation. Beginning in 1970, he arranged for a series of meetings with groups of security analysts in cities across the country, and later with the investment officers of financial institutions. Each meeting would include a presentation on the company and its prospects, along with background on the water utility industry as a whole.

(continued . . .)

(. . . continued)

At the time the investor relations program began, the common stock of American was selling at a price about 30 percent below "book value," the per-share value of its assets. As the communication effort took hold, the price of the stock began to rise. By the mid-1980s, the stock price reached a level somewhat above book value. Furthermore, as the company presented the financial community with the facts about the industry, the price of the shares of other water companies rose as well. One day the president of another publicly-held water company remarked to Gubanich, "The price of our stock keeps going up and up, and I can't figure it out. We haven't done anything."

"You can thank us," Gubanich replied. "In promoting our industry, we're raising the price of your shares."

mediary to handle that kind of transaction. So, in 1969, 38 American subsidiaries sold a total of more than $55 million in bonds to American Commonwealth. Using these bonds as collateral, American Commonwealth in turn sold $50 million of its own bonds to investors, and the refunding problem was solved.

In 1973, with inflation mounting and construction at record levels, bank debt reached a total of nearly $100 million. By 1976, using the new financing device and carefully limiting additional construction, bank debt had been reduced to just over $11 million.

E Pluribus Unum

If the consolidation of financings by subsidiary companies provided important savings, consolidation of the companies themselves offered even greater benefits. The number of subsidiary operating companies of American Water Works in 1967, the year

John Gubanich joined the company, was 87, ranging from one in Arizona to 29 in Pennsylvania. The personnel of a typical small system might consist of a business manager, a production superintendent and a distribution superintendent, along with supporting labor and clerical staff. The personnel of another system nearby would consist of a similar group with the same skills, and the one next to that of the same. Thus the staffs of a dozen independently operated water systems might total 60 or more people, whereas if their efforts were pooled, the same work could be handled by perhaps half that many.

This arrangement persisted as long as it did because, as noted, state regulatory commissions had traditionally taken a tolerant approach to operating expenses. As long as Small Company A was approximately as efficient as Small Company B, and as long as both companies were asking for about the same costs this year as they did last, the regulators would tend to accept these costs as "normal" and allow both companies to recover them in their rates. But when the point was reached where even a highly efficient company had difficulty recovering its full costs from regulators who were under increasing pressure to keep rates down, there was suddenly an incentive that did not exist before to find new ways of cutting those costs.

The most obvious way to cut costs was to consolidate small units into larger ones. The first major consolidation occurred in 1970, when 12 operating companies in New Jersey were combined under the name of the New Jersey Water Company. Two years later, 17 companies were merged into another new entity, the Western Pennsylvania Water Company. The following year, 15 companies in central and eastern Pennsylvania became the Keystone Water Company. By 1983, the year Gubanich retired, the number of American subsidiaries had been reduced to 33.

Now not only was the total number of people holding management positions substantially reduced, but it was also possible to develop a higher level of technical and financial skill in the managers that remained. An added advantage was the fact that the consolidated companies, with their greater assets and bank balances, had the ability to negotiate better terms for short term credit when that was needed.

Paralleling the move to consolidate operating companies was the consolidation of technical facilities. As water quality problems became more numerous and safety requirements stricter, and as equipment for detecting contaminants in the water became more sophisticated and sensitive—and expensive—the skills required and the equipment needed for monitoring water quality became more than individual water companies, or even consolidated companies, could support. So in 1980 the company began gradually consolidating its testing facilities in one systemwide laboratory in Belleville, Illinois.

Operation Upgrade

Here, once again, solving one set of problems created another. All the changes that were occurring—the merger of operating companies, the creation of a central testing lab, the newly strengthened budgeting and regulatory efforts, not to mention the increased use of data processing—had one requirement in common: more highly qualified people to lead and staff the new organization.

This need prompted the development of an in-house training program designed to broaden the perspective and sharpen the skills of people already on staff. The training occurred at various levels. For example, everybody who repaired pumps might be called together to pool their knowledge and agree on the most efficient way of repairing pumps. At another level, the local operating people who had responsibility for water quality might be called together and given instruction in dealing with emergencies so they would have less need to call for a specialist to make a trip from headquarters to handle a crisis.

The centerpiece of the training effort was a week-long program designed to give every supervisor and professional in the organization a broader knowledge of the business and the company's approach to it, along with improved skills in managing work and motivating people. In addition, John Gubanich saw the training sessions as a vehicle for leadership—providing the troops with a chance to meet the company's top bosses face to face and to hear their management philosophy and business goals. He put a high priority on these encounters. Of the approximately 75 management training sessions that were held while he was president, Gubanich took part in all but one or two.

Anatomy of a Crisis

The annual reports of the American Water Works Company from the mid-1960s through the early 1980s provide a vivid picture of an organization sailing along confidently—perhaps a little overconfidently—through easy times, then gradually feeling the impact of a radically changed environment, struggling to mount a response, and finally regaining control of the situation.

The report for 1963 declared, "The officers and directors of the company are proud and happy to report that . . . consolidated income reached the highest level ever attained from operations." The following year, "For the ninth year in the last ten, net income from operations established a new record." The report for 1965 announced one of the company's "most successful years." "Consolidated revenues, quantities of water sold and net income from operations all again established new records."

In 1966, "The steady growth pattern characteristic of the American Water Works system continued. . . . Consolidated revenues, quantities of water sold and net income from operations all again reached higher levels than before." But now a more somber note crept in. These gains were "largely nullified by the sharply increased cost of money and the increase in outstanding debt and preferred stocks incurred to finance system growth."

In the report for 1967, the opening statement was bravely upbeat: "Consolidated net income was the highest in history, amounting to $23,332,320." But this statement was quickly qualified.

Thirteen million dollars had come from the sale of the Alexandria property. Net income from actual operations—the delivery of water—was only $10.2 million, down from the $11.5 million of the year before, the first decline in operating income in 11 years. The report added:

> The failure of added revenues to offset rising costs of operation and capital confirms and emphasizes the necessity for the concentrated and extensive attention our management devotes to attaining appropriate adjustments in rates for water service.

In 1968 consolidated income from operations eked out an increase of less than $80,000 over the $10,200,865 of 1967, a rise of just one penny a share. The reason given for this performance was the loss of revenues resulting from the sale of the Alexandria property. However, the report conceded that the situation also "rather clearly emphasized the regulatory lag problem which we confront in our continuing efforts to establish more equitable prices for our product." That was John Gubanich's first year as treasurer.

The next year, "despite the highest levels of product delivery and revenue ever attained," income from operations declined again. "Notwithstanding unprecedented effort, we simply were unable to offset the inflationary spiral in operating and capital costs."

The report for 1970 told a different story. Now the efforts of Gubanich were beginning to bear fruit. The company reported "the greatest increase in revenues ever realized in one year." This, plus tight control of costs, including a sharp reduction in construction spending, yielded an increase in net income from operations of no less than 17 percent. "The added revenues produced by the diligent pursuit of regulatory approval for higher rates for water service," the report added, "were responsible for more than 75 percent of the total increase in 1970 operating revenues."

The following year similar efforts produced an increase in operating income of another 19 percent. For 1972, the twenty-fifth anniversary of the acquisition of control of American Water Works by John H. Ware, Jr., the company reported still another year of progress. Now, however, it was more restrained. Income from operations increased, but by only 6 percent, as the rate of inflation accelerated, fueled in part by the newly aggressive pricing policies of the Arab oil producing countries.

The next year, 1973, was the year of the Yom Kippur War and the Arab oil embargo. As interest rates skyrocketed and the rate of inflation moved into double digits, and as the company's construction budget reached a record high, operating income declined by 11 percent.

In the early part of 1974, with inflation continuing to mount and some forecasters predicting worldwide economic collapse, it looked as though the Gubanich Express had been derailed. But in the words of the annual report, "The disheartening results we reported for the first three months of 1974 evoked a searching reappraisal." Stringent cost reduction held the increase in operating expense for the year to only 5 percent, the work force was reduced by 287 people, and the construction budget was slashed by $22 million. The result was a stunning turnaround. Despite the enormous pressures, operating earnings for the year as a whole actually increased to $1.64, almost 8 percent higher than the $1.52 per share of 1973.

In 1975, with inflation and interest rates moderating and construction still held to a minimum, operating earnings increased by another 16 percent. (Jack Barr took early retirement at the end of that year, to be succeeded by John Gubanich.) In 1976 the gain again was 16 percent. From 1977 through 1982 the earnings growth continued at an average annual rate of almost 13 percent. In 1983, the year Gubanich retired, operating earnings rose by no less than 33 percent, a very nice going-away present indeed.

Big Brother Was Watching

From the moment he became president in 1975 until the day of his retirement in 1983, John Gubanich was working under the critical eye, the dominant personality, and the tendency to second-guess his successor of Jack Barr, as he continued to watch from his catbird seat on the board. In the words of one observer, each time Gubanich would raise an issue or propose an action at a meeting of the board, "Jack interjected his comments, and instead of listening to John, everybody would turn and listen to the old pro."

"Jack was the dominating factor, there was no question about that," Gubanich recalls. "When I was speaking to the board or the executive committee, I was really speaking to one individual. Depending on how he would react, that would be it."

Explanations of the situation varied. "Maybe it was jealousy on the part of Jack," suggests one director. In the view of another: "When John Gubanich was talking as CEO, Jack Barr would ask questions. And as with all those situations, the fellow who was there before and came up with the company knew the way they used to do it. Jack had grown up in the company and knew the company from A to Z and knew how everything should work."

Other members of the board were not entirely pleased with Barr's behavior. "I will say," one of them observed afterward, "that in the eyes of the board members, John had their support. They were disappointed that Jack kept sitting there. I could sense that over a period of time. They wanted the president to do his thing and not be overridden."

But no one spoke up to challenge Barr. Furthermore, despite the continuing tension, "It was not detrimental to the company to any degree," in the words of one member of management, "because John Gubanich was strong enough and the rest of us went about our business running the company in spite of that situation."

Curiously, it appeared that the tension between the two was largely confined to the boardroom. On other occasions, Gubanich recalls, when he and Barr were traveling, or having dinner together, or discussing business on a one-to-one basis, the relationship was harmonious enough. It was only in the forum of the board meetings, when Barr saw the mantle of leadership that he had worn so long shifting to a successor, that he would resist.

Ultimately, Barr came to acknowledge the contribution Gubanich made. In an interview several months before his death, he commented, "I hired John and brought him into the company, but

I didn't realize how smart he was, I guess. He did an outstanding job of taking over at a time when revenue was so scant and we needed rate increases badly—and by God, he drove at it, and unquestionably he deserves credit and recognition for that."

Jack Barr remained a member of the board until a few months after Gubanich retired. Then he retired as well. "I guess he was quite tired by that time," John Gubanich observes.

At the time of his retirement, Gubanich could have chosen to remain a member of the Board. He refused. "I wouldn't do that to my successor," he explained.

FIFTEEN

"He Did Me a Favor"

The successor in question was Jim LaFrankie, the former junior manager at Alexandria who had managed to get Jack Barr lost in the Pentagon parking lot, and later had angered him by putting people into little squares and boxes on an organization chart. Of Gubanich's decision not to remain on the board, LaFrankie observed, "He did me a favor. You cannot have an ex-president sitting there if he can't back away and help rather than hinder."

James Vincent LaFrankie was born in 1927 in Elizabeth, Pennsylvania, near Pittsburgh, attended the local high school, where he was president of the student council, and in February 1945 enlisted in the Marines. In 1947, his hitch being over, he was released to inactive duty and entered the University of Pittsburgh on the GI Bill of Rights, intending to study journalism. Here he picks up the story:

> In 1948 a young lady named Theresa Brennan was office manager for a little water company called the Monongahela Valley Water Corporation, which was located in my hometown. Theresa inquired of our family if there was anybody interested in working there part-time. That was my first knowledge that there was such a thing as a water utility.*

*The Monongahela Valley Water Corporation was a subsidiary of the American Water Works Company, inherited from the old American Water Works & Electric, although it is unlikely that the young ex-Marine was aware of that fact or, at the time, that he cared.

I agreed to go down and talk to them, and I started work on February 14, 1948, drawing work-order sketches. Drawing work-order sketches was a matter of tracing with carbon paper from distribution maps and adding extensions of pipe and so forth. After working there for maybe a year, while still attending the University of Pittsburgh, I began to do various other types of things in that office. I remember we used to run "3.60, 3.60, 3.60, 3.60" on the adding machine, three dollars and sixty cents being the minimum charge for three months of water service.

My impression of a water system in those days—and it didn't change for 15 years—was "the dirty little pump station under the bridge," and that was the image the general public had. It came from the fact that most pump stations were located on a river and the pump stations were fired with coal. They had coal piles and people shoveling coal into steam boilers to drive pumps. The Monongahela Valley Water Corporation was no different. I worked at the pump station and watched how people inventoried the coal. That was my first recollection of this business.

Electrification of the water industry began in the 1950s. They electrified the pump stations and took down the smokestacks. Today you will see very few smokestacks at any of our pump stations. They've all been taken down. The coal bins are gone, the boiler rooms are either gone or used for storage.

I worked at the Monongahela Valley Corporation for two years at 90 cents an hour, which I guess was minimum wage at that time, while going to Pitt. In October 1950, I was called back into the Marine Corps, having been in what we called the inactive reserve. There was an immediate need for a military buildup for the Korean War, so all reserves were called back.

In 1951, I was released and came back home, and rather than return to Pitt right away, I went back to this water utility and took the same job. However, Ray Wendell, who at that time was in charge of that area, came down and asked me if I would be interested in working for American Water Works Service Company as a construction inspector.

None of the companies in those days had sufficient personnel to watch individual construction jobs beyond normal work requirements. So we had a group of construction inspectors in the Service Company, and they moved from job to job, measuring concrete, looking at pipeline performance, seeing if a contractor's work was what it should be.

I started work as a construction inspector on a filter expansion at the Monongahela Valley plant. Then I became involved in large pipeline construction in South Pittsburgh and Riverton, Pennsylvania.

You run into funny relationships in these jobs because you become involved with contractors, who have always been looked on with suspicion. I'll never forget one instance where my boss sent me out to replace an inspector who they were sure was not spending sufficient time on a particular job. And I went out there and found this young man in a bar with shiny eyes, and I said to him, "Joe, I've got news for you. I am supposed to be replacing you on this job." They couldn't even get hold of the guy to tell him he was through.

And my job in going out there was to check and see how much rock excavation there had been on the job. This fellow apparently had been approving tremendous quantities of rock excavation. Well, if you can have in your contract a price for rock excavation that is sufficient, hell, you can forget about laying the pipe. You can just get paid for removing a lot of rock.

These were the kinds of things that created a need for conscientious pipeline inspectors or concrete inspectors or what have you. Someone's got to oversee the contractor and confirm that he's complying with specifications.

After doing various construction jobs, in 1953 I was asked if I would be interested in going to Alexandria, Virginia, to inspect a pipeline job. So I didn't go back to Pitt; instead I went to Virginia on January 1, 1954.

Six months later I married Nancy Wiegel, a girl from back home. Nancy and I had known each other for a long time. We lived just a few houses apart. She was five years younger and a prom queen, and I guess coming home from the Marine Corps I was attracted to a prom queen, and she says she was always attracted to Marine uniforms. So we hit it off, and in June 1954 we got married and moved into an apartment in Alexandria.

I worked on the pipeline in Alexandria, then moved to

"Now We've Got You, You SOB"

Between a construction contractor and a construction inspector, there is what is known as an adversary relationship. The contractor's profit depends on finishing the job as quickly and at the lowest cost possible. The inspector's responsibility is to see that the contractor has met all requirements and standards spelled out in the contract. Correcting any deficiency noted by the inspector means extra work and expense—and therefore lower profit—for the contractor.

Jim LaFrankie recalls one occasion when the adversary relationship took a dramatic turn:

> One of my early encounters with a contractor occurred in western Pennsylvania. The contractor was installing a 36-inch concrete pipe. The pipe went under the Monongahela River and then up the side of a fairly steep hill, 600 or 700 feet high.
>
> Pre-stressed concrete cylinder pipe requires an internal inspection to make sure the joints have been properly sealed. On this particular project I was having a running controversy with a large, burly foreman we'll call "Tony" about the way the work was being done. At the close of each day's work, I would get on a dolly—like the ones auto mechanics use for rolling around under automobiles—and the foreman would lower me down the pipe with a rope to inspect the joints. This particular day, he had installed about 200 feet of pipe almost vertically up the side of the mountain. I recall being lowered on the dolly to the very bottom. After the inspection, I'll never forget being pulled up almost to the top and then having Tony flash his light down and, while holding a large knife against the rope say, "Now we've got you, you SOB. You're heading for the bottom of the river!"
>
> Tony had no intention of cutting the rope—I guess—and after that we became friends.

another job there, and another. So instead of going back to Pittsburgh after six months, which was the original plan, I stayed for the whole construction period of our new facilities in northern Virginia.

I became involved in management in 1956. Ken Earnhardt was assistant manager in Alexandria when I arrived. In '56 he moved to Palmyra, New Jersey, and I replaced him as assistant manager.

Three years later the battle for control of the company's properties in Fairfax County began. Young Assistant Manager Jim LaFrankie was drawn into the fray as Jack Barr's lieutenant, providing LaFrankie, as he put it later, "with a chance to be associated on a daily basis with the president of the company." However, the Battle of Alexandria was not his only concern:

During this period in Virginia, we were raising a family of seven children, and I was attending night school at Georgetown University. That became a hassle toward the end. Three nights a week for five years steady, including summer school, I went back and forth to Georgetown, and graduated with a bachelor of science in business management in 1964.

When the Alexandria condemnation case was finally settled, LaFrankie was offered the post of assistant division manager back in Pittsburgh:

I had some apprehension about leaving Virginia. I was well known in the community after the condemnation, so I had other opportunities there. I thought about it for quite a while and Nancy and I talked to the kids about it. And we finally decided to make the move to Pittsburgh. I hoped at the time that more would come from the move than heading a division there, although I was never promised anything as to future opportunities. I took it as it came.

I went to Alexandria from western Pennsylvania—supposedly for six months—in 1954. Thirteen years and seven children later, we left Virginia and returned to western Pennsylvania.

[251]

Passing the Torch

Jim LaFrankie's career at American began only months after John Ware took control of the company and received its first significant boost when he caught the eye of Ray Wendell, whose own career had been advanced through his association with Ware. LaFrankie's progress was further helped as a result of working with Jack Barr, who had also been Ware's protege and continued on a day-to-day basis his contact with the Boss. Yet the curious fact is that even though Ware continued as head of the company for 13 years after LaFrankie joined it, he and LaFrankie never met. By now the elder statesman of the water business—the news media would soon begin calling him the "Water King"—Ware was occupied with buying and selling properties, pursuing his dream of the Aqueduct project and spending time with his grandchildren. Although he was often in western Pennsylvania during the period when LaFrankie first went to work there and visited northern Virginia more than once to inspect a project with which LaFrankie was involved—and the two may now and then have been within a few hundred yards of one another—Ware had no cause to deal directly with the young ex-Marine, one of many junior employees at the time, as LaFrankie prepared sketches for extending water mains, rang up "3.60, 3.60, 3.60, 3.60" on the adding machine, and inspected pipeline projects.

Thus, while the stamp of John Ware on the American organization remained strong, and his memory was vivid, Jim LaFrankie, who was now to lead the enterprise, was separated from the Founding Father not only by time, temperament, and education, but also by an intervening generation of managers and managing experience.

Maintaining the Balance

When Jim LaFrankie, an operations man, moved up to replace John Gubanich, a financial man, LaFrankie's old job as president of the Service Company was filled by Loren Mellendorf, another financial man, thus maintaining the historic balance between operating and financial skills in the management of the company. However, it would not be accurate to categorize Mellendorf as simply "another financial man." He was different, both in experience and style, from either John Gubanich or Jack Barr, his predecessors in the senior financial role. His inclination was more toward negotiated solutions than one-man decisions; his approach tended to be more consultative than argumentative.

Loren D. Mellendorf was born in Indianapolis, Indiana, in 1925, attended local high school, and upon graduation in 1943—at the height of World War II—joined the Army. Discharged as a corporal in December 1945, he entered Butler University in Indianapolis on the GI Bill of Rights. Following are his recollections:

> At Butler the first four semesters were what they called the University College, which was a liberal arts education. Philosophy, psychology, the whole gamut of the liberal arts. Then in your junior and senior years you went into your specialized field. So I concentrated on the business area and just loaded up with all the accounting courses they had.

Mellendorf graduated in August 1948, then went to work in the Indianapolis office of Peat Marwick, Mitchell & Company, the same accounting firm in whose Philadelphia office John Gubanich began his career. Almost ten years later, in February of 1958, Mellendorf left Peat Marwick to join the Indianapolis Water Company.

> When I started with Indianapolis Water, I had been so concentrated in public accounting that I knew a lot about a lot of different businesses and really very little about the water business.
>
> The man I worked for there, Ralph Swingley, who eventually became president of the company, immediately had me visit every piece of property the company owned, explain why they owned it and what it did. I went through all the departments of the company to understand what the source was, what kind of water rights we had, the treatment

process, the distribution by pumping, the booster stations and all the problems of broken mains. This fellow, over a period of time, exposed me to every aspect of water utility operation.

In September of 1966, after 8½ years with Indianapolis Water, Loren Mellendorf accepted a job with American Water Works, where he became manager of finance in the Eastern Region Office, in Haddon Heights, New Jersey.

My major responsibility was to get the rate increases filed and get the needed revenues for all the companies in that region. In most cases I presented the rate-of-return testimony myself. Water companies tended to hire outside consultants to do that. I guess I felt that someone with the company ought to do a better job than an outside consultant.

In 1975, when John Gubanich succeeded Jack Barr as president, Mellendorf was made treasurer of both the parent company and the service company. At this point, he recalls:

I moved from rates into the more typical financial function—financial planning, dividend increases, looking at cash flow, how to get the debt level paid down, monitoring financial performance, some involvement with security analysts.

Eight years later, in January of 1984, when Gubanich retired and Jim LaFrankie took his place, Loren Mellendorf was named president of the Service Company—as well as executive vice president and a director of the parent company. As to his role:

I may not be as knowledgeable about each area of water utility operations as the people who do the work there, but I think I have a working knowledge of all the operations. So it's a matter of dealing with the people who have, let's say, the "precise skills" in each area and trying to create an atmosphere that permits everyone to do what they do best.

[254]

"And That Was the End of It. We Were Captured"

During his army service, Loren Mellendorf was a "company aid man"—a medic. "You were given rudimentary medical training," he explains, "and then a helmet with a red cross on the front of it and sent up to the front lines with no gun."

Experience as an Army medic would not ordinarily be considered a prerequisite for a career in the water business, but during his military service young Mellendorf did learn one lesson useful to a future manager of any sort. He has vivid memories of a situation that demonstrated the critical importance of communication and coordination between units of the same organization.

> In January of '45 we went up to the front from Strasbourg to a little village near the Rhine. I don't even remember its name.
>
> We were infantry. We had an antitank unit attached to us. One day the Germans were coming across open fields, and these tanks were throwing shells in and everything was popping all around us. And when the sun started to set, our antitank unit took off. I don't know whether they were short of fuel or what. But we were left up there basically with rifles, with people coming at us with tanks.
>
> So we got holed up in different houses around the village. A group of us were down in a cellar. And ultimately the Germans just parked a tank down the block and blew the corner of the house away. Then the infantry stormed the house and . . . I forget the words they used, but it was like "*Rauschmitten*. American soldiers, *kommen zie hier.*"
>
> The lieutenant in charge of the company went up the stairs. Another medic and I were down there with a wounded guy. Then everybody went up but the three of us, and the lieutenant told the Germans we were down there, and they told us to come up, so we carried the guy up. And that was the end of it. We were captured.

Mellendorf was a prisoner for five months, then, after the war ended in Europe in 1945, spent several months in a hospital recovering from hepatitis.

Smooth Transition

In the transfer of leadership from John Gubanich to Jim La-Frankie, in contrast to the earlier shift from Barr to Gubanich, there was no clear-cut separation between one regime and the next, no abrupt change in policy or program. One reason for this difference was that there was greater continuity of people. When Jack Barr retired, his entire generation of senior managers left with him. During the eight years of Gubanich's tenure, by contrast, Jim LaFrankie, as his deputy, was involved in developing and carrying out the policies and programs he was to inherit. Meanwhile, Loren Mellendorf, who in turn was to become LaFrankie's deputy, was playing an increasingly important role in matters of finance. Furthermore, Gubanich took over at a time of crisis, when major change was virtually demanded. LaFrankie and Mellendorf, on the other hand, took charge when the efforts of the preceding eight years were paying off and inflationary pressures had moderated. Thus the challenge to the new team was not to turn everything upside down again, but to fine-tune and perfect existing programs and to make use of now more plentiful resources in building for the longer term.

Even so, there were differences, reflecting not only the contrasting backgrounds of the two men, but also the historic tension between the financial and operating points of view. As noted earlier, John Gubanich, the financial man, characterizes his tenure as "a period of profit motivation." In other words, the bottom line. He quickly adds that the bottom line can be served only if the interests of customers and employees as well as stockholders—the three *equal* sides of the corporate triangle, he stresses—are taken care of. Nonetheless:

> I always advocated to our people, to our managers, supervisors, employees, to be successful, you must be profitable. You need profits to succeed, and I used the example of Penn Central, W.T. Grant. When they went into bankruptcy, the bankruptcy affected not only the investor, but it affected the employees, it affected the communities they served, the sup-

pliers, the whole realm. So profits are necessary. To be successful, you profit.

In the words of Jim LaFrankie:

I was the head of the Service Company when John Gubanich was chosen to be president, and I would be the first to agree that I was not ready at that time to assume the responsibilities of chief executive. John Gubanich was. It was necessary to establish the value of budgetary planning and controlling expenditures. And that's what was done.

But a period of increasing environmental concerns and consumerism demands something other than a strictly bottom-line approach. I agree that bottom-line numbers are a necessity, but without quality of service and harmony in a community, you don't have to worry about the numbers on the bottom line, because they won't be there. If you provide quality service, build the facilities and develop community relations to the point where the community wants you there, the bottom line is going to come about. You have to work at it, but it's going to come about.

There's an easy way to get out of this business. Just let the service go to hell and tell the community you don't give a damn about anything, and you will get out of this business real quick. If a particular community is upset about quality of service or quality of management, we couldn't go there for an anniversary celebration and tell them that we have provided service for 100 years and then go for another rate increase.

With his operating background, LaFrankie also put major emphasis on being out among the troops—counseling, cajoling, trouble shooting, cheerleading:

I can hire financial people, I can hire engineers and water quality people. Someone once asked me, "Jim, what is your job?" I said that my job is to see that 3,800 people do what they're supposed to do, when they're supposed to do it . . . and with enthusiasm.

[257]

The last part is the hard part. You can have people do things with the proper timing, but if they aren't enthusiastic about it or don't want to do it, you aren't going to accomplish a thing.

They're Taking Over the Neighborhood

The program of consolidating operating companies continued under LaFrankie. Between 1984 and 1991, the number of subsidiaries decreased from 33 to 21 as companies were combined. But the focus was changing. Increasingly it went beyond simply putting a number of small companies together into one big company. Now the goal was not merely the consolidation of properties already in the company's hands but "regionalization"—that is, acquiring small water systems adjacent to the company's existing properties with the purpose not only of achieving additional volume of sales but of making American the dominant supplier to a given geographic region.

Both economics and technology—or more accurately, the economics of technology—encouraged this trend. As problems of water supply become more pressing, and as safety and environmental regulations become stricter, the cost of complying with the regulations becomes higher and less affordable for the small, independent supplier. Thus there is increasing incentive to sell out to a larger neighbor, which has the resources to provide the necessary skills and facilities. In addition, state regulatory authorities are not merely recommending, but more and more often are compelling smaller systems, public or private, to merge with or sell out to larger entities when the burden of meeting the new standards becomes too great.

Interestingly, this is an area where a private company has both greater motivation to acquire a smaller neighbor than a municipal system does, and greater freedom to do it. A municipality is normally concerned primarily with serving those customers who live—

and vote—within its limits, and there are often restrictions in the charter that prevent it from borrowing money to acquire additional property. A private company, by contrast, has no such impediments to acquiring peripheral operations that would not only make it more efficient, but also more secure in its status as supplier to a region.

Protecting the Assets

In the case of Jim LaFrankie, the motivation for moving aggressively to become a regional supplier rested not simply on calculations of economic and political advantage, but on painful memory. The primary lesson of the Battle of Alexandria was that he who hesitates can lose his water company. Because American failed to secure its position as regional supplier to northern Virginia, a public authority, like the proverbial camel, got its nose under the tent, then proceeded to take over one of the company's choicest properties. In LaFrankie's words:

> Decisions we make today reflect our past experience. The experience I had in Virginia had a lot to do with my thoughts on where the organization ought to go. The regionalization concept became timely, and for me that went back to the problem of Alexandria. I realized that if we don't pull it together, somebody else will.
>
> When I talk to the American board about what we ought to be doing besides providing quality service, I say we need to protect our existing assets. So I have fostered and encouraged this concept of acquisition of peripheral companies, and you can see it every day now in what's taking place as we acquire one here, one there, this municipality, that one, always in the general vicinity of our operations. And what that's doing is protecting the assets, because you are firming up a solid nucleus of an organization and you are becoming accepted as a regional supplier.

God Bless American

Along with the program of regionalization, there was another change, begun in the early 1970s and continued since. That was the shift from a traditional posture of attempting to downplay the connection of a local company with its American parent to one of spotlighting and promoting that connection. The names of the consolidated companies reflect this approach: Kentucky-American, New Jersey-American, Virginia-American, California-American. Here is what Jim LaFrankie has to say about it:

> I can remember back to the days when they didn't want the community to know who we were or what we were doing. I can remember being sent to one community or another and told, "Jim, tell 'em we want to stay in business, but don't tell 'em who we are." There was something in the philosophy back then that we should play down the fact that American Water Works was the parent, the owner, and dividends were being paid to the parent company. For some reason this was frowned upon. Today we have opened that up as our biggest asset, and we emphasize that here is a group of professionals providing a vital service to the community.
>
> So we have made a complete turnaround. Instead of the dirty little pump station under the bridge, we have become a sophisticated service organization. We want the trucks clean. We want visibility. We want professionalism. We have come the full route from being a collection of strictly local operations with no clear public image, to telling the community here's who we are and what we can do for you.

Home at Last

Still another change, symbolizing in concrete terms—and steel and glass as well—both the LaFrankie approach to management and the new company image and outlook, was the completion in November 1987 of a modern corporate headquarters building in Voorhees, New Jersey, a suburb of Philadelphia.

A list of the headquarters locations of the American company reads like the trajectory of a tumbleweed. Over the course of more than a century, depending on varying circumstances of geography, law, finance, economics and personal preference, the company and its chief predecessors have claimed as head office no fewer than 21 locations in five states. The headquarters of the original Kuhn Brothers construction company was Connellsville, Pennsylvania, where the Kuhn brothers lived. As the enterprise evolved from a primary concern with building water systems to the ownership and management of a far-flung collection of properties, and the name was changed to American Water Works & Guarantee, the head office was moved to McKeesport, Pennsylvania. A few years later the headquarters was shifted to Pittsburgh, where transportation was better and access to investors more convenient. Then in 1899, after New Jersey passed the first holding company act, permitting one corporation to control another without owning 100 percent of its stock, the legal headquarters of the company was moved to that state, in order to take advantage of the opportunities created by the new law. However, its operating headquarters remained in Pittsburgh.

In 1914, American Water Works & Guarantee became insolvent as a result of its ill-advised investments in western irrigation projects, and control passed to the group headed by H. Hobart Porter. The management then moved the legal headquarters of the newly constituted company, now called American Water Works & Electric, to Virginia, because of the more liberal protection provided to companies in trouble by the laws of that state. Then as the public utility boom of the 1920s gained momentum and the management decided to expand the company rather than liquidating it, the operating headquarters was moved to what was then the center of the world in financial terms, 50 Broad Street in New York, just down the block from Wall Street. Meanwhile, in 1927, the legal headquarters was shifted from Virginia to Delaware, where the law made possible a saving on taxes. Later, when the new American Water Works company was created, its legal headquarters was also located in Delaware, while its operating headquarters remained at 50 Broad Street.

While all this was going on, young John Ware, born in Philadelphia, at age 16 took charge of the J. Elliot Shaw Electric Company at 632 Arch Street in that city. A few years later, sensing brighter opportunity to the west, he moved to Lancaster, Pennsylvania, where he first established the J. H. Ware Engineering Company and then the Farmers Electric Company at 45 North Duke Street.

Some time after that, having built up his properties in the Lancaster area, Ware moved again, locating both his home and his headquarters in the little farm town of Oxford, Pennsylvania, about 50 miles southwest of Philadelphia. In 1933, having sold his electrical holdings, he took charge of the faltering National Water Company, located in Philadelphia. Then in 1938, in the interest of saving on rent, he moved his headquarters back to Oxford. "Mr. Ware owned the gas company down there," Jack Barr recalled. "The gas company in turn owned a building on the main street of town that was split between the Pennsylvania Liquor Control board and the offices of the gas company. In the back was a garage—it was a sizable building. He decided to convert that garage into offices for his water companies."

The eight years between 1942 and 1950 involved no fewer than six changes of location. In 1942, after John Ware purchased the Northeastern Water & Electric Company, he transferred the headquarters of his other water holdings to the operating headquarters of Northeastern in New York City. (However, the legal headquarters of Northeastern was also located in Delaware.) That arrangement ended in 1946 when the operating headquarters was moved to Camden, New Jersey. But the very next year, after Ware took control of American Water Works, the combined operating headquarters was again transferred to New York, to the American offices at 50 Broad Street. Then in 1950 the head office was shifted back to Philadelphia, first to 121 South Broad Street, then in 1955 to a newly constructed office building at Three Penn Center. (During all this time the legal headquarters of both companies remained in Delaware. However, in 1956, again in the interest of saving on rent, the Delaware office was moved from downtown Wilmington to a small building constructed for that purpose in the nearby suburb of Greenville.)

Although the company's operating headquarters was now located in the most modern office building in Philadelphia, the premises were by no means lavish. "In the early days," recalled Howard Carlock, "we made no pretense of trying to look successful, with fancy offices. In 1955 we still had some furniture that went back to the old water company offices in Pittsburgh in 1913. We had carpet on the floor only in a small selected area for the executives."

From 1955 to 1976 the operating headquarters remained at Three Penn Center, the longest stay in one place in the modern history of the company. But in the early 1970s, with all costs under pressure and John Gubanich relentless in his quest for savings, the decision was made to move the operating headquarters out of Philadelphia once again, this time to nearby Haddon Heights, New Jersey. "We decided we didn't need to be downtown for our type of operation because we weren't selling anything," Carlock explains. "Our product was water. It was sold through the water companies. Anyone who ever visited our offices through all those years was selling *us* something."

However, as often happens, as the headquarters staff continued to grow, it soon became necessary to rent additional office space in the town of Evesham, nearby.

Governing from the Saddle

During most of his time as president of the parent company, Jack Barr was also president of the Service Company. This resulted in a kind of shuttle existence. While he was wearing his Service Company hat, he would work at the company's operating headquarters, which at that time was still in Philadelphia. However, when he wanted to put on his corporate hat—to sign documents or hold a

[263]

board meeting—he would get into his car and drive 45 miles to the corporate office outside of Wilmington.

After Barr retired in 1975, his hats were divided. Now John Gubanich, who inherited the president's hat, worked out of the corporate office in Wilmington, while Jim LaFrankie, who wore the Service Company hat, continued to work in Haddon Heights. In 1983, after LaFrankie became president of the parent company, he in turn moved his office to Wilmington.

At this point the situation of the chief executive resembled that of the chieftain of one of the ancient nomadic tribes of central Asia. He was essentially "governing from the saddle." His day might start with a meeting with the financial people in Haddon Heights. Then he would drop by the office in Evesham for a conference with the water quality director. Next would come an hour-long drive to Wilmington to catch up on paperwork, lunch in Philadelphia with a member of the board of directors, and finally back to Haddon Heights for a meeting with Loren Mellendorf, the president of the Service Company, all the while playing telephone tag with various subordinates.

During the early Gubanich years, there was neither time nor cash to spare on considerations of physical arrangement. By the mid-1980s, with financial pressures abated and profit margins restored, the time had come to remedy the situation. So in the fall of 1986 ground was broken for a $4.7 million headquarters in Voorhees, and on November 4, 1987, the building was dedicated. At the same time, the Delaware office was sold, and for the first time in 60 years the corporate and operating headquarters of American were located in the same place.

"I guess I will take credit some day," LaFrankie observes, "for having said, 'Let's get this organization into one building so we can be a close-knit group.' I want to talk to our people without being on the phone all day."

In contrast to the earlier situation, the new building is carpeted throughout, and there is no trace of furniture of 1913, except for the desk said to have belonged to Samuel Insull, a souvenir of John Ware's encounter with that famous tycoon.

Broadening the Board

Another feature of the post-Barr era was a shift in the composition and influence of the company's board of directors. When John Ware took control of American Water Works in 1947, its board included representatives from the highest levels of the worlds of management, law and finance. In a few years, these had been replaced by friends and business associates of Ware. Then as he faded from the scene, the board's membership was increasingly influenced and its proceedings dominated by Jack Barr. In 1974, the year Barr retired, the American board included four "inside" members—directors who were also members of Barr's management team—and only one or two who could provide an outsider's perspective.

A trend to broaden the membership began in 1975, with the accession to the presidency of John Gubanich. In that year Samuel H. Ballam, Jr., president of the Fidelity Bank of Philadelphia and of its parent company, Fidelcor, Inc., was elected a member, along with Arthur E. Bone, president of the UGI Corporation, a gas and electric utility. But as long as Barr remained on the board, his presence continued to be the dominating factor. With the simultaneous retirement of Barr and the accession of Jim LaFrankie, there was room for the contribution of a broader board. Moreover, a series of retirements made room for additional outside members. In 1983, Elizabeth Gemmill, at that time a senior vice president of the Girard Bank of Philadelphia, replaced her father, Kenneth Gemmill, who had become a major shareholder at the time of the retirement of John Ware. In 1984, William F. Hyland, senior partner of the New Jersey law firm of Riker, Danzig, Scherer, Hyland & Peretti, former attorney general of the state of New Jersey and a former public utility commissioner, was elected. In 1985, Nelson G. Harris, president and CEO of the Tasty Baking Company, joined the board and later became vice chairman. Ross A. Webber, a professor of management at the University of Pennsylvania's Wharton School, joined the board in 1986, and in 1987, Henry G. Hager, senior partner of the law firm of Liebert, Short & Hirshland, president of the Insurance Federation of Pennsylvania and a former state senator, was elected. In 1990, William O. Albertini, vice president and chief financial officer of Bell Atlantic Corporation, joined the board.

By 1990 the number of management members on the board had been reduced to two—LaFrankie and Mellendorf—while the number of outsiders had increased to six, representing a diversity of backgrounds and points of view.

Meanwhile, a new generation of Wares was coming up as well. John Ware IV, the son of John Ware 3rd, served the Board from 1975 until 1990. Rhoda Ware Cobb, a daughter of Willard Ware, joined in 1976. Marilyn Ware Lewis, daughter of John 3rd, became a member in 1982, and Nancy Ware Pascal, another daughter of Willard, in 1984. Paul W. Ware, who had succeeded his father, John 3rd, as president of Penn Fuel Gas Company, served on the board from 1982 to 1986, and was elected again in 1990.

Symbolic of the new trend was the election in 1985 of Samuel H. Ballam as chairman of the board, upon the retirement of John Ware 3rd. A product of the University of Pennsylvania and the Advanced Management Program of the Harvard Business School, Ballam, in addition to his banking career, was a director of a number of other companies and a leader in a wide variety of civic, charitable and public interest organizations.

Sam Ballam retired as chairman in 1988, to be succeeded by Marilyn Ware Lewis. The former owner and editor of weekly newspapers, and president of KLS Educational Systems, a school for learning-disabled children, and a director of the Penn Fuel Gas Company, Marilyn Lewis also followed her father, John Ware 3rd, into political life. She was successively chairman of the Lancaster County Republican Committee, a member of the Pennsylvania State Republican Committee and, in 1985–86, chairman of the statewide Scranton for Governor Committee. She thus represents not only the continuing involvement of the Ware family in the affairs of the company, but a background extending well beyond the water business.

Jim LaFrankie, newly elected president of American, confers with
Board Chairman John H. Ware, 3rd, before a 1984 board meeting.

Sam Ballam, a Philadelphia
banker and director of several
other companies, served as a
director of American from 1975
to 1990 and as chairman of the
board from 1984 to 1987.

Loren Mellendorf, who joined
American as treasurer of the
eastern subsidiaries in 1966, was
president of the Service
Company and executive vice
president of the parent
company from 1984 to 1991.

American Water Works Company's corporate headquarters was in this building in Greenville, Delaware, from 1956 to 1987.

This building in Haddon Heights, New Jersey, has been the headquarters of the Eastern Region of American Water Works Service Company since the mid-1960s.

The American Water System Corporate Center in Voorhees, New
Jersey, dedicated in 1987.

Jim LaFrankie (*left*), Marilyn Lewis and Loren Mellendorf watch stock
prices from the floor of the New York Stock Exchange during a visit
in 1989.

Top left: George Johnstone, an engineer who joined the company in 1966, was named president of American Water Works Service Company and president-elect of the parent company in 1991.

Top right: Ed Limbach joined the American System as a management trainee in 1964 and moved through the ranks to become a vice president of the parent company in 1990.

Left: Jim Barr joined the American System in 1961 in New Jersey and was named treasurer of the parent company in 1984, a vice president in 1987 and chief financial officer in 1991.

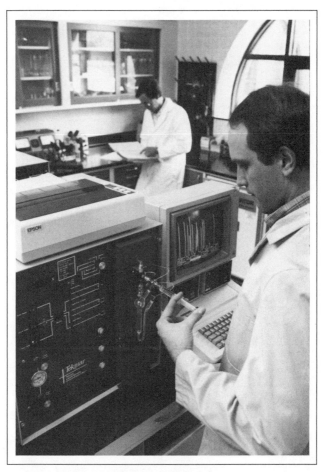

By the 1980s the large companies in the American System had developed their own sophisticated water quality labs, like this one in Pittsburgh, to supplement work done at the System's analytical and research lab in Belleville, Illinois.

A new storage tank ready to go on-line at Davenport, Iowa, in 1986.

The American Water Works Company Board of Directors in 1991 included (*from left*), *standing*, Ross A. Webber; Nelson G. Harris; James V. LaFrankie, President; Loren D. Mellendorf; and *sitting*, Paul W. Ware; Rhoda W. Cobb; William F. Hyland; William O. Albertini; Marilyn W. Lewis, Chairman; Nancy W. Pascal; Elizabeth H. Gemmill; and Henry W. Hager.

Directors of American Water Works Service Company in 1991 included (*from left*), *sitting*, Glen W. Thornburg; Robert W. Greaves; Gerald C. Smith; William R. Cobb; Dillard L. Edgemon; and *standing*, Edward W. Limbach; George W. Johnstone; Loren D. Mellendorf, President; James V. LaFrankie, Chairman; W. Timothy Pohl; and J. James Barr.

SIXTEEN

And Tomorrow . . .

Now entering the second century of its existence under one or another variation of the American Water Works name, the company by 1990 had passed the $500 million mark in revenue and was approaching $2 billion in assets. It was moving steadily ahead in the professionalism of its staff, in the technical quality of its facilities, and in the strength of its position in its market communities. But if the history of its first hundred years teaches anything, it is that the water business—or indeed any business—is no more static in the 1990s than it was in the 1890s, or the 1920s, the 1930s or the 1950s. Nor is it any more insulated from the forces at work in the society around it.

Any broad look at the problems of water and water supply in the last decade of the twentieth century reveals a dramatic contrast of detail, an arresting sameness in long-term implications:

• For generations the communities on Long Island in New York have drawn their water from a gigantic underground "aquifer," a water-bearing bed of gravel. Now the demand is so great that the underground reservoir is being drawn down to the point where there is danger that salt water will seep in, destroying the supply. The suggestion has been made that to remedy the situation a massive system of pipes and pumps be installed, through which water from the Hudson River can be pumped into the aquifer during periods of reduced demand, replenishing its supply.

• In the Boston area, the growth of demand for water has outrun the existing supply. One proposed solution to the problem is to tap the waters of the Merrimac River to the north and the Connecticut River to the west—a proposal that has aroused bitter opposition on the part of communities in those areas.

• In Colorado, water requirements have become so great that cities have begun to bid for the water rights of farmers on nearby irrigated land—providing lawns and swimming pools for the residents of urban areas, but leaving affected farmland to revert to desert.

• In one area of the Central Valley of California, irrigation has provided bumper crops to farmers. But the runoff from the irrigated land, carrying fertilizer and other agricultural chemicals, has accumulated nearby, destroying or deforming wildlife and endangering drinking water supplies. A proposal has been made to run a costly pipeline to the Pacific Ocean to carry the contaminants away. The alternative would be either to abandon agriculture in that district, or simply to give up on the wildlife and move the people away.

Water people, Jim LaFrankie included, are quick to point out that in global terms there is really no shortage of water. The earth has the same amount of water it has had for the last 10,000 years. The problem is what it has always been: getting the water from where it is available to where it is needed, and providing it in a condition that is both palatable and safe.

Perhaps someday solar energy or superconductivity or low-temperature nuclear fusion will permit the economical desalination of seawater or the recycling of wastewater on a massive scale. The suggestion has even been made that icebergs be floated down from the Arctic to meet the requirements of coastal cities. This gives rise to the vision of a latter-day John Ware appearing some bright morning as commodore of a fleet of tugboats hauling a great mountain of ice into Delaware Bay to meet the needs of thirsty citizens.

But that will not be for a while, and what is certain in the meantime is that the cost of water is bound to rise, as communities reach out to more distant sources, as processing to assure public safety increases, and as competing users bid up the price.

The question of price has particular significance for investor-owned water companies. A century of experience has shown that whenever rates go up sharply there is likely to be talk of the public takeover of a private system. Will this trend threaten the future of the investor-owned segment of the industry? The possibility provides a strong argument for a continuing program of regionalization. If one small community challenges a region-wide entity, it is likely to discover it has taken on a formidable opponent.

There undoubtedly will be periodic calls for the community takeover of one system or another. But, as already noted, it is one thing for a politician to propose the takeover of the local water company and another to mobilize the money and public support required to do it. "They can try," Jim LaFrankie observes. "They might succeed. But they would find it very difficult."

Straws in the Wind

Furthermore, there are indications that the public, which has historically assumed that water should be free, or something close to it, may be beginning to realize that a reliable supply of good-quality water no longer comes cheap. Recently the citizens of the Boston area, while opposing increases in rates for electricity and gas, have not complained about comparable increases in their water rates, apparently convinced by publicity surrounding their current water problems that an increase in cost is both inevitable and necessary.

But that is not the only straw in the wind. Recently local governments across the country have begun to encounter problems in constructing the expensive new water facilities required to comply with stricter environmental standards or to meet increasing demand. Federal grants to assist with such projects have largely dried up; state subsidies are dwindling; local debt levels are approaching saturation. So a number of communities have begun to explore the possibility of finding private partners to design, finance, construct and then operate the facilities they need.

This "new" approach to providing water service is in fact a curious throwback. The terms of financing and management are remarkably similar to those devised by John Ware in the late 1930s to take advantage of the opportunities created by the Municipal Authorities Act. And the identical pattern—of designing, financing, constructing and then managing local water facilities—was the essential reason for being of the original American Water Works & Guarantee Company in the 1880s, and the key to its growth and success.

Progress in developing these public-private partnerships has been slow. Negotiations with municipal authorities, unfamiliar with such novel relationships and reluctant to give up power, have proven tedious and complex. So far, across the country, only a handful of such arrangements have been agreed to. Nonetheless, the need is compelling and alternatives are few. So perhaps it will turn out that in the late twentieth century, as in the late nineteenth, a significant opportunity will develop for private business to turn a profit by stepping in and offering a service that local government is unable to provide.

As Long as People Are Gathered . . .

A few miles north of the Dead Sea, in what was once the Land of Canaan and today is known as the Occupied West Bank, a gushing spring has flowed since before human memory, fed by the rains on the hills above, creating a circle of sparkling green in the bleak Judean wilderness. From immemorial time, animals have come to the spring. As early man migrated out of Africa, human beings came to the spring as well, and then settled there, since it offered the only reliable supply of water for miles around. As trade routes grew and agriculture developed, more and more people gathered near the spring, until they created what today we call a city, which in time came to be called Jericho. Archaeologists have discovered remnants of walls at Jericho dating as far back as 8000 B.C., more than six millennia before Joshua blew his fabled trumpet.

In the ten thousand years since the first walls of Jericho were built, much has changed, but the fundamentals remain the same. Where there is water, people gather. Where people are gathered, there is a need for water. Where there are few people, arrangements for providing water, if any are required, are simple. Where there are more people, there is a need to organize.

It was not ordained by Heaven that any given institution should provide the water for a particular place. It has usually been the dominant institution of the society in question. In ancient Babylon, control over the water system on which that civilization depended was exercised by priests, who are said to have developed the science of astronomy in order to predict seasonal variations in flow, to have created mathematics to control and measure water use, and to have invented writing in order to keep records. As long as Rome was a republic, water was provided by the Republic; after it became an empire, the Empire took over that function. In France, the water system that supplied the Palace of Versailles was constructed on the order of the King, and paid for out of his treasury.

The earliest arrivals in the New World provided for their own individual needs at first; then, as settlements grew, they engaged in cooperative efforts equivalent to a "bucket brigade." As these measures were outgrown, private initiatives stepped in to fill the gap. When these in turn proved inadequate, municipal government tended to take over. But then, as industry spread across the land and cities by the dozen exploded into pell-mell growth, municipal authorities were often too weak to meet the new demand, and private business, certainly the dominant institution in that era, stepped in again. Since then, in a kind of cyclic pattern, in cities that grew beyond a certain size, municipal government has tended to take over once more. But in situations where a community has been unable or unwilling to take on the task of improving or expanding its supply, private efforts have continued to be an efficient way, and arguably the most efficient way, to provide the necessary service.

What is certain in any case is that as long as people are gathered together in cities, they will find a way to see to it that water—good water—continues to flow.

[271]

APPENDIX A

Selected Financial Data

The table on the next two pages gives a consolidated summary of selected financial data for American Water Works Company, Inc., and subsidiary companies. The second page includes data for Northeastern Water Company, which merged with American on August 17, 1962.

American Water Works Company, Inc., and Subsidiary Companies

(Dollars in thousands except per share amounts)

For the years ended December 31,	1990	1985	1980	1975	1970	1965	1960
Revenues							
Water service							
Residential	$308,698	$235,932	$146,130	$100,590	$64,429	$43,193	$26,717
Commercial	129,360	95,904	54,468	36,112	22,008	14,351	9,929
Industrial	44,406	37,113	26,296	18,487	13,043	9,625	7,226
Public and other	68,802	50,879	29,622	19,234	14,864	10,845	7,479
Other water revenues	3,925	2,200	1,335	966			
Subtotal	555,191	422,028	257,851	175,389	114,344	78,014	51,351
Sewer service	10,157	6,560	2,442	1,291	749	517	
Authority management fees	5,350	1,102	802	527	68	539	
Total revenues	$570,698	$429,690	$261,095	$177,207	$115,161	$79,070	$51,351
Water sales (million gallons)							
Residential	98,069	93,919	92,273	87,045	80,684	58,710	39,548
Commercial	56,442	53,602	50,389	46,349	39,603	28,635	21,343
Industrial	34,804	38,112	48,057	50,327	57,622	50,813	43,050
Public and other	23,539	22,750	23,131	21,189	22,451	18,594	13,902
Total water sales	212,854	208,383	213,850	204,910	200,360	156,752	117,843
Customers (thousands)	1,514	1,436	1,367	1,325	1,229	1,075	812
Total assets	$2,092,596	$1,383,015	$1,026,389	$851,081	$678,247	$516,953	$341,032
Net income	$57,088	$58,377	$22,999	$14,995	$11,197	$11,201	$5,601
Earnings per common share	$1.85	$1.91[a]	$0.77	$0.48	$0.33	$0.34	$1.53
Common dividends paid per share	$0.80	$0.50	$0.24	$0.16	$0.14	$0.14	$0.20
Market price of common share at year end[b]	$16.00	$16.07	$2.75	$2.16	$3.35	$4.50	$2.47

[a]Influenced by an extraordinary item in 1985.
[b]Market prices have been adjusted for stock splits in 1987, 1985 and 1965.

[274]

American Water Works Company, Inc., and Subsidiary Companies

(Dollars in thousands except per share amounts)

For the years ended December 31,	1955	1950	1947
Revenues			
Water service			
Residential	$18,052	$12,058	$10,574
Commercial	7,667	5,991	5,341
Industrial	5,382	4,192	3,961
Public and other	5,496	4,110	3,670
Other water revenues			
Subtotal	36,597	26,351	23,546
Sewer service			
Authority management fees			
Total revenues	$36,597	$26,351	$23,546
Water sales (million gallons)			
Residential			
Commercial			
Industrial			
Public and other			
Total water sales	121,193	111,928	104,716
Customers (thousands)	772	743	663
Total assets	$286,799	$215,450	$183,275
Net income	$3,773	$2,748	$2,276
Earnings per common share	$0.98	$1.39	$0.84
Common dividends paid per share	$0.13	$0.15	$0.00
Market price of common share at year end	$1.13	$1.19	$0.99

Northeastern Water Company

	1960	1955	1950	1947
Revenues				
Water service				
Residential	$3,317	$2,592	$2,074	
Commercial	694	501	439	
Industrial	249	271	230	
Public and other	586	534	479	
Other water revenues				
Subtotal	4,846	3,898	3,222	
Sewer service	288	181		
Authority management fees	430			
Total revenues	$5,564	$4,079	$3,222	$2,833
Water sales (million gallons)				
Residential	5,732			
Commercial	1,770			
Industrial	1,515			
Public and other	874			
Total water sales	9,891	9,303	8,019	7,543
Customers (thousands)	105	100	92	86
Total assets	$53,608	$50,179	$40,891	$39,846
Net income	$1,815	$1,144	$1,182	$739
Earnings per common share	$2.25	$1.21	$1.27	$0.62
Common dividends paid per share	$0.30	$0.25	$0.35	$0.00
Market price of common share at year end				

Subsidiary Companies

The companies in the following list have at one time or another been part of the American Water System. The abbreviation "I." indicates the year the company was incorporated. "J." refers to the year the company joined the American Water System, if it was not in the original American Water Works & Electric group. "D." indicates the year a company was dissolved (usually by merger into another company), and "S." the year it was sold. Companies that were part of the Community Water Service or Northeastern system are identified as follows: Community (C) and Northeastern (N).

Alexandria Water (VA)   I. 1936; D. 1972.
Alton Water (IL)   I. 1850; D. 1984.
Armstrong Water (PA)   I. 1886; D. 1972.
Ashtabula Water Works (OH)   I. 1928; D. 1977.
Atlantic County Water (NJ)   I. 1915; D. 1971.
Bangor Water (PA)   I. 1884; J. 1936; D. 1974. (C)
Bernards Water (NJ)   I. 1903; D. 1972.
Berwick Water (PA)   I. 1818; J. 1936; D. 1974. (C)
Biglerville Water (PA)   I. 1908; J. 1963; D. 1974. (N)
Birmingham Water Works (AL)   I. 1885; S. 1952.
Bluefield Valley Water Works (WV)   I. 1916; J. 1965.
Bluefield Valley Water Works (WV)   I. 1883; D. 1947.
Butler Water (PA)   I. 1877; D. 1973.
Cairo Water (IL)   I. 1886; J. 1936; D. 1983. (C)
California-American Water   I. 1966; J. 1966.
Canawacta Water Supply (PA)   I. 1899; J. 1936; D. 1974. (C)
Citizens Water (PA)   I. 1886; J. 1936; D. 1973. (C)
Citizens Water Service (PA)   I. 1923; J. 1963; D. 1970. (N)
City of New Castle Water (PA)   I. 1902; D. 1970.
City Water Company of Chattanooga (TN)   I. 1909; D. 1973.

Clairton Water (PA)   I. 1941; J. 1947; D. 1950.
Clarion Water (PA)   I. 1887; J. 1971; D. 1973. (N)
Clark's Summit Water (PA)   I. 1893; J. 1936; D. 1974. (C)
Clinton Water Works (IA)   I. 1906; D. 1985.
Clymer Water Service (PA)   I. 1886; J. 1963; D. 1973. (N)
Cohasset Water (MA)   I. 1886; J. 1936; D. 1950. (C)
Commonwealth Water (NJ)   I. 1915.
Commonwealth Water and Light (NJ)   I. 1904; D. 1969.
Connecticut-American Water   I. 1977; J. 1977.
Connellsville Water (PA)   I. 1883; D. 1973.
Consumers Water of Montrose (PA)   I. 1892; J. 1963; D. 1974. (N)
Davenport Water (IA)   I. 1930; D. 1985.
Dedham Water (MA)   I. 1876; J. 1936; S. 1985. (C)
Delaware River Water (NJ)   I. 1902; J. 1963; D. 1966. (N)
Delaware Valley Water (NJ)   I. 1888; J. 1966; D. 1971.
Dorchester Water (MD)   I. 1913; J. 1936; D. 1960. (C)
Dravosburg Water (PA)   I. 1941; J. 1947; D. 1950.
East St. Louis and Interurban Water (IL)   I. 1916; D. 1978.
Elizabeth Township Water (PA)   I. 1941; J. 1947; D. 1950.
Ellwood Consolidated Water (PA)   I. 1926; J. 1971; D. 1973. (N)
Florida Water   I. 1961; J. 1968; D. 1978.
Forward Township Water (PA)   I. 1941; J. 1947; D. 1950.
Frenchtown Water (NJ)   I. 1900; J. 1963; D. 1971. (N)
Glassport Water (PA)   I. 1941; J. 1947; D. 1950.
Glenville Power & Water (WV)   I. 1903; J. 1947; D. 1963.
Grafton Water (MA)   I. 1886; J. 1959; S. 1988. (N)
Gravity Water Supply (PA)   I. 1917; J. 1969; D. 1973.
Greenwich Water (CT)   I. 1880; J. 1936; D. 1977. (C)
Greenwich Water System (CT)   I. 1925; J. 1936. (C)
Hallstead Water (PA)   I. 1892; J. 1947; D. 1973. (C)
Hampton Water Works (NH)   I. 1889; J. 1960. (N)
Hendersonville Water (PA)   I. 1946; J. 1968; D. 1970.
Hershey Water (PA)   I. 1913; J. 1977.
Hills Station Water (PA)   I. 1946; J. 1968; D. 1970.
Hingham Water (MA)   I. 1879; J. 1936. (C)
Huntington Water (WV)   I. 1917; D. 1986.
Hyde Park Water (PA)   I. 1922; J. 1936; D. 1949. (C)
Ideal Beach Water (NJ)   I. 1912; J. 1950; D. 1965. (N)
Illinois-American Water   I. 1916.
Indiana-American Water   I. 1887.
Inter-Township Water (PA)   I. 1938; J. 1963; D. 1964.
Jamesburg Water (NJ)   I. 1908; J. 1963; D. 1971. (N)
Jefferson Township Water (PA)   I. 1941; J. 1947; D. 1950.
Joplin Water Works (MO)   I. 1893; D. 1983.
Junction Water (NJ)   I. 1889; J. 1963; D. 1971. (N)
Kentucky-American Water   I. 1973; J. 1973.

Keystone Water (PA)   I. 1974; J. 1974; D. 1986.
Kokomo Water Works (IN)   I. 1887; D. 1984.
Lakewood Water (NJ)   I. 1944; J. 1963; D. 1971. (N)
Laurel Springs Water Works (NJ)   I. 1930; J. 1963; D. 1965. (N)
Lawrence County Water (OH)   I. 1928; D. 1978.
Lexington Water (KY)   I. 1927; J. 1936; D. 1973. (C)
Lincoln Township Water (PA)   I. 1941; J. 1947; D. 1950.
Marion Water (OH)   I. 1923; J. 1936; D. 1981. (C)
Maryland Water Works   I. 1935; J. 1963; D. 1983. (N)
Massachusetts-American Water   I. 1978.
Massachusetts Water Supply   I. 1893; J. 1960; D. 1978.
Mifflin Township Water (PA)   I. 1941; D. 1950.
Missouri-American Water   I. 1984.
Monmouth Consolidated Water (NJ)   I. 1926; D. 1987.
Monongahela City Water (PA)   I. 1886; J. 1936; D. 1973. (C)
Monongahela Valley Water (PA)   I. 1897; D. 1971.
Morgantown Water (WV)   I. 1927; D. 1951.
Morris Water (PA)   I. 1901; J. 1963; D. 1970. (N)
Moshannon Valley Water (PA)   I. 1970; D. 1974.
Mountain City Water (PA)   I. 1883; J. 1936; D. 1974. (C)
Mount Jewett Water (PA)   I. 1890; J. 1936; D. 1973. (C)
Muncie Water Works (IN)   I. 1885; J. 1936; D. 1973.
Myerstown Water (PA)   I. 1895; J. 1936; D. 1950. (C)
Mystic Valley Water (CT)   I. 1887; J. 1960; D. 1978. (N)
Neptunus Water (NJ)   I. 1901; J. 1963; D. 1971. (N)
New Castle Water (PA)   I. 1970; D. 1973.
New Jersey Water   I. 1925; J. 1936; D. 1973. (C)
New Jersey Water Service   I. 1905; J. 1963; D. 1973. (N)
New York-American Water   I. 1983.
Noroton Water (CT)   I. 1901; D. 1978.
Norristown Water (PA)   I. 1925; J. 1963; D. 1972.
North Little Rock Water (AR)   I. 1937; D. 1960.
Northumberland Water (PA)   I. 1892; J. 1936; D. 1974. (C)
Ocean City Sewer Service (NJ)   I. 1893; J. 1963; D. 1971. (N)
Ocean City Water Service (NJ)   I. 1892; J. 1963; D. 1971. (N)
Ocean County Water (NJ)   I. 1929; D. 1971.
Ohio-American Water   I. 1977.
Ohio Cities Water   I. 1928; J. 1936; D. 1980. (C)
Old Dominion Water (VA)   I. 1924; D. 1974.
Osceola Water Supply (PA)   I. 1889; J. 1936; D. 1969. (C)
Palmyra Water (PA)   I. 1921; J. 1936; D. 1974. (C)
Paradise Valley Water (CA)   I. 1949; J. 1969.
Pekin Water (IL)   I. 1886; J. 1981; D. 1982.
Pennsylvania State Water   I. 1927; J. 1936; D. 1966.
Peoria Water (IL)   I. 1967; D. 1984.
Peoria Water Works (IL)   I. 1898; J. 1936; D. 1967. (C)

Pollock Water Service (CA)   I. 1965; J. 1966; D. 1970.

Port Chester Water Works (NY)   I. 1883; J. 1936; D. 1983. (C)

Prince William Water (VA)   I. 1966; D. 1975.

Providence Water (PA)   I. 1922; J. 1963; D. 1964.

Punxsutawney Water Service (PA)   I. 1920; J. 1963; D. 1973. (N)

Ramey Water (PA)   I. 1909; J. 1936; D. 1962. (C)

Richmond Water Works (IN)   I. 1926; J. 1947; D. 1983.

Riverton and Palmyra Water (NJ)   I. 1888; J. 1963; D. 1966. (N)

Riverton Consolidated Water (PA)   I. 1904; J. 1963; D. 1986. (N)

St. Joseph Water (MO)   I. 1879; J. 1936; D. 1983.

St. Marys Water (PA)   I. 1889; J. 1936; D. 1969. (C)

Salisbury Water Supply (MA)   I. 1915; J. 1960. (N)

Seymour Water (IN)   I. 1889; J. 1981; D. 1983.

South Pittsburgh Water (PA)   I. 1904; D. 1972.

Spring Water Company of Kane (PA)   I. 1887; J. 1936; D. 1973. (C)

Sullivan County Water (PA)   I. 1912; J. 1971; D. 1976.

Tennessee-American Water   I. 1973.

Terre Haute Water Works (IN)   I. 1924; D. 1983.

Texarkana Water (TX)   I. 1904; D. 1949.

Thompson Borough Water (PA)   I. 1891; J. 1972; D. 1974.

Uniontown Water (PA)   I. 1938; J. 1936; D. 1973. (C)

Vandergrift Water (PA)   I. 1895; J. 1936; D. 1950. (C)

Village Water (CA)   I. 1960; J. 1967; D. 1970.

Virginia-American Water   I. 1973.

Virginia Water   I. 1948; D. 1958.

Wannacomet Water (MA)   I. 1880; J. 1936; D. 1988. (C)

Warren Water (PA)   I. 1881; D. 1972.

Washington Water (NJ)   I. 1881; J. 1963; D. 1971. (N)

Waynesburg Water (PA)   I. 1886; J. 1936; D. 1968. (C)

West Elizabeth Water (PA)   I. 1941; D. 1949.

Western Pennsylvania Water   I. 1972.

Westland Water (PA)   I. 1946; J. 1973; D. 1974.

West Norristown Water (PA)   I. 1912; J. 1963; D. 1964.

West Penn Water (PA)   I. 1924; J. 1963; D. 1974. (N)

West Virginia Water   I. 1965; D. 1985.

White Deer Mountain Water (PA)   I. 1899; J. 1936; D. 1974. (C)

Whitpain Water (PA)   I. 1932; J. 1963; D. 1964.

Wichita Water (KS)   I. 1911; S. 1957.

Yardley Water (PA)   I. 1969; D. 1974.

Retired Managers, Executives and Directors

The following is a list of retired managers, executives and directors who left a mark on the post–World War II company, either in the records or in the memory of those interviewed for this history. We include the list by way of recognizing their contribution. It is somewhat subjective and may be incomplete, for which we apologize.

Paul E. Aberli Born 1899; joined system, 1926; manager, American Water Works Service Company, 1959–64; retired 1964; died 1987.

Frank P. Agulia Born 1925; Harvard University, AB, 1945; joined system, 1953; vice president–water quality, American Water Works Service Company, 1980; retired 1980.

Clyde H. Albert Born 1928; joined system, 1947; district manager, Western Pennsylvania Water Company, 1985–89; retired 1989.

Francis B. Alberts Born 1933; joined Gettysburg Authority, 1961; manager, Gettysburg, 1961–89; district manager, Keystone Water Company, 1973–81; retired 1989; died 1990.

Elwood H. Aldrich Born 1894; University of Illinois, BSCE; joined system, 1933; vice president and chief engineer, American Water Works Service Company, 1947–59; retired 1962; died 1965.

Marshall A. Anderson Born 1910; University of Illinois, BS; joined system, 1946; vice president, American Water Works Company, 1953–74; director, 1953–74; retired 1974.

Clarence C. Arbogast Born 1904; joined system, 1923; manager, Alton Water Company, 1968–69; retired 1969.

Edward A. Baier   Born 1917; joined system, 1939; manager, Joplin Water Company, 1976–77; retired 1977; died 1978.

Frederick W. Baker   Born 1916; joined system, 1937; district manager, Keystone Water Company, 1948–81; retired 1981.

Samuel H. Ballam, Jr.   Born 1919; director, American Water Works Company, 1975–89; chairman, 1985–88; president and chief executive officer, Fidelity Bank, 1971–78.

Orville L. Banz   Born 1917; joined California Water and Telephone, 1945; president, California-American Water Company, 1976–80; retired 1980.

Samuel J. Bargh   Born 1905; Bowdoin College, BS, 1921; joined American Water Works & Electric Company, 1927; division manager, 1939–55; retired 1955; died 1957.

John J. Barr   Born 1913; joined system, 1932; president, American Water Works Company, 1960–75; retired 1975; director, 1948–84; died 1987.

Ralph B. Bartlett   Born 1920; joined system, 1965; manager–finance, American Water Works Service Company, 1978–85; retired 1985.

Russell D. Bartlett   Born 1916; University of Maine, BS; joined system, 1948; manager, Davenport Water Company, 1969–80; retired 1980.

John W. Behee   Born 1919; joined system, 1936; manager, Pittsburgh District, Western Pennsylvania Water Company, 1971–75; retired 1975.

Albert I. Bennett   Born 1932; Stevens Institute of Technology, ME; joined system, 1961; director of engineering, Western Region, American Water Works Service Company, 1979–87; retired 1987.

Otto J. Biehl   Born 1919; joined system, 1966; vice president, personnel, American Water Works Service Company, 1966–79; died 1979.

Donald F. Bixler   Born 1899; Massachusetts Institute of Technology, BS; joined system, 1926; chief mechanical engineer, American Water Works Service Company, 1957–62; retired 1962; died 1984.

Arthur E. Blood   Born 1902; joined system, 1924; manager, Terre Haute Water Works, 1951–64; retired 1964; died 1981.

Arthur E. Bone   Born 1914; director, American Water Works Company, 1975–85; president and chairman, UGI Corporation.

[281]

Edward J. Boulton   Born 1915; joined system, 1936; manager, Citizens Water Service Company, 1956–69; died 1969.

Glenn E. Boulton   Born 1902; joined system, 1920; manager, The St. Joseph Water Company, 1957–67; retired 1967; died 1990.

Thomas G. Braman   Born 1907; Bowdoin College, AB, 1929; joined system, 1933; vice president and manager, South Pittsburgh Water Company, 1963–71; retired 1971; died 1989.

Edward C. Bratton   Born 1915; joined system, 1950; director of tax accounting, American Water Works Service Company, 1975–76; died 1976.

Horace W. Breece, Jr.   Born 1920; Swarthmore College, BA; joined system, 1954; comptroller, American Water Works Company, 1970–84; vice president–accounting, American Water Works Service Company, 1980–85; retired 1985.

Charles A. Briggs, II   Born 1909; director, American Water Works Company, 1956–82; retired senior vice president, County Trust Company of New York; died 1983.

Howard H. Briggs   Born 1903; New York University, BS, 1925; joined system, 1925; treasurer, American Water Works Service Company, 1959–68; retired 1968; died 1989.

Robert W. Bruce   Born 1923; Pomona Junior College, AS; joined system, 1968; vice president–finance, California-American Water Company, 1979–83; retired 1983; died 1986.

Allen J. Brumbaugh   Born 1921; Earlham College, AB, 1943; joined system, 1946; manager, Riverton Consolidated Water Company, 1969–86; retired 1986.

Harold N. Burd   Born 1908; joined system, 1920; manager, Commonwealth Water Company, 1962–73; retired 1973.

Donald T. Burr   Born 1916; joined system, 1946; Eastern Pennsylvania Division manager, American Water Works Service Company, 1978–81; retired 1981.

Pierson J. Butcher   Born 1915; joined system, 1946; manager, West Virginia-American Water Company, 1968–80; retired 1980.

Howard J. Carlock   Born 1916; New York University, BCE, 1938; joined system, 1949; vice president–engineering, 1980–84; vice president–real estate development, 1985–88; retired 1988.

James G. Carns, Jr.   Born 1906; joined system, 1927; vice president and manager, East St. Louis and Interurban Water Company; died 1971.

Stephen C. Casteel Manager, East St. Louis and Interurban Water Company, 1950s; died 1980.

Thomas W. Coleman Born 1900; Chattanooga College of Law, BSME; joined system, 1925; manager, Commonwealth Water Company, 1950–65; retired 1965; died 1977.

James F. Conroy Born 1903; joined system, 1948; resident engineer, American Water Works Service Company, 1966–68; retired 1968.

Robert J. Cooke, III Born 1944; joined system, 1963; manager, Uniontown-Connellsville District of Western Pennsylvania Water Company, 1970–89; died 1989.

Vernon B. Corle Born 1904; joined system, 1929; manager, New Castle Water Company, 1951–62; retired 1962; died 1983.

Charles W. Coughenour Born 1905; joined system, 1922; manager, Connellsville Water Company, 1944–61; retired 1961; died 1961.

James C. Crenshaw Born 1901; Clemson A&M, BSME; joined system, 1928; assistant division manager, New England Water Service Corporation, 1960–63; died 1963.

Jesse E. Curry, Jr. Born 1922; joined system, 1941; district manager, West Virginia-American Water Company, 1980–84; retired 1984.

James E. Cypher Born 1919; joined system, 1947; manager, Hingham Water Company 1969–81; retired 1981; died 1986.

C. Samuel Daley Born 1920; Gettysburg College, BA; joined system, 1955; special services accountant, American Water Works Service Company, 1980–85; retired 1985.

Joseph A. Daley, Jr. Born 1915; joined system, 1939; director–accounting, Eastern Region, American Water Works Service Company, 1973–80; retired 1980.

Paul G. Dannels Born 1915; joined system, 1940; district manager, Western Pennsylvania Water Company, 1950–80; retired 1980.

Robert S. Dawson Born 1914; joined system, 1937; vice president and manager, West Virginia Water Company, 1968–81; retired 1981; died 1990.

John B. Delaney Born 1914; joined system, 1959; director–public relations, American Water Works Company, 1965–79; retired 1979.

Clarence H. Dickey Born 1888; University of Iowa, LLB, 1915; joined American Water Works & Electric Company, 1927; vice president, American Water Works Company and Northeastern Water Company, 1947–53; retired 1953; died 1971.

William J. Dixon Born 1905; Carnegie Institute of Technology, ME; joined system, 1934; manager, St. Mary's Water Company, 1945–69; retired 1969; died 1984.

Francis D. Donahue Born 1898; joined system, 1930; manager, Monongahela Valley Water Corporation, 1930–63; retired 1963; died 1969.

Philip H. Dowdell Born 1900; Hamilton College, BS; joined American Water Works & Electric Company, 1924; manager, The Alexandria Water Company, 1957–64; retired 1964; died 1980.

Arnold C. Doxsey Born 1909; Purdue University, BS, ME; joined system, 1933; chief mechanical engineer, American Water Works Service Company, 1962–74; retired 1974.

Thomas C. Earl Born 1915; Tulane University, BE, ME; joined system, 1959; chief engineer, American Water Works Service Company, 1961–76; retired 1976.

Kenneth B. Earnhardt Born 1914; Cornell University, CE, 1936; joined system, 1937; Eastern Division manager, American Water Works Service Company, 1968–79; retired 1979.

Elmer F. Eld Born 1905; joined system, 1925; manager, Old Dominion Water Corporation, 1926–70; retired 1970; died 1970.

Gordon N. Ells Born 1924; joined system, 1957; manager, Hampton Water Works Company, 1971–82; died 1982.

Roy N. Farley Born 1914; joined system, 1945; district manager, West Virginia Water Company, 1957–77; retired 1977.

Edward Feldman Born 1905; district manager, New Jersey Water Company, 1957–66; retired 1966; died 1982.

Elizabeth M. Flaherty Born 1920; joined The Noroton Water Company, 1938; district manager, Connecticut-American Water Company, 1972–83; died 1983.

Martin E. Flentje Born 1897; University of Iowa, BS, MS; joined system, 1927; chief sanitary engineer, American Water Works Service Company, 1959–62; retired 1962; died 1976.

Garnet E. Foor Born 1906; joined system, 1929; treasurer and secretary, New England Division, American Water Works Service Company, 1967–71; retired 1971.

Charles A. Forrest, Jr. Born 1913; joined American Water Works

& Electric Company, 1934; manager, Massachusetts Water Works Company, 1950–68; retired 1969; died 1985.

Robert B. Freeman   Born 1902; Brown University, 1924; joined American Water Works & Electric Company, 1928; assistant chief engineer, 1941–47; vice president, American Water Works Service Company, 1947–57; retired 1957.

Frank R. Freestone   Born 1910; joined system, 1927; manager, Ocean City Water Service Company, 1966–69; retired 1969; died 1988.

Maurice B. Frost   Born 1903; Massachusetts Institute of Technology, BSCE; joined system, 1930; planning engineer, American Water Works Service Company, 1962–68; retired 1968.

A. Kenneth Fuller   Born 1911; joined system, 1946; district manager, California-American Water Company, 1972–76; retired 1976; died 1981.

William B. Gamble, Jr.   Born 1910; Grove City College, BS; joined system, 1955; vice president, American Water Works Company, 1957–75; director, 1967–74; retired 1975; died 1984.

Stephen J. Gannon   Born 1901; joined system, 1921; manager, The Noroton Water Company, 1936–66; retired 1966; died 1972.

Joseph J. Garland   Born 1901; joined system, 1928; vice president, American Water Works Service Company, 1958–66; retired 1966; died 1991.

Edward A. Geehan   Born 1889; joined system, 1917; vice president, American Water Works Service Company, 1946–59; retired 1959; died 1969.

Kenneth W. Gemmill   Born 1910; director, American Water Works Company, 1958–82; partner, Dechert, Price & Rhoads, Philadelphia attorneys.

Robert T. Genovesi   Born 1928; Villanova University, BS, Economics; joined system, 1955; corporate secretary, American Water Works Service Company, 1968–72.

William J. Gillespie   Born 1920; joined system, 1947; manager, Dedham Water Company, 1982–85; died 1985.

Kenneth A. Glenz   Born 1918; joined system, 1936; vice president–operations, American Water Works Service Company, 1980–83; retired 1983; died 1985.

Frank F. Gordon   Born 1915; joined Water Utilities Service Corporation, 1940s; controller, New Jersey Division, 1949–58.

Anthony H. Greco   Born 1910; joined system, 1931; New Jersey Division manager, American Water Works Service Company, 1951–63; died 1963.

Edward M. Griffin   Born 1917; joined system, 1966; manager, Muncie Water Works Company, 1973–79; retired 1979.

John A. Gubanich   Born 1919; University of Notre Dame, BSC, 1949; joined system, 1967; president, American Water Works Company, 1975–83; director, 1974–83; retired 1983.

William D. Hall   Born 1922; joined system, 1959; director–risk & materials management, American Water Works Service Company, 1978–84; retired 1984.

J. Earl Hampson   Born 1910; joined system, 1926; district manager, Western Pennsylvania Water Company, 1952–73; retired 1973.

William S. Harris   Born 1924; Cornell University, BCE, 1945; joined system, 1948; vice president–administration, American Water Works Service Company, 1983–86; retired 1986.

Wilford J. Hays   Born 1911; joined system, 1966; president, California-American Water Company, 1966–70; division manager, American Water Works Service Company, 1971–76; retired 1976; died 1983.

James F. Heagy   Born 1916; Pennsylvania State University, BS, 1941; joined system, 1954; forester, American Water Works Service Company, 1967–78; retired 1978.

John W. Heiney   Born 1913; Lehigh University, BS; joined system, 1935; division manager, American Water Works Service Company, 1957–60.

James F. Heyworth   Born 1904; joined system, 1928; manager, Davenport Water Company, 1958–69; retired 1969; died 1979.

Lloyd B. Hillyer   Born 1919; joined system, 1945; manager, Coronado District, California-American Water Company, 1976–86; retired 1986.

Edwin O. Horner   Born 1901; Baltimore Polytechnic Institute; joined system, 1928; division manager, Municipal Management Company, 1950–62; died 1962.

Harry M. Iverson   Born 1907; Syracuse University, BS; joined system, 1946; comptroller, American Water Works Service Company, 1952–55; died 1955.

Ernest E. Jacobson   Born 1901; University of Iowa, BSE; joined American Water Works & Electric Company, 1931; manager, Lexington Water Company, 1939–66; retired 1966; died 1968.

[286]

John M. Jennings   Born 1911; Syracuse University, BS; joined system, 1937; director–system data processing, 1975–76; retired 1977; died 1989.

Max K. Jones   Born 1901; University of Iowa, BSC; joined system, 1926; manager, Huntington Water Corporation, 1950–66; retired 1966; died 1980.

Arthur P. Jost   Born 1907; joined system, 1926; manager, Ocean County Water Company, 1951–65; retired 1965; died 1989.

Frank J. Kavanaugh   Born 1931; Manhattan College, BBA; joined system, 1970; vice president–accounting, California-American Water Company, 1979–88; retired 1989.

Robert W. Kean, Jr.   Born 1922; director, American Water Works Company, 1962–78; president, Elizabethtown Water Company, 1960–72.

John T. Kearns   Born 1913; University of Iowa, BSCE; joined system, 1950; water quality superintendent, American Water Works Service Company, 1973–74; retired 1974; died 1983.

William H. Kellett   Born 1911; joined system, 1955; manager, Bangor District, Keystone Water Company, 1960–76; retired 1976.

James M. Kelly   Born 1928; Pennsylvania public utility commissioner, 1967–77; joined system, 1979; vice president–regulatory practices, American Water Works Service Company, 1980–83; resigned to accept appointment as U.S. district court judge.

Joseph M. Kendra   Born 1920; joined system, 1958; manager, The Salisbury Water Supply Company, 1973–84; retired 1984; died 1991.

Samuel E. Kerr   Born 1900; joined system, 1929; division comptroller, American Water Works Service Company, 1963–65; retired 1965; died 1981.

Jack H. King   Born 1921; University of Illinois, BS; joined system, 1943; manager, Commonwealth Water Company, 1964–84; retired 1984.

Louis C. Krueger   Born 1906; joined system, 1922; manager, New Castle Water Company, 1955–71; retired 1971; died 1984.

Howard M. Landers   Born 1904; joined system, 1920; manager, Uniontown Water Company, 1965–69; retired 1969; died 1972.

John W. Lawrence   Born 1902; joined system, 1945; manager, Alton Water Company, 1959–67; retired 1967; died 1981.

George K. Leary   Born 1907; University of Vermont, BS; joined system, 1927; manager, Citizens Water Company of Washington, Pennsylvania, 1955–72; retired 1972; died 1982.

Carl W. Lintner Born 1917; joined system, 1958; district manager, New Jersey Water Company; retired 1980.

Elmer E. Long Born 1921; joined system, 1941; manager, Alton Water Company, 1969–81; retired 1982; died 1989.

John H. Long Born 1920; Juanita College, BS; joined system, 1946; New England Division manager, American Water Works Service Company, 1963–74; retired 1981; died 1987.

Dennis Lord Born 1914; joined system, 1948; manager, Richmond Water Works Corporation, 1967–71; died 1971.

James W. Luengene Born 1900; joined system, 1920; manager, New Jersey Water Company, 1950–65; retired 1965; died 1979.

Frank J. McAndrew Born 1902; joined system, 1937; division manager, American Water Works Service Company, 1960–67; retired 1967; died 1980.

Theodore R. McDaniel Born 1922; University of Kentucky, BS; joined system, 1950; manager, Haddon District, New Jersey Water Company, 1967–84; died 1984.

William D. MacDonald Born 1916; joined system, 1938; manager at Norristown and vice president, Keystone Water Company, 1965–81; retired 1981.

William B. MacIndoe Born 1898; joined Water Utilities Service Corporation, 1928; secretary, Northeastern Water Company, 1947–63; retired 1963.

W. James MacIntosh Born 1901; director, American Water Works Company, 1947–74; senior partner, Morgan, Lewis & Bockius, attorneys, 1967–1975; died 1989.

Linn E. Magoffin Born 1923; University of California, Los Angeles, BSCE; joined system, 1946; district manager, California-American Water Company, 1980–85; retired 1986.

Clarence F. March Born 1900; joined system, 1919; vice president, Municipal Management Division, American Water Works Company, 1963–69; retired 1969.

Joseph W. Matlavage Born 1898; joined system, 1929; manager, Municipal Management Company, 1942–68; retired 1968; died 1986.

John L. Matthews Born 1898; joined system, 1922; manager, New Jersey Water Company, 1960–63; retired 1963; died 1965.

Oliver B. Merrill, Jr.   Director, American Water Works Company and Northeastern Water Company, 1947–50; partner in law firm of Sullivan & Cromwell.

Donald R. Metzger   Born 1914; University of Colorado, BSME; joined system, 1940; assistant manager–engineering, American Water Works Service Company, 1973–76; retired 1976.

Robert F Miller   Born 1909; joined system, 1940; assistant treasurer, American Water Works Service Company, 1960–67; retired 1967.

W. Ray Mize   Born 1910; joined system, 1934; manager, The Terre Haute Water Works Corporation, 1964–73; retired 1973.

Clinton D. Moon   Born 1895; joined system, 1927; manager, New Jersey Water Company, 1950–60; retired 1960; died 1968.

Clinton D. Moon, Jr.   Born 1920; joined system, 1940; district manager, Western Pennsylvania Water Company, 1962–85; retired 1985.

James G. Moore   Born 1918; University of Pennsylvania Law School, LLB; joined system, 1965; director–system risk management, American Water Works Service Company, 1972–79; retired 1979.

George G. Morrow   Born 1892; joined system, 1927; manager, Peoria Water Works Company, 1940–57; retired 1957; died 1960.

John H. Murdoch, Jr.   Born 1886; Washington & Jefferson College, BA, 1909; joined system, 1917; vice president and counsel, Water Works Service Company, 1917–49, American Water Works Service Company, 1949–56; retired 1956; died 1966.

John B. Murphy   Born 1914; joined system, 1940; regional manager, American Water Works Service Company, 1974–77; retired 1978; died 1986.

Howard H. Myers   Born 1905; joined system, 1942; manager, Clinton Water Works Company, 1954–67; retired 1968; died 1985.

George W. Naylor   Born 1909; Carnegie Institute of Technology, CE; joined system, 1933; manager, Riverton Consolidated Water Company, 1951–70; retired 1980.

Clifford Newbauer   Born 1923; joined system, 1952; manager, Clinton Water Works Company, 1972–88; retired 1988.

Oscar A. Newquist   Born 1904; Washington & Jefferson College, BS; joined system, 1926; vice president and manager, Monmouth Consolidated Water Company, 1953–69; retired 1969; died 1973.

John O. Newton   Born 1901; manager, Joplin Water Company, 1950s; retired 1960s.

John P. O'Boyle   Born 1924; St. Francis College, BS; joined system, 1955; manager, Virginia-American Water Company, 1967–78; retired 1978; died 1978.

Cecil M. O'Day   Born 1920; State University of Iowa, BSCE; joined system, 1954; vice president, American Water Works Service Company, 1976–86; retired 1986.

Earl G. Ohlson   Born 1909; joined system, 1927; purchasing agent, American Water Works Service Company, 1960–73; retired 1973.

Theodore E. Olson   Born 1911; joined system, 1938; district manager, Western Pennsylvania Water Company, 1950–76; retired 1976.

Edgar F. Orpin   Born 1908; joined system, 1925; manager, Wannacomet Water Company, 1947–70; retired 1970; died 1970.

Earl J. Patterson   Born 1919; joined system, 1945; director–rates and revenue, Pennsylvania Region, American Water Works Service Company, 1974–89; retired 1989.

Justus W. Patterson   Born 1899; joined system, 1929; assistant division manager, American Water Works Service Company, 1949–64; retired 1964; died 1971.

George E. Paul   Born 1911; Rensselaer Polytechnic Institute, BSCE; joined system, 1936; chief construction engineer, American Water Works Service Company, 1956–60; retired 1976.

Lloyd H. Payne   Born 1906; joined system, 1925; manager, Punxsutawney Water Service Company, 1950–71; retired 1971.

Earl J. Pierce   Born 1898; joined system, 1919; manager, Davenport Water Company, 1946–58; retired 1958; died 1989.

John L. Plummer   Born 1916; director, American Water Works Company, 1955–86; president, Plummer Precision Optics.

Albert F. Porzelius   Born 1886; University of Missouri, BSCE; joined system, 1911; manager, City Water Company of Chattanooga, 1922–56; retired 1956.

Jerome Powers   Born 1892; Rutgers College, CE, 1914; joined system, 1922; division manager, Water Works Service Company, 1939–49, American Water Works Service Company, 1949–57; died 1957.

William H.H. Putnam Born 1905; Alabama Polytechnic Institute, BS; joined system, 1922; Central Division manager, American Water Works Service Company, 1956–70; retired 1970.

Homer Reed Born 1889; director, American Water Works Company, 1954–75; director, Northeastern Water Company, 1951–63; Philadelphia realtor; died 1984.

Rudolf C. Reese Born 1904; joined system, 1946; mechanical technician, American Water Works Service Company, 1962–66; retired 1966; died 1973.

Lawrence T. Reinicker Born 1894; Cornell University, BSCE; joined system, 1927; president, American Water Works Company, 1953–54; vice chairman of the board, 1955–58; retired 1959; died 1967.

John A. Rich Born 1920; joined system, 1941; manager, Port Chester Water Works, 1971–83; retired 1983.

Howard C. Richards Born 1903; Pennsylvania State College, ME; joined system, 1924; manager, The Alexandria Water Company, 1936–57; retired 1968; died 1983.

Henry A. Riddle, Jr. Born 1920; University of Pittsburgh Law School, LLB; joined system, 1953; corporate secretary, American Water Works Company, 1967–85; retired 1985.

Vance E. Rigling Born 1911; joined system, 1934; manager, American Water Works Service Company, 1949–54; retired 1954.

George C. Roberts Born 1943; University of Delaware, MBA; joined system, 1971; secretary and assistant treasurer, American Water Works Company, 1985–87.

James L. Rodgers, Jr. Born 1923; Cornell University, BSCE; joined system, 1954; system company president, American Water Works Service Company, 1978–83; retired 1983.

Milton B. Rodgers Born 1895; joined system, 1932; vice president, Water Utilities Service Corporation, 1932–53; retired 1953; died 1957.

Charles P. Rogers Born 1916; joined system, 1933; manager, Bristol County Water Company, 1957–78; retired 1978.

John T. Rooney Manager, Monongahela Valley Water Corporation, 1950s.

Gerald E. Rowley Born 1914; joined system, 1941; district manager, Western Pennsylvania Water Company, 1969–77; retired 1977.

Russell F. Ruhp Born 1908; joined system, 1926; manager, The Salisbury Water Supply Company, 1950–73; retired 1973; died 1978.

John Salamon Born 1913; joined systsem, 1945; district manager, Western Pennsylvania Water Company, 1973–78; retired 1978.

Earl C. Schwalm Born 1911; joined system, 1928; assistant manager, Central Division, American Water Works Service Company, 1969–74; died 1974.

Russell J. Sharp Born 1897; joined system, 1940; president, New England Water Service Corporation, 1960–62; retired 1962.

L. Edward Sharpe Born 1889; joined system, 1929; comptroller, American Water Works Company, 1947–52; retired 1952; died 1984.

Herman L. Shiflett Born 1899; joined system, 1928; manager, Water Works Board, City of Birmingham, 1956–57; died 1957.

William C. Shoemaker Born 1902; joined system, 1923; manager, Richmond Water Works Corporation, 1954–62; retired 1962; died 1986.

James E. Simon Born 1921; Boston University Law School, JD; joined system, 1974; corporate secretary, American Water Works Service Company, 1974–83; retired 1983.

Morton S. Simon Born 1916; joined system, 1947; manager, Virginia-American Water Company, 1973–83; retired 1983.

E. Clinton Smith Born 1905; Columbia University, BA; joined system, 1957; manager, Western Division, American Water Works Service Company, 1965–70; retired 1970; died 1987.

Frank J. Smith Born 1923; joined system, 1965; manager, Maryland-American Water Company, 1978–85; retired 1985.

Richard L. Snider Born 1925; joined system, 1948; manager, Shore District, New Jersey Water company, 1976–83; died 1983.

Elmer S. Steelman Born 1892; joined system, 1911; manager, Ocean City Water Service Company, 1950–57; retired 1957; died 1964.

Milton Steelman, Jr. Born 1914; joined system, 1936; district manager, New Jersey Water Company, 1966–78; retired 1979; died 1982.

John G. Storer Born 1910; joined system, 1936; manager, Keystone Water Company, 1973–75; retired 1975; died 1979.

Wesley P. Thornburg   Born 1891; joined system, 1917; manager, Armstrong Water Company, 1948–56; retired 1956; died 1961.

Edwin S. Tillotson   Born 1909; joined system, 1927; manager, Tennessee-American Water Company, 1956–74; retired 1974; died 1981.

Richard B. Tompkins   Born 1901; joined system, 1929; vice president–rates & research, American Water Works Service Company, 1960–66; retired 1966; died 1985.

Charles Trowbridge   Born 1890; University of Illinois, BSME; joined system, 1917; chief sanitary engineer, American Water Works Service Company, 1920–55; retired 1955; died 1974.

Daniel E. Troxell   Born 1925; joined system, 1952; operations manager, Western Pennsylvania Water Company, 1979–87; retired 1987.

Thomas A. Tunney   Director, Northeastern Water Company, 1947–60; director, American Water Works Company, 1948–60; partner in the firm of Tunney & Hodge.

Ralph L. Tyler   Born 1902; University of Maryland, AS; joined system, 1932; assistant division manager, American Water Works Service Company, 1959–64; retired 1964; died 1984.

Harold H. Waddel   Born 1910; joined system, 1959; management assistant, American Water Works Service Company.

Eugene H. Wagner   Born 1906; joined system, 1925; manager, Connellsville Water Company; retired 1971; died 1987.

Herbert L. Walborn   Born 1920; joined system, 1957; manager, Municipal Management Division, American Water Works Company, 1980–85; retired 1985.

Guy Waldrop   Born 1900; Georgia School of Technology, BSEE; joined American Water Works & Electric Company, 1926; assistant chief engineer, American Water Works Service Company, 1957–65; retired 1965.

Jacob T. Wankmuller   Born 1910; New York University, MCE; joined system, 1951; vice president, American Water Works Service Company, 1967–73; retired 1975.

John H. Ware, Jr.   Born 1888; chairman of the board, Northeastern Water Company and American Water Works Company, 1947–60; died 1963.

John H. Ware, 3rd   Born 1909; University of Pennsylvania, 1929;

chairman of the board, American Water Works Company, 1960–84; chairman, Penn Fuel Gas Company, 1960–88.

Willard M. Ware   Born 1910; University of Pennsylvania, 1931; director, American Water Works Company, 1953–82; vice chairman, 1970–82; died 1984.

Raymond T. Wendell   Born 1909; University of Michigan, MS; joined system, 1939; vice president and director, American Water Works Company, 1959–73; retired 1974.

Eugene R. Westbrook   Born 1916; joined system, 1941; district manager, Keystone Water Company, 1956–78; retired 1978; died 1981.

Raymond S. Whaite   Born 1911; joined system, 1950; district manager, Keystone Water Company, 1973–76; retired 1976; died 1987.

Willis J. Williams   Born 1911; joined system, 1933; district manager, Western Pennsylvania Water Company, 1973–76; retired 1976.

Otis W. Withington   Born 1904; joined system, 1937; manager, Mystic Valley Water Company, 1960–69; retired 1969; died 1976.

Glenn A. Woodhouse   Born 1891; University of Michigan, BCE, 1914; joined system, 1925; chief supervising engineer, American Water Works Service Company, 1925–56; retired 1956.

Joseph O. Yates, Jr.   Born 1923; Virginia Polytechnic Institute, BSCE; joined system, 1950; manager, Connecticut-American Water Company, 1984–86; retired 1986.

APPENDIX D

Officers of American Water Works Service Company, 1991

Chairman of the Board	James V. LaFrankie
President	Loren D. Mellendorf
Senior Vice President–Financial Services	J. James Barr
Senior Vice President–Operating Services	George W. Johnstone
Senior Vice President–Corporate Development & Governmental Affairs	Edward W. Limbach
Regional Vice President–Eastern	William R. Cobb
Regional Vice President–Western	Robert W. Greaves
Regional Vice President–Southern	Dillard L. Edgemon
Regional Vice President–Pennsylvania	Gerald C. Smith
Regional Vice President–Mid-America	Glen W. Thornburg
General Counsel	W. Timothy Pohl
Vice President–Operations	Michael J. Caponigro
Vice President–Finance	Bruce E. Tillotson
Vice President–Engineering	Daniel L. Kelleher
Vice President–Risk Management	Michael J. Kowalsky
Vice President–Water Quality	Richard H. Moser
Vice President–Information Systems	Akiva F. Pipe
Vice President–Accounting	Simon S. Stock, Jr.

Vice President–Human Resources	Richard Strahlman
Vice President–Corporate Communications	T. Ward Welsh
Vice President–Corporate Services	W. Timothy Pohl
Assistant Vice President–Accounting/ Auditing	Robert D. Sievers
Treasurer	J. James Barr
Secretary	W. Timothy Pohl
Comptroller	Simon S. Stock, Jr.
Assistant Treasurer	Bruce E. Tillotson
Assistant Secretary	George W. Johnstone
Assistant Comptroller	Robert D. Sievers

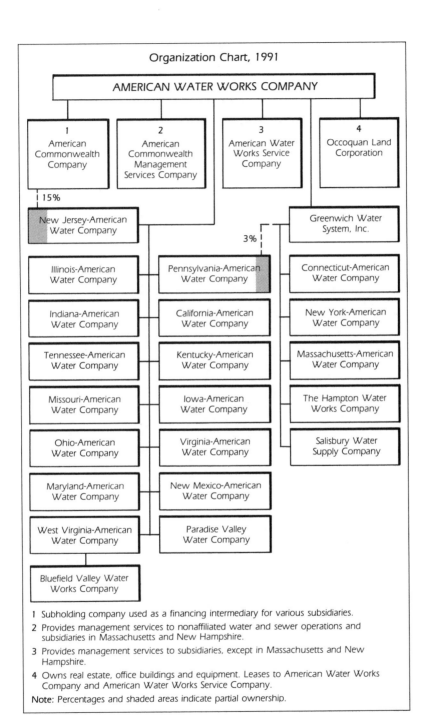

Organization Chart, 1991

AMERICAN WATER WORKS COMPANY

1 American Commonwealth Company

2 American Commonwealth Management Services Company

3 American Water Works Service Company

4 Occoquan Land Corporation

15%

New Jersey-American Water Company

Greenwich Water System, Inc.

3%

Illinois-American Water Company

Pennsylvania-American Water Company

Connecticut-American Water Company

Indiana-American Water Company

California-American Water Company

New York-American Water Company

Tennessee-American Water Company

Kentucky-American Water Company

Massachusetts-American Water Company

Missouri-American Water Company

Iowa-American Water Company

The Hampton Water Works Company

Ohio-American Water Company

Virginia-American Water Company

Salisbury Water Supply Company

Maryland-American Water Company

New Mexico-American Water Company

West Virginia-American Water Company

Paradise Valley Water Company

Bluefield Valley Water Works Company

1 Subholding company used as a financing intermediary for various subsidiaries.

2 Provides management services to nonaffiliated water and sewer operations and subsidiaries in Massachusetts and New Hampshire.

3 Provides management services to subsidiaries, except in Massachusetts and New Hampshire.

4 Owns real estate, office buildings and equipment. Leases to American Water Works Company and American Water Works Service Company.

Note: Percentages and shaded areas indicate partial ownership.

[297]

Acknowledgments

The preparation of this history was made possible through the sponsorship, encouragement—and a considerable measure of patience—on the part of James V. LaFrankie, president of American Water Works, who also provided firsthand recollections at key points of the story. The considerable task of assembling documents and pictures, identifying key sources, searching out facts and overseeing production of the book was undertaken by T. Ward Welsh, vice-president for corporate communications. The following were generous with their time, knowledge and memories, submitting to a series of interviews that provided much of the material central to the story:

Marshall A. Anderson, Samuel H. Ballam, Jr., the late John J. Barr, the late Howard H. Briggs, Howard J. Carlock, Rhoda Ware Cobb, John B. Delaney, Thomas C. Earl, Kenneth B. Earnhardt, Kenneth W. Gemmill, John A. Gubanich, William S. Harris, George W. Johnstone, the Honorable James M. Kelly, Elizabeth Kuiper, Marilyn Ware Lewis, the late W. James MacIntosh, Loren D. Mellendorf, Richard H. Moser, Martha Ware Odom, Nancy Ware Pascal, John L. Plummer, William H.H. Putnam, George H. Roberts, E. Clinton Smith, John H. Ware, 3rd, John H. Ware, IV, Rhoda Chambers Ware and Raymond T. Wendell.

Henry A. Riddle, Jr., assisted in verifying facts from corporate records. Elizabeth Hovinen and Timothy Cross provided additional research. Various members of the Wall Street community were helpful in clarifying financial matters. The Free Library of Philadelphia; the Boston Public Library; the Chatham, New Jersey,

Public Library; the Morris County, New Jersey, Library; and the library of Dean Junior College in Franklin, Massachusetts, were also generous in making available facilities for reference and checking.

G.C.

Index

About the Author

When Gilbert Cross was 19 years old, his ambition was to become a writer, so the U.S. Navy, with the logic peculiar to the military, sent him to the Harvard Business School. After recovering from his initial stage fright, he distinguished himself by publishing humorous verses about the school's famous "decision-making process" in the student newspaper. Following a stint as a Navy paymaster in the mountains of southeast China, he returned to Harvard on the GI Bill, completed an MBA, then enrolled at the Creative Writing Center of Stanford University.

Next came an apprenticeship in journalism on a small country daily in eastern Oregon, where he had his first encounter with a controversy involving water: the debate over public versus private development of the resources of the Columbia River. The water issue carried him to Washington, to the office of a congressman, where he employed his literary skills in pushing legislation through the congressional mill. This was followed by a stint as a speechwriter for the secretary of state and the White House, where he again found himself at the ringside of a controversy involving water: the nationalization of the Suez Canal in retaliation for the withdrawal of U.S. support for the Aswan Dam on the Nile.

Cross has contributed to *Fortune, Holiday, Look, Esquire* and *Reader's Digest* on topics ranging from innovative uses for computers to the wit and wisdom of Jimmy Hoffa. He has also written speeches for the chief executives of General Foods, Chemical Bank and TRW, and is co-author of a book entitled *The Game of Wine*, which he describes as "a Harvard Business School approach to the decision about which wine to serve with the lamb chops." Cross lives in Franklin, Massachusetts, with his wife, Patricia, an editor and former English teacher, who often corrects his punctuation.